MW00654162

THE GRACE OF "NOTHINGNESS"

The Grace of "Nothingness"

Navigating the Spiritual Life
WITH
Blessed Columba Marmion

BY FR CASSIAN KOENEMANN, OSB

Angelico Press

First published in the USA
by Angelico Press 2021
Copyright © Fr Cassian Koenemann, OSB 2021

All rights reserved:
No part of this book may be reproduced or transmitted,
in any form or by any means, without permission

For information, address:
Angelico Press, Ltd.
169 Monitor St.
Brooklyn, NY 11222
www.angelicopress.com

ppr 978-1-62138-809-8
cloth 978-1-62138-810-4

Book and cover design
by Michael Schrauzer

CONTENTS

PREFACE

IT IS RIGHT AND JUST TO GIVE THANKS TO THE FATHER, Son, and Holy Spirit for everything. It is also fitting to proclaim that my parents, Dennis and Diane, dedicated their lives to Betsy and me, making time for our every activity, from the days of my leading the neighborhood parade of numbers as "Zero the Hero" to my current pursuit of writing a book about nothingness. Betsy, who is the model of what it means to be a good sibling, and Mike are also surer supports than any brother could have. The first context for this book is, then, a loving family.

Saint Louis Abbey and Saint Louis Priory School are the next most important contexts for this book. I came under the teaching and influence of the Benedictines in seventh grade, entering into a rich Catholic environment, a rigorous academic setting, a monastic culture, and a classical education that pushed literature, Latin, and French. I had great teachers.

The stability and spirituality of the monks ensured that the fire of the Holy Spirit could always be felt at Saint Louis Abbey. I eventually made the abbey my home and was accepted by my teachers as a brother. My brothers have challenged me, hopefully purified me, spiritually, intellectually, and emotionally. In short, this book would not have happened in any other context, not to its present degree of development on any of those levels. The community always knows the real person, good and bad, and I am most grateful for the patient ways that my brothers have endured my extraverted, choleric excesses. Gregory, Thomas, Linus, Ralph, Benedict, Finbarr, Laurence, Symeon, Gerard, Mark, Dominic, Augustine, Michael, Ambrose, Aidan, Francis, Sixtus, Andrew, Cuthbert, Edward, Athanasius, Hugh, and Philip; y'all are special to me.

Twenty years ago, first while walking to the National Shrine of the Immaculate Conception, I couldn't stop puzzling over the chapter of the *Imitation of Christ* entitled "How Man Has No Personal Goodness of Which to Boast," especially over the lines "Can nothing boast of its nothingness? This would be the height of vanity!"[1] For a young man with the besetting sin of vanity, this topic was a challenge; for an insecure friend of God with both positive and negative experiences of his nothingness, it was a revelation. For

---

1   Thomas à Kempis, *The Imitation of Christ*, trans. Leo Sherley-Price (London: Penguin Books, 1952), 146.

those who have guided my soul, it's probably been much work and tedium. Gregory Mohrman, OSB, Mark Hargreaves, OSB, and Greg Mikesch deserve much credit for prudently guiding my soul and giving me confidence at various times. Just last week I said to Msgr. Mikesch, "Well, I guess that's why I wrote a book about overcoming self-reliance." With a kind laugh and an understanding smile, he simply replied, "That may be relevant."

It is said that every theologian has his own tension with God that he needs to explore. I needed to explore the grace of nothingness, and God blessed me with the most perfect director for it in Paul Murray, OP. Our time together was much more than a capstone experience for a license in spiritual theology at the Angelicum. I could finally express myself because I finally felt as if I had someone who could fully receive and process my tensions and my ways of making sense of them. Father Paul is world-class, and he proved that in his personal approach as much as in his life-changing lessons. I am also grateful for his permission to analyze one of his interactions with Saint Teresa of Calcutta in this work.

There is a miracle of Providence here to report. When I was fixated on reading the Doctors of the Church, Cardinal Raymond Burke doggedly kept after me to read a twentieth-century Benedictine author who connected with my interests. In trying to persuade me to read and write on Marmion, he even bought me my first book by Marmion. I eventually found in this suggestion a heaven-sent resolution of my tension with God and much more. Deo gratias.

After my time at seminary, this work deepened and reached a new level of synthesis when Sr Marysia Weber, RSM, DO provided me with supervision when I became prior; Bishop Robert Hermon and Jane Guenther administered healing and deliverance to me and later welcomed me into the Diocese of Saint Louis's healing and deliverance team; and Dr Michael Sy put me through his "torture chamber" and supported me in my darkest times. Yes, it was all a grace.

To Lauren, Kevin, BJ, Stephen, Ryan, Steve, Joey, Terry, Rob, JR, Hillary, Austin and Stephanie, Ryan and Lauren, Dustin and Tasha, Adam and Gretchen, Paul, Andrew, Debbie, Sr Marie Fe, Lawrence, Tricia, Jen, Karen, Cassian D., Toni, David, Boniface, Paul, Luigi, Bartholomew, Selamawit, Claire Thérèse, Sr Catherine Marie, Lamar, Michael and Janine, Ann, Laurie, Judy, Jerry and Judy, the frequenters of the festive Roman dinners, and many more; life is "nothing" without friends.

The eighth graders reminded me that I'm just a big eighth grader; the eleventh graders kept me motivated to help the next generation to thrive; the twelfth graders patiently endured and helped me to refine earlier versions of this book in my course on friendship with God. Those who allowed me to accompany them spiritually provided a context in which the Holy Spirit could help each of us. The mature and open adults in my night school on spirituality, Abbot Mathew Stark, and some elders gave me confidence that the time was right to publish. Father Augustine Wetta gave me expert tips on writing. Cesar Azrak reliably made my first draft bleed. John Riess and the readers of Angelico Press fortunately love Marmion. The good folks at Angelico have taken care of getting this book into its final form.

It is my privilege to bring out some nearly lost treasures from the saints and a spiritual master of the early twentieth century, Blessed Columba Marmion, OSB, to add some new insights and updates to that tradition, and to bring them together in a contemporary Benedictine playbook about grace and transformation in Christ (cf. Mt 13:52).

INTRODUCTION

"I AM NOTHING." (YOU ARE, TOO.) CATHOLIC MYSTICS from Saint Bernard of Clairvaux to Saint Teresa of Calcutta have repeatedly used such language. Does it express a truth? Is it merely a hyperbole that expresses a mystical feeling? Or is it simply a statement of low self-esteem? If it expresses a truth, does it express a philosophical truth about our existential dependence on God or a theological truth about our dependence on God's power at work in us, what Catholics call grace? To answer these questions, I have turned to Blessed Columba Marmion, OSB, a twentieth-century monk (1858–1923) attentive to his interior response to God's felt presence, the principles that undergird the spiritual life, his own nothingness, and the spiritual benefits that resulted from having accepted his nothingness. His theology built upon his own experience of having felt his nothingness, especially whenever he perceived himself as miniscule relative to God's unbounded majesty. Still, he strove to understand and explain those experiences in a theological way. For example, in his books he made a refrain of Jesus's statement in John 15:5b, "Apart from me, you can do nothing." For Marmion, "to be nothing" was an expression of humility that credited God for being at work in him. Since Jesus had made him a friend and enabled him to live a godly life, Marmion was not considering himself a piece of trash or a loser. You too can welcome God's friendship, and you too can release intense gifts of the Holy Spirit in your life. In fact, God wants to cut you free from any false conceptions of yourself or him that make you feel miserable. Jesus has an exquisite compassion for you, personally, and so you will not feel the weight of ultimate failure. To accept your nothingness, therefore, is not a negation of self or an expression of low self-esteem — love is good, and we are all loveable. It is, rather, a way of finding yourself, your proper graces, your poise. The accent of this work is, then, upon the *grace* of "nothingness."

Let us briefly consider God's scheme and the place of humility within it. "This is the will of God, your sanctification" (1 Thess 4:3). Since God perfectly acts upon His desires, God actively works to make each person, already precious in his eyes, more like himself. The Father sent his Beloved Son into the world to adopt us and grant us a close friendship with him.

The Holy Spirit, Bond of love between the Father and Son, inhabits us, if we will it, forming us over time into union with God, in the fullest measure in the hereafter though in part in the here and now. Yet to respond fully to God's invitation, we need to remove the obstacles we have placed to union with God, most notably the obstacle of self-reliance. We do not make ourselves worthy of God and we all come incomplete and imperfect before God. Instead of trying to win God or solve our problems by our own unaided power, let us humbly trust in the Omniscient's help for us, allowing God to heal, transform, and perfect us.

Consider the spiritual life in terms of canoeing down a river similar to the one depicted in Thomas Cole's "Voyage of Life" paintings. This book attempts to offer some targeted advice for those wanting to progress beyond some particularly turbulent ranges in the spiritual life. In relying on themselves alone, some who are excessive in the spiritual life (i.e., those filled with presumption) rush into ill-chosen chutes, only to be overturned. As for those given to defect in the spiritual life (i.e., those given to faintheartedness), they maneuver so timidly as to be swamped by the waves. Marmion's blend of dogmatic and spiritual insights offers an approach that can rescue you from wreck and/or help you to navigate these dangers.

To recognize yourself "to be nothing" requires theological preparation, for this self-description is only appropriate on the mystical level, not the literal one. Thankfully, Marmion has left behind many dogmatic indications and some mystical traces by which we can assemble a cogent understanding of this type of humility. This book begins, then, in chapter one, by analyzing the ways by which "being nothing" connects with his thoughts on God, Christ, and Christian anthropology. It notes that Jesus, the God-Man, is our model for such humility, for Jesus credited the Father for all of the good in his life. So, to say we are nothing is merely to recognize Christ is the Vine and we are the branches. Without him, we can do nothing (cf. Jn 15:1–5). Yet with him, we can "do all things" (Phil 4:13).

The second chapter compares the insights gained in the first to the use of this term and related terms in the Catholic tradition. It reveals Marmion's approach to be an excellent expression of humility that is deeply rooted in the Catholic tradition and efficacious in opening a person to transformative graces. This chapter also speculates that Marmion's approach reinforced that of Saint Thérèse of Lisieux — to whose cause for canonization Dom Marmion contributed. These first two chapters help to ground this type of humility in trustworthy sources, giving you the confidence that you too can make it through the challenges of humility.

The third chapter presents practical spiritual advice relative to difficulties associated with humility and a deep trust in God. If you want immediate results and you find it tedious to read through the theological underpinnings for practical advice, please skip directly to this final chapter, the heart of this work. If you find it really tedious to read theology, just save this book on your device or shelf until some divine touch, failure, or cataclysmic disaster finally humbles you. If, though, you fear humility because you fear your true worth may be lacking, "Fear not, therefore, you are of more value than many sparrows" (Mt 10:31).

The practical advice here offered is simple: you will progress in your relationship with God and in God's gifts by adopting a humble confidence in his favoritism toward you, his adopted child by baptism. Why is this so? Since each Mass provides enough grace to make each person into a saint, and since you and I are not there yet, we need to review our reception of those graces. Within the work of generally removing our obstacles to God's work in us, many of us need to purify our hearts of interior obstacles to God, in order to participate more fully in the graces of the sacraments. With regard to common interior difficulties, some people overcomplicate their ascetical and spiritual lives; some neglect the process of deep healing and interior renewal; and even some souls who seek God with a balanced singlemindedness struggle too long through dark nights of the soul designed to break them of self-reliance. Marmion's advice cuts through the error of relying on ourselves alone and the difficulties related to that error, allowing us, by God's help and at God's pace, to progress most efficiently. Of special note, Blessed Columba's teaching about humility touched Saint Teresa of Calcutta, and so this chapter also explores the ways in which she confirmed this teaching by rejoicing at her nothingness.

In brief, Blessed Columba Marmion's simple practical advice to us is:

1) tend to God in Himself (through standard exterior conformity to Christ and his Church),

2) accept your nothingness (as a liberating interior disposition that overcomes self-reliance), and

3) have confidence in God (to heal you, bless you, and take you, his glorious one, to his heart).

Before we begin, let us pray:

> Father, your Beloved Son taught that
> I can do nothing without him, it is too true,
> yet Saint Paul also taught I can do all things with Jesus;
> clothed in Jesus, I trust in your work
> to sanctify me, your adopted child;
> moved by the Holy Spirit, I ask you to give me
> yourself as my great reward;
> so, I ask for the graces necessary to deepen
> my friendship with you and to heal others:
> please deliver me from what gives me misery,
> from false perceptions of me and you;
> give me the discernment to know what to do,
> the humility to avoid presumption,
> and the trust in your favor — indeed, your favoritism —
> toward me to avoid faintheartedness,
> so that I may be present in a gifted way
> to you and to others at all times.

ABBREVIATIONS

used to indicate the works of Blessed Columba Marmion

L'Âme: *Le Christ Vie de l'Âme*
Soul: *Christ the Life of the Soul*

Mystéres: *Le Christ dans Ses Mystéres*
Mysteries: *Christ in his Mysteries*

Moine: *Le Christ, Idéal du Moine*
Monk: *Christ the Ideal of the Monk*

Prêtre: *Le Christ, Idéal du Prêtre*
Priest: *Christ: The Ideal of the Priest*

Sponsa Verbi (French): *Sponsa Verbi: La Vierge consacrée au Christ*
Sponsa Verbi (English): *Sponsa Verbi: The Virgin Consecrated to Christ*

L'Union: *L'Union a Dieu: D'après les Lettres de Direction
de Dom Columba Marmion*
Union: *Union with God: Letters of Spiritual Direction
by Blessed Columba Marmion*

Correspondance: *Correspondance: 1881–1923*
Letters: *The English Letters of Abbot Marmion, 1858–1923*

The quotations from the Bible were taken from
the Revised Standard Version (RSV).

CHAPTER I

Nothingness:

THE BIBLICAL AND
DOGMATIC UNDERPINNINGS

LET US FIRST ALLOW MARMION'S COMMENTA-
tors to introduce his special blend of dogmatic and spiritual
insight, before exploring the ways in which he was careful to
connect his spiritual counsels to Biblical texts and dogma. In the biography
of Marmion's spiritual son Pie de Hemptinne, Marmion was described as
having had "a rare quality: the professor of dogma had the gift to make
[others] savor the revealed truths and draw from them mystical conclusions."[1]
Indeed, Marmion so integrated dogma with spirituality that Eugene Boylan commented that Marmion's mission was to give "a perfect synthesis of
Christian dogma in its relation to the spiritual life."[2] With regard to Blessed
Columba's dogmatic approach to spiritual theology, T. O'Herlihy goes so
far as describing Marmion as "a revolutionary [who] started a new order of
theological synthesis as applied to mystical theology, which has been since
imitated by many."[3] Raymond Thibaut was Abbot Columba's secretary,
ghostwriter, and biographer; and, as such, his assessment of Columba's
dogmatic approach to spiritual direction offers invaluable insight into the
spiritual theology here reviewed. Of it, Thibaut wrote, "Direction, as he
understands and practices it, is a work of light. He lights up the path of
perfection before enlisting souls to walk in it. Darkness and error are the
first obstacles to be dispersed . . . . Dom Marmion never forgets this. By turn
of mind, by inmost conviction, he always makes his practical conclusions

---

1   Monk of Maredsous, *Une Âme Bénédictine: Dom Pie de Hemptinne*, 5th ed. (Paris:
Desclée De Brouwer, 1922), 33. Also published after Marmion's death in a revised and
expanded version as: Monk of Maredsous, *Dom Pie de Hemptinne, Moine de Maredsous:
Un Disciple de Dom Marmion*, 9th ed. (Namur, Belgium: Maredsous, 1941), 41 [my trans-
lation]. It is notable that these words were published during Marmion's own lifetime,
under his own permission.
2   Eugene Boylan, "Benedictine Influence in the Doctrine of Abbot Marmion," in
Abbot Marmion: An Irish Tribute, ed. Monks of Glenstall (Westminster, MD: Newman
Press, 1948), 54.
3   T. O'Herlihy, "Abbot Marmion as Spiritual Director," in ibid., 107.

flow from the light of his principles."[4] Let us, then, examine Marmion's principles with regard to this topic.

THE RELEVANT PRINCIPLE: TO FOLLOW CHRIST IN HIS BEING OF GRACE

At some level, you are intrigued at the idea of becoming like Jesus, though perhaps without all of the sacrifice. If you already recognize that you were made in the image of God (cf. Gen 1:27), you may have at least some vague notion that you want to embody God's attributes more perfectly, reflect his glory a little more in this world. Adding some Christian reflection to it, you may want to pattern your life on that of the Trinity by becoming a more perfect gift of self. The basic principle behind any of these points of view is to accept Christ Jesus, the Word Incarnate, as the archetype of a perfect life.

Yet we cannot conform ourselves to Christ's godly actions without the supernatural grace and gifts of the Holy Spirit to do so, and this subtlety is lost on many Christians. We must go beyond imitating Christ to releasing and reactivating the supernatural gifts he left us. In the transformation offered by the Holy Spirit, we must reveal the Kingdom of God in all its power, as Jesus did. So, the full expression of the relevant principle in Marmion's spirituality is that we must first avail ourselves of the transformative power of God before trying to imitate him in his virtues: "The imitation of Christ Jesus in His Being of grace and in His virtues is the substance of holiness for us,"[5] wrote Marmion. Given that Christ Jesus left us both an example and the supernatural means for following that example, it would be folly to attempt the former without the latter: "Some souls imagine, more or less subconsciously, that they can resemble Christ by imitating His virtues by their own efforts. This is a great illusion."[6]

---

4 Raymond Thibaut, preface to *Union with God: Letters of Spiritual Direction by Blessed Columba Marmion*, selected and annotated by Raymond Thibaut, trans. Mary St. Thomas (1834; rpt. Bethesda, MD: Zaccheus Press, 2006), xvii–xviii (hereafter *Union*).

5 Columba Marmion, *Christ the Life of the Soul*, trans. Nun of Tyburn (1925; rpt. Tacoma, WA: Angelico, 2012), 58 (hereafter *Soul*); see also Paolo Maria Gionta, *Le Virtù Teologali nel Pensiero di Dom Columba Marmion* (Roma: Edizioni Università della Santa Croce, 1998), 341.

6 Columba Marmion, *Christ: The Ideal of the Priest*, trans. Matthew Dillon (1952; rpt. San Francisco: Ignatius, 2005), 48 (hereafter *Priest*). Also see Columba Marmion, *Christ in his Mysteries*, trans. Alan Bancroft, British ed. (Leominster, UK: Gracewing, 2009), 445–50 (hereafter *Mysteries*); Marmion, *Priest*, 37–39, 299ff; Columba Marmion, *Christ the Ideal of the Monk*, trans. unknown (Ridgefield, CT: Roger A. McCaffrey, 1952), 20–22 (hereafter *Monk*).

Here is our guide's assessment of the situation:

> A man can imitate the Exemplar who is Christ in two ways. He can strive to do so by a wholly natural labor as when one imagines oneself reproducing the human ideal presented by a hero or an individual one likes or admires. There are some souls who think that is the way in which one should imitate our Lord and reproduce in us the features of His adorable person. The "imitation" of Christ that such a path leads to is an imitation conceived according to our human ideas.
>
> That is to lose sight of the fact that Christ is a divine model. His beauty and his human virtues have their roots in His divinity, and draw all their splendor from His divinity. Aided by grace, we can and assuredly ought to bring all our efforts to understanding Christ and to modeling our virtues and our actions on His; but only the Holy Spirit, "Finger of God's right hand," is capable of reproducing in us the true image of the Son — because our imitation has to be an imitation of a super-natural order.[7]

While some non-Catholics deny the supernatural effects of divine adoption, Marmion was here probably addressing a fault within his primary audience of spiritually minded Catholic men and women, rather than making an apologetic point.[8] In fact, he was addressing those Catholics who nonetheless fail to turn to God for help prior to acting. Such self-reliance, also known as Semipelagianism, is a practical refusal to have "an imitation [of Christ] of a super-natural order."[9]

In his opening chapters of *Christ the Life of the Soul*, Marmion set out to heal the deep wounds created by the confusion of this heresy. In the first chapter, he established the *objective* divine plan for divine adoption; in the third, the *subjective* principle for accepting the supernatural means for following Christ's example.[10] In this regard, Marmion was trying to recall Christians to an earlier, simpler spirituality: "[The early Christians] lived by this doctrine, *Christus . . . vita vestra* [Christ . . . your life] (cf. Col 3:4), and that

---

7 Marmion, *Mysteries*, 31.
8 On the topic of the foundations of self-reliance in today's world, see Gionta, *Le Virtù Teologali*, 111: "In fact, after centuries of anthropological philosophy, the common mentality encloses happiness within mundane horizons, holding that man is able to reach the realization of himself with his own proper forces or at least thanks to the contribution of society." My translation.
9 Marmion, *Mysteries*, 31.
10 Cf. Marmion, *Soul*, 21ff., 58.

is why their spiritual life was at once so simple and bore so much fruit."[11] As for those who fail to accept the supernatural means for following each of Christ's virtues, Marmion had this to say: "For years, their lives have been as it were cramped, they have been often depressed, hardly ever contented, forever finding new difficulties in the spiritual life."[12] Marmion continued by explaining that a transformation occurs upon overcoming self-reliance:

> Then one day God gives them the grace of understanding that Christ is our All, that He is the Alpha and Omega (Apoc 22:13), that out of Him we have nothing, that in Him we have everything, for everything is summed up in Him. From that moment all is, as it were, changed for these souls; their difficulties vanish like the shades of night before the rising sun. As soon as Our Lord, the true Sun of our lives, Sol justitiae [Sun of justice] (Mal 4:2), fully illumines these souls, they unfold, mount upwards and bear much fruit of holiness.[13]

In sum, "It is in Christ, and no longer in self, that these souls seek the source of their holiness,"[14] for they surrender to God's grace and God's plans for them.

Now, the necessary condition for accepting Christ as our all is to accept our insufficiency. As long as we try to solve our problems by own strength, we do not trust that "we can find that strength in the grace that the satisfactions of Christ have merited for us."[15] The key to the process is to look to God for help:

> What, then, can prevent us from becoming saints? If, on the day of the Last Judgment God asks us: "Why have you not reached the height of your vocation? Why have you not attained the holiness to which I was calling you?" we shall not be able to reply: "Lord, my weakness was too great, the difficulties were insurmountable, the trials beyond my strength." God would reply to us: "On your own, it is but too true that you could do nothing. But I have given you my Son; in Him you lacked nothing of what was necessary for you. His grace is all-powerful, and through Him you could have united yourself to the very source of life."[16]

---

11 Ibid., 43.
12 Ibid., 44.
13 Ibid.; Columba Marmion, Le Christ Vie de l'Âme, 17e mille ed. (Paris: Desclée, De Brouwer, 1919), 42 (hereafter L'Âme).
14 Marmion, Soul, 44.
15 Ibid., 58.
16 Marmion, Mysteries, 456.

Sanctity, in other words, has nothing to do with merely following Christ's example. For Marmion, "ALL OUR SANCTITY CONSISTS IN BECOM- ING BY GRACE WHAT JESUS CHRIST IS BY NATURE, THE CHILD OF GOD."[17] In turning your insufficiency over to God, you accept to be overwhelmed by the power of God.

Finally, "[to imitate] Christ Jesus in His Being of grace" requires that the Bible be the primary source text for the investigation and Christ be the archetype for the resulting spiritual disposition. Let us begin with our review of Jesus's words on this topic with a selection of his high priestly prayer to the Father in the Gospel of John:

> I have manifested thy name to the men whom thou gavest me out of the world: thine they were, and thou gavest them to me, and they have kept thy word. Now they know that everything that thou hast given me is from thee; for I have given them the words which thou gavest me, and they have received them and know in truth that I came from thee; and they have believed that thou didst send me. (Jn 17:6 – 8)

As a gloss on this passage, Marmion taught, "The Word Incarnate insists that we recognize that he receives everything from His Father; so often has He repeated it to His disciples! Our declaring it with Him is therefore pleasing to Him."[18] Jesus was not always as explicit, but Jesus did repeatedly make statements similar to the content above. Abbot Columba offered an array of proof texts for this point of view. In *Christ in His Mysteries*, he cited John 6:57, "As the living Father sent me, and I live because of the Father"; and John 5:19, "Truly, I say to you, the Son can do nothing of his own accord, but only what he sees the Father doing; for whatever He does, the Son does likewise."[19] In *Christ the Ideal of the Monk*, he cited: John 17:7, "Now they know that every- thing that thou hast given me is from thee"; John 7:16, "My teaching is not mine but his who sent me"; John 8:28b, "I do nothing on my own authority but speak thus as the Father taught me"; John 8:50, "Yet I do not seek my own glory; there is One who seeks it and he will be the judge"; John 14:10, "The words that I say to you I do not speak on my own authority; but the Father who dwells in me does his works"; and John 17:10, "All mine are thine,

---

17 Columba Marmion, "Retreat at Hayward's Heath, August 1905," quoted in M. M. Philipon, *The Spiritual Doctrine of Dom Marmion*, trans. Matthew Dillon (London: Sands & Co., 1956), 98.
18 Marmion, *Mysteries*, 52.
19 Ibid., 47–48.

and thine are mine; and I am glorified in them."[20] Marmion's attentiveness to Jesus's words about his relation to his heavenly Father had a two-fold purpose: to demonstrate a Biblical warrant for Christ's self-understanding about his graces and, more importantly, to indicate the ways in which Jesus modeled for us the need to receive everything from the Father and attribute everything to the Father. In requesting the graces necessary for imitating Christ's actions and in acknowledging our graces, we allow divine gifts to flow freely. We then begin to follow Jesus in the fullest measure.[21]

At this point, it may help to pause from the theory to apply this principle and experience its effects firsthand. Try these prayers both now and in your daily life: *Father, I know that everything in your Son came from you, please send me, your adopted son / daughter in Christ, the help to [insert your petition].* Alternatively, *Lord Jesus, I am nothing without you, please work through me to [insert your petition].* Finally, *Come Holy Spirit, work through me to [insert your petition].* It's great to offer these prayers in general ways, such as to be a better Christian or to be a good parent, but try to apply them to something very specific, such as "speak through me during this important upcoming conversation." These prayers can lead you into privileged moments where God's grace and the gifts of the Holy Spirit can be easily discernible, even, in a sense, palpable. If I could offer you one takeaway only, it would be to incorporate prayers such as these into your daily life.

THEOLOGICAL REFLECTIONS

How, then, is the Word the archetype for attributing our gifts to the Father? In *Christ in His Mysteries*, Marmion discussed three "functions" for the Second Person of the Trinity, and those functions will serve well to organize our initial theological and Christological responses to this question.[22]

The first function identifies that the Word receives all from the Father, the Fountainhead of the Trinity, as from a Source.[23] Marmion explained it thus:

> When we say of a man that he is someone's son, we establish two
> different things: his individual human nature and his position
> of being a son. It is not so within the Trinity. The Son is really
> and truly identified with the Divine nature (which He possesses
> in an indivisible way with the Father and the Holy Spirit). What

---

20 Marmion, *Monk*, 203–4.
21 Cf. Marmion, *Soul*, 58.
22 Cf. Marmion, *Mysteries*, 47ff.
23 Cf. ibid., 47.

distinguishes Him from the Person of the Father, what properly speaking constitutes His Personality, is not being God, but being Son. And, as a Divine Person, He is nothing but the Son, entirely the Son, and that uniquely. He is (if I may express it thus) a Living Sonship; He is "oriented" entirely towards the Father.

And in the same way that the Father proclaims His ineffable fecundity — "You are my Son; I have begotten you this day" (Jn 6:58), the Son knows that He is Son, that the Father is the Fountainhead, His Source, and that everything comes from the Father. There (if one may put it like this) is the first "function" of the Word.[24]

In saying, "The Son is really and truly identified with the Divine Nature (which He possesses in an indivisible way with the Father and the Holy Spirit),"[25] Marmion excluded any Subordinationalist or Arian misunderstandings about the Word being less than the Father in his divine Person.[26]

From that foundation, Marmion discussed the Word's relation of Sonship as having the trait of having received everything from the Father. In *Christ the Ideal of the Monk*, Marmion described this relation of filiation in these words that correspond well with the remaining content on this function in *Christ in His Mysteries*:

> The Son, even as God, holds everything from the Father. *Omnia quae dedisti mihi abs te sunt* [Now they know that everything that thou hast given me is from thee] (Jn 17:7). The Son, in beholding His Father, can say to him that all that He is, all that He has, all that He knows, is from His Father because He proceeds from Him, without there being between the First and Second Person, either inequality, or inferiority, or succession of time. This is one side of the mystery.[27]

So, while Marmion excluded from the Second Person of the Trinity any causal dependency on the Father,[28] he saw the relationship between the

---

24 Ibid.
25 Ibid.
26 On Arian misunderstandings, see Thomas Aquinas, *Summa Theologica*, trans. English Dominican Province (Notre Dame, IN: Ave Maria, 1948), iii, q. 16, a. 8: "Now the Arian heretics said that Christ was a creature and less than the Father, not only in his human nature, but even in His Divine Person."
27 Marmion, *Monk*, 203. For similar thoughts, see Marmion, *Mysteries*, 47–49.
28 About causal dependency, see *Summa Theologica*, i, q. 33, a. 1, ad 1: "The Greeks use the words cause and principle indifferently, when speaking of God; whereas the Latin Doctors do not use the word cause, but only principle. The reason is because principle is a wider term than cause; as cause is more common than element. For the first term

Father and the Son as one in which "the Son, even as God, holds everything from the Father."[29]

These reflections have an application in our spiritual lives. If we are to reflect the image of the Word, we too must express our gratitude for having received everything.

According to Marmion, "The second 'function' of the Word is to be, as Saint Paul says, the image of the Father: 'The image of the invisible God' (Col 1:15)";[30] it can be summarized in these words: "The Eternal Father, in beholding His Son, sees in Him the perfect reproduction of His own divine attributes. The Son reflects perfectly, as in a 'spotless mirror' (Ws 7:26), all that the Father gives Him."[31] This function complements the first by highlighting the other side of the mystery, i.e., of the substantial equality the Son has always shared with the Father and the Holy Spirit. Together these two functions note that the Word is both full of divine Being and also in relation to the Father (and the Holy Spirit).

CHRISTOLOGICAL REFLECTIONS

The other side of this second function of the Word reflects upon the Word Incarnate's role of being the Image of God for us: "Therefore the Word, when become incarnate, reveals the Father to us, manifests God to us."[32] In moving the discussion from the inner life of the Trinity to the mission of the Second Person, Marmion transitioned into Christological reflections. The starting point for these Christological reflections is the way in which Jesus offers to the world a perfect, unmarred image of the Father: "Christ translates all the perfections of the Father into human actions, into language accessible to our poor minds. Let us always remember [these] words: 'Whoever sees me, sees my Father' (Jn 14:9)."[33] This function, then, is in part a reflection on Jesus's divine nature.

The third function is, "The Word is to relate Himself to the Father by love."[34] By way of this function, Marmion explained that the Incarnate

---

of a thing, as also the first part, is called the principle, but not the cause. Now the wider a term is the more suitable it is to use as regards God (q. 13, a. 11), because the more special terms are, the more they determine the mode adapted to the creature."
29   Marmion, Monk, 203.
30   Marmion, Mysteries, 49.
31   Ibid.
32   Ibid.
33   Ibid., 50.
34   Ibid., 51.

Word accepted all of his sufferings and humiliations out of love for the Father's will. [35] This function brings into account Christ's human nature and is similar to Aquinas's explanation of Christ's threefold subjection to the Father: as possessing a degree of goodness inferior to the Father, as having become a servant who is subservient to the Father, and as one obedient to the Father. [36] The hymn in Philippians best expresses these truths:

> Have this mind among yourselves, which was in Christ Jesus, who, though he was in the form of God, did not count equality with God a thing to be grasped, but emptied himself, taking the form of a servant, being born in the likeness of men. And being found in human form he humbled himself and became obedient unto death, even death on a cross. Therefore God has highly exalted him and bestowed on him the name which is above every name, that at the name of Jesus every knee should bow, in heaven and on earth and under the earth, and every tongue confess that Jesus Christ is Lord, to the glory of God the Father. (Phil 2:5–11)

Despite having had the plenitude of Divinity, Jesus Christ, true God and true man, acted in humble, human fashion. In this regard, Marmion taught that Christ came above all to teach men self-effacement rather than heroic virtues. To be more precise, perhaps Jesus came to teach men self-effacement as a "heroic virtue," i.e., as the heroic humility that leads to accepting the pain of life manfully without using it as a pretext for improper behavior. [37]

How did Marmion understand Christ's self-effacement? Marmion's restatement of this hymn answers that question, for he replaced the words "taking the form of a servant" and "being born in the likeness of men" (Phil 2:5–11) with an emphasis on being nothing: "Because this Son, though wholly God, brought Himself down to nothing so as to sanctify His mystical body: 'Therefore God . . . has exalted Him' (cf. Phil 2:9)." [38] To understand this choice, let us consider another place in which Marmion used nothingness to express the way in which Jesus receives everything from the Father. The following sentence is from Bossuet's pen, but Marmion made it his own by quoting it: "Nothing of Himself, nothing for Himself, [Jesus] only does

---

35   Ibid., 51; cf. ibid., 51ff.
36   For Aquinas's explanation of Christ's threefold subjection to the Father, see *Summa Theologica*, iii, q. 20, a. 1.
37   On Christ coming to teach humility and self-effacement as "heroic" virtues, see Marmion, *Monk*, 211–12.
38   Marmion, *Mysteries*, 465.

that which the Father reveals to Him, and all that the Father does, He also does, but yet He does it in a like manner, with the same dignity and the same perfection, because He is the Sole-begotten Son, God of God, perfect God of perfect God."[39] From these two instances alone, it is clear Marmion saw Jesus as the archetype for accepting our nothingness.

But what did Marmion mean by being nothing? Also, what did Christ mean in saying, "Truly, I say to you, the Son can do nothing [ουδεν] of his own accord [αφ'εαυτου — literally, 'by himself'] but only what he sees the Father doing; for whatever he does, that the Son does likewise" (Jn 5:19) and "I can do nothing [ουδεν] on my own authority [απ' εμαυτου — literally, 'by myself']" (Jn 5:30)?[40] To solve this question, we must understand the Christological principles that led to Christ's perfect humility. While contemporary Christians are accustomed to thinking of Christ as humble, it must be noted that humility is a revealed attribute of God. Whereas strength is an expansive attribute that finds its pure perfection in the Almighty, a humble God seems, at first sight, to be a contradiction in terms, for humility is by definition restrictive. Indeed, Christ's humility was probably a mixed perfection, a type of perfection that occurs among men rather than in pure form in God.[41] Serge-Thomas Bonino argues this point in saying that to be humble is to be subservient and to be subservient is not a divine attribute.[42] We Christians must strive to understand the way in which this exceedingly Christian virtue was modeled for us in Christ, so as to accept divine friendship and produce, via grace, supernatural virtue.

For answers in seeking this virtue, we turn to two of Marmion's Christological arguments: first, an analysis of Christ's virtue of religion; and second, an analysis of the operation of grace in Christ, in whom all operations proper to man are found.[43]

---

39 Bossuet, *Meditations on the Holy Gospel* (NP: Publisher Unknown, Date Unknown), quoted in Marmion, *Monk*, 97.

40 Cf. Max Zerwick and Mary Grosvenor, *A Grammatical Analysis of the Greek New Testament*, 5th ed. (Roma: Editrice Pontificio Istituto Biblico, 1996), 300–301, John 5:19, 30; Eberhard Nestle and Erwin Nestle, *Novum Testamentum Graece*, ed. Barbara Aland et al., 28th revised ed. (Stuttgart: Deutche Bibelgesellshaft, 2012), 308–9; John 5:19, 30.

41 Cf. James Fox, "Divine Attributes," in *The Catholic Encyclopedia*, vol. 2 (New York: Robert Appleton Company, 1907), last accessed October 23, 2014. http://www.newadvent.org/cathen/02062e.htm.

42 Cf. Serge-Thomas Bonino, "De Deo Uno" (lecture, Pontifical University of Saint Thomas in Urbe, Rome, 2014).

43 In *Sponsa Verbi*, Marmion made an unsuccessful Christological argument for Christ's attribution of everything to God. The second chapter of *Sponsa Verbi* was dedicated to a way in which the human nature in Christ is the spouse of the Word; in it Marmion

Marmion's Understanding of Christ's Virtue of Religion

Let us consider the primary objection to the mystical usage of nothingness that this book proposes. When a person renders praise to God, either in an unformed way or in ways revealed by God, we say that he is exercising the virtue of religion. Since man, ignorant of revelation, can offer an unformed (or misinformed) praise of God, to analyze Christ's virtue of religion gives some insights into whether the acceptance of our nothingness could be purely the result of a natural awareness of God's greatness. In other words, do we really need a Catholic theology of grace to understand phrases such as "I am nothing" in relation to God? This exploration also takes us into the interesting field of speculations on Christ's psychological feeling of His nothingness in the light of the Father's majesty and offers us insights into the ways in which the felt presence of God can provoke this expression of humility.

---

argued: "Having then nothing, belonging to nothing, the human nature in Jesus 'adhered to the Word with all its powers'"; Columba Marmion, *Sponsa Verbi: The Virgin Consecrated to Christ*, trans. Francis Izard (Saint Louis, MO: B. Herder, 1925), 27. In Marmion's reflections, the human nature of Christ "acts" in a personified way in the drama of receiving the Word. Marmion exclaimed, "What an absolute possession of the humanity by the Word, yet also what an absolute surrender [*donation plénière*] of itself by the human nature, and in its free acts, what a transport of love towards the Word!" Marmion, *Sponsa Verbi*, 28. That argumentation is a bit forced, for the human nature of Christ could neither have preceded the Incarnation nor have chosen to accept the Word. Yet, while Marmion was there guilty of having projected attributes back onto a fabricated ontological principle of a personified human nature that accepted, so to speak, the Word, we can still appreciate his desire to highlight our need, as creatures, to accept the Word; cf. *Sponsa Verbi*, 31–32. We can also learn from his mistakes. Based upon the clarification in Marmion, *Sponsa Verbi*, 32, n. 1, this faulty principle seems to have been the basis for Marmion's easily misunderstood recommendation that we should sublimate our personality into Christ. As the human nature of Christ gained, so to speak, its personality from the Word by submitting to it, so too we purportedly gain by sublimating our personality, as evidenced by these words from his spiritual direction: "You are called to be united to the Word as His S. Humanity, that is to say, in deep adoration and annihilation of your personality — His humanity had no human personality — and consequently, all its powers belonged immediately & exclusively to the Word"; Columba Marmion, "Letter to a Nun, 27 September 1920," in *The English Letters of Abbot Marmion, 1858–1923*, vol. 4 of *Benedictine Studies* (Baltimore, MD: Helicon, 1962), 206 (hereafter *Letters*). While some of this counsel may be salvageable based upon other principles of asceticism associated with the term nothingness, it certainly must be purified of any extreme tendency to deny completely a person's God-given personality. Elsewhere in Marmion's writings, it is clear that he does not negate a person's personality, in the psychological sense of the word: "There are no two of you exactly the same. And so it is with prayer: there are no two souls who have quite the same way of praying or talking with God. One can give, therefore, only a general outline of procedure in this matter of prayer. God adapts His approach to the individual character"; Marmion, "Conference, Maredret, May 9, 1911," quoted in Philipon, *Spiritual Doctrine*, 164.

Undoubtedly, Jesus offered to the Father a religious response unique among men.[44] Here is Marmion's take on it:

> This intimate contemplation produced in our divine Master the constant need to abase [*s'anéantir*] Himself before the infinite majesty. The activity of His soul consisted principally in ineffable adoration. "He that sent Me is with Me, and He hath not left Me alone" (Jn 8:29). These were the sentiments of Jesus, and this constant contact with the divinity not only maintained His soul in an attitude of profound abasement [*abaissement*] but served also to arouse in Him a thirst to sacrifice Himself for each one of us.[45]

For Marmion, abasement (at times literally "self-naughting" in the original French) and self-offering were the only appropriate responses to the knowledge Jesus had of the Father's role in his life. In other words, Christ, in beholding the Beatific Vision as one fully human, felt a sense of his nothingness, even though he was constantly cognizant of the Father's and the Spirit's love for him, the Incarnate Word, as one who is also fully God.

We too can have this sense of nothingness when God draws close to us, for God's Goodness and Perfection are simply so superior that human nature feels small in comparison. How reassuring this insight is! Since God's presence can indeed weigh heavy on us, this insight encourages us to accept such experiences with greater confidence.

The above passage also specifically demonstrates that Marmion understood Jesus as having had the obligation, common to men, to exercise the virtue of religion. When read independently of the rest of Marmion's theology, the above statement could give the impression that anyone could engage in this self-naughting in comparison to God.

Later in this text, Marmion explained that we, adopted children of God, must also exercise the virtue of religion as a way of giving God proper sovereignty: "He came into this world to teach men to glorify the Father and to acknowledge His sovereignty. If He wishes that they render to Caesar the things that are Caesar's, it is in order to establish more forcibly the rights of the Most High: 'Render to God the things that are God's' (Mk 7:17)."[46] We creatures owe much to God. Marmion, quite surprisingly, held that our

---

44 Cf. Marmion, *Priest*, 151.
45 Ibid., 152–53; Columba Marmion, *Le Christ, Idéal du Prêtre*, 11e mille ed. (Namur: Abbaye de Maredsous, 1952), 141 (hereafter *Prêtre*).
46 Marmion, *Priest*, 154.

natural dependence on God could serve as enough justification for "self-abasement [*abaissement*] . . . as far as annihilation [*jusqu'à l'anéantissement*]."[47] Since we were created *ex nihilo* and since we cannot add to God's being or goodness, philosophy or natural theology could, strictly speaking, label man as nothing in such reflections — even though man is good, created in God's image. Yet this feeling of our nothingness is just the beginning of a reality that has a fuller sense under the content of revelation.

Let us here pause a moment to bring this investigation into the virtue of natural religion into contact with contemporary American culture. Leonard Cohen's secular "Hallelujah," covered by many artists, has become a cultural icon.[48] Why does this "broken hallelujah" resonate so much with the soul of our time? The song's musicality and poetry are highly attractive, especially in a subdued setting at the end of a day, but it is probably the secular medium of this song that speaks broadly in a pluri-religious environment. The Jewish roots of the song are evident, and yet it is re-sung by so many diverse voices as a secular ode to an unknown or estranged God: "If there is a God above." It expresses a need, seemingly both for believers and non-believers. If a non-believer, who is "spiritual-but-not-religious," were to sing this song to an indeterminate God, then it would express the natural virtue of religion (using the term decoupled of any allegiances or obligations). Even if this interpretation of how some people may sing this song were askew in some way in this particular instance, to think of a secular hallelujah gives us a sense of what natural religious expression may look like these days. Bringing this aside back to our topic, could someone who is spiritual-but-not-religious say he is nothing without God? Sure. You can also tell me the view from America's highest monument is great; I agree, but it's not nearly as great as the view from the plane. (Also, I don't like swaying in the trams as they navigate the parabola.)

It must be acknowledged that Marmion himself did not always make fine distinctions when he spoke of his own nothingness. While many of his comments about his nothingness have an explicit or implied fuller sense of this term, others were lacking that clarity. For example, in *Christ the Ideal of the Priest*, he simply stated, "The virtue of religion prostrates us before

---

47   Marmion, *Soul*, 245; Marmion, *L'Âme*, 383.
48   See Leonard Cohen, "Halleluiah," last accessed August 12, 2020. https://www.leonard-cohen.com/video/hallelujah; Rolling Stone, "How Leonard Cohen's 'Hallelujah' Brilliantly Mingled Sex, Religion," last accessed August 12, 2020. https://www.rollingstone.com/music/music-news/how-leonard-cohens-hallelujah-brilliantly-mingled-sex-religion-194516/.

[God's] infinite majesty. It makes us say: 'You, my God, are everything, and I am nothing.'"[49] Yet he clarified that this statement cannot express a mere "passing sentiment" but must express a disposition or virtue (i.e., a habit).[50] Central to the virtue of religion, as its fundamental act, is adoration, which he defined as "the entire submission of man, who thus acknowledges his nothingness before the absolute sovereignty of God."[51] He continued this definition thus: "Adoration means looking at God and humbling oneself."[52] These phrases, however, especially in English, could belong to any religion and could be understood in a philosophical or natural way. Since God upholds our being, we creatures are dependent on Him, are nothing without Him; yet Marmion's relationship with God and expressions about it went beyond that limited sense of the term.

Considering Marmion had in previous paragraphs been discussing the Christian expression of the virtue of religion, he may indeed have intended these statements to include some acknowledgement of the Christian anthropology.[53] Is the disposition of nothingness merely part of the natural virtue of religion? In the third part of the chapter on humility in *Christ the Ideal of the Monk*, Marmion outlined more specifically the way by which the virtue of religion alone, moved by a profound reverence, should provoke a sense of abasement, annihilation of self, and nothingness; to that argument, however, he added the additional attribute of crediting our graces and intrinsic justification to God.[54] So, Marmion indeed had more than abasement before divine majesty in mind when thinking of the principles underpinning his words about nothingness. In this regard, it is worth noting that Marmion stressed the necessity of acknowledging our supernatural dependence: "In the supernatural order our dependence is no less absolute. 'Without Me you can do nothing'

---

49 Marmion, *Priest*, 148.
50 Ibid.
51 Ibid., 150.
52 Ibid.
53 Cf. ibid., 147–48.
54 Cf. Marmion, *Monk*, 223–28. Pages 227–28 build upon previous supernatural references: "The Holy Spirit harmonises the two sentiments, the one of fear, the other of piety; and their accord causes the soul, selfless as it is before God and the neighbor, to be yet assured of the divine grace that comes to it through Christ, in Whom it finds everything which of itself it lacks. This invincible assurance fills it with the very power of God, and thus renders its life altogether fruitful. Knowing that without Christ it can do nothing, *sine me nihil potestis facere* (Jn 15:5), it knows with the same certainty that it can do all things as soon as it leans upon Him: *Omnia possum in eo qui me confortat* (Phil 4:13). Humility is the secret of its strength and vitality."

(Jn 15:5)."[55] He was also clear about the way in which our relationship with God must indeed go beyond natural religion:

> We shall therefore no longer have only the simple relationship of creatures with God; we are not only to unite ourselves with Him through homage and the duties of a natural religion founded on our position as created beings. With nothing of that relationship being destroyed, and no part of those duties being diminished, we shall enter into a more intimate relationship with God, that of children, one that will create in us special duties towards a Father whom we love: "Be imitators of God, as very dear children" (Eph 5:1–2). A relationship and duties wholly super-natural, these, because they go beyond what is required of our nature, beyond our nature's rights; and because it is only the grace of Jesus that makes them possible.[56]

For Marmion, therefore, a relationship with God should never be merely natural. Both Christ and each Christian (as an adopted son or daughter of God through grace) are always in supernatural relationship with the Father. When a Christian accepts being nothing, he makes such a disavowal of his or her own supernatural merits within the larger context of needing to attribute his or her graces to God. Therefore, the natural virtue of religion, founded only upon a sense of our nothingness, fails to found the fuller acceptance of it. Furthermore, our Christian virtue of religion, to be discussed soon, must account for any revelation from God on this matter.

Marmion's Understanding of Grace in Christ

In order to understand the full dogmatic weight behind the mystical shorthand term of nothingness, we must try to grasp all of the mystical principles related to it, including the erudite one that Christ himself had during his life on earth the same graces we can have. Unfortunately, with reference to Christ, Marmion did not elaborate on such a principle, beyond citing the Biblical warrant for it. He did, however, indicate a theology of grace in Christ. That this point of view was operative for Marmion is not surprising, given two facts: first, Catholic theologians had nearly universally accepted such a point of view;[57] and second, Marmion had studied his

---

55   Marmion, Priest, 275.
56   Marmion, Mysteries, 449.
57   Cf. F. Ocáriz, L. F. Mateo Seco, & J. A. Riestra et al., The Mystery of Jesus Christ: A Christology and Soteriology Textbook, trans. Michael Adams and James Gavigan (Dublin: Four Courts, 1994), 182.

dogmatic theology under Father Francis Satolli, "a leading Thomist scholar, who encouraged the young Marmion to throw himself into a study of the Summa of Saint Thomas Aquinas."[58] In place of arguments by Marmion in this regard, one proof text and two references suffice as evidence for it. For example, Marmion wrote, "The humanity of Jesus also in its incomparable dignity received from the Father all that it is; an inexhaustible effusion of divine life flowed constantly from the bosom of the Father to Jesus, by virtue of which He possessed in all plenitude sanctifying grace, infused charity, the virtues, and the gifts of the Spirit."[59] Unfortunately, Marmion offered little else about a theology of grace in Christ beyond these passing acknowledgments of it. These references, though, are sufficient to prove he accepted the common theology of grace in Christ.

Marmion also acknowledged that Christ needed to possess those graces so as to bestow them on us. This was clear from his rephrasing of Philippians 2:5-7, "This Son, though wholly God, brought Himself down to nothing so as to sanctify His mystical body."[60] This is an application of Thomas Aquinas's (and others') view of the *gratia capitis* ("the grace of the head"), which states that the mystical Body of Christ, the Church, has received its graces from the fullness of grace possessed by its Head, Christ.[61] It is an explanation of John 1:14, 16: "And the Word became flesh and dwelt among us, full of grace and truth; we have beheld his glory, glory as of the Son from the Father. . . . And from his fulness have we all received, grace upon grace." So Christ, in Marmion's view, came not merely to give the virtue of religion as a man but to bestow, from His fullness of grace, supernatural sanctification upon us. Christ, then, is indeed the archetype of how humanity must understand sanctification as a gift. He became nothing, in

---

58 Mark Tierney, Blessed Columba Marmion: A Short Biography (Blackrock: Columba Press, 2000), 21; for Saint Thomas's treatment of the subject, see Aquinas, Summa Theologica, iii, q. 7-8, p. 2059ff.

59 Marmion, Priest, 243; for similar ideas, see: Marmion, Soul, 113, 121.

60 Marmion, Mysteries, 465; the text of Marmion, Mysteries, 449, examined on the previous page, is another proof text: "It is only the grace of Jesus that makes [our supernatural relation and duties] possible."

61 For a clear example of Marmion's acceptance of the *gratia capitis*, see Marmion, Soul, 69 (quoted below on 106-7) and Marmion, Mysteries, 99: "There is not one grace that has not been paid for by the love and blood of Jesus." In this regard, Marmion followed the *gratia capitis* of Summa Theologica, iii, q. 8 (entitled, "Of the grace of Christ, as He is the Head of the Church"), 2069ff. For a detailed historical account of this theology, see Ocáriz, The Mystery of Jesus Christ, 175-94, esp. 184ff. For a detailed assessment of Marmion's use of the *gratia capitis*, see Gionta, Le Virtù Teologali, 58ff., esp. 60ff., 246-48.

a mystical shorthand and hyperbolic manner of speaking (cf. Phil 2:9), so that we might receive grace.[62] He became nothing so we might learn how properly to attribute our graces to God by accepting our own nothingness with regard to divine merits.

REFLECTIONS ON CHRISTIAN ANTHROPOLOGY

If you were lost like last year's Easter egg in the last section, you can rejoice that the hardest parts of the dogmatic theology are now over and that this study becomes easier now that we turn to Saint Paul's teaching about our dependence on God for supernatural power. Marmion expressed the link between his theological reflections and his reflections on Christian anthropology with the following words:

> In a very real, a very true sense, we are divinely begotten by grace. With the Word, we can say: "O Father, I am your son, I have come forth from you." The Word says this necessarily, by right, He being of His essence God's only Son. But we — we can only say it through grace, in our capacity of adopted children. The Word says it from all eternity; but we say it in the sphere of time, though the decree of that destiny is eternal. For the Word, what He says indicates no more than a relation of origin with the Father. For us, there is added a relation of dependence. But for us, as for Him, it is a true childship; we are, by grace, God's children. The Father wills that, despite our unworthiness, we give Him the name of "Father": "Because you are sons, God has sent the Spirit of His Son into our hearts, crying 'Abba, Father'" (Gal 4:6).[63]

In truth, it is only with Jesus that we dare to say, "Our Father," and we only follow Jesus's example of sonship in analogous or adopted ways.

The Biblical data for this section come from the works of Saints Peter and Paul on grace. Let us first hear from Saint Peter:

> His divine power has granted to us all things that pertain to life and godliness, through the knowledge of him who called us to his own glory and excellence, by which he has granted to us his precious and very great promises, that through these you may escape from corruption that is in the world because of passion, and become partakers of the divine nature. (2 Pt 1:3–4)

---

62 Cf. Marmion, *Mysteries*, 465.
63 Marmion, *Mysteries*, 54.

THE GRACE OF "NOTHINGNESS"

In sum, when we allow God's power to be at work in us, we allow his glory and goodness to become evident in our lives, even to the point of showing forth godliness.

Saint Paul reflected further on the topic of God's power at work within us. In the opening lines of Ephesians, he writes: "He destined us in love to be his sons through Jesus Christ, according to the purpose of his will, to the praise of his glorious grace which he freely bestowed on us in the Beloved" (Eph 1:5–6). Saint Paul also asked his disciples, "What have you that you did not receive?" (1 Cor 4:7). The Apostle himself gave various answers about his self-understanding of God's power at work in him: "I have been crucified with Christ; it is no longer I who live, but Christ who lives in me" (Gal 2:19–20); "But by the grace of God I am what I am, and his grace toward me was not in vain" (1 Cor 15:10); "Three times I besought the Lord about this, that it should leave me; but he said to me, 'My grace is sufficient for you, for my power is made perfect in weakness'" (2 Cor 12:8–9); "I can do all things in him who strengthens me" (Phil 4:13); and "Now to him who by the power at work within us is able to do far more abundantly than all that we ask or think, to him be glory in the church and in Christ Jesus to all generations, for ever and ever. Amen" (Eph 3:20–21).

Marmion interpreted this Biblical data with the words, "All that is good in us, all that is meritorious for eternal life comes from God through Christ: *sufficientia nostra ex Deo est* [our sufficiency is from God] (cf. 2 Cor 12:9)."[64] This line from Marmion clearly and succinctly indicates a fact seen throughout his spirituality, namely that Christ has given us the ability to cooperate with the power of God. We, in following Saint Paul's teaching on the subject, call this divine power "grace."[65]

In a beautiful passage from a letter to someone that he was accompanying spiritually, Marmion specified that a person's true richness derives from the merits of Christ working in her:

> Oh, my dear child, I would wish to engrave on your heart, in let-
> ters of gold, this truth, that no matter how great our misery, we

---

64 Marmion, *Soul*, 71; see also: Marmion, *Monk*, 222; Marmion, "Letter to a Benedictine nun of Ventor, no. 3," in *Letters*, 201; and Tierney, *Blessed Columba Marmion*, 148
on the way in which Marmion followed a classic Thomistic scheme in articulating his
Catholic understanding of the Christian anthropology.

65 Cf. *Catechism of the Catholic Church* (Washington: Libreria Editrice Vaticana, 1994),
n. 1996: "Grace is favor, the free and undeserved help that God gives us to respond
to his call to become children of God, adoptive sons, partakers of the divine nature
and of eternal life."

are infinitely rich in Jesus Christ, if we unite with Him, if we lean on Him, if we realize constantly by a firm living faith that all the value of our prayer, & of all that we do, comes from His merits in us. All this is contained in two texts: "Without me you can do nothing" (Jn 15:5). "I can do all things in Him who strengthens me" (Phil 4:13).[66]

Here Marmion expressly endorsed the Catholic view canonized at the Council of Trent that our supernatural merits are due to Christ.[67] God intrinsically transforms (justifies) us by adopting us.[68] In accepting this adopted childhood, we, according to the standard Thomistic framework followed by Marmion, receive sanctifying grace,[69] welcome the presence of the indwelling Spirit[70] (indeed, indwelling Trinity), acquire the theological virtues,[71] and infuse our natural virtues with a supernatural character aimed at higher supernatural ends.[72] Since we attribute this transformation

---

66 Marmion, "Letter to an Irish sister of Mercy, no. 3, 2 July 1896," in *Letters*, 55.
67 See Heinrich Denzinger, *Enchiridion symbolorum definitionum et declarationum de rebus fidei et morum: Compendium of Creeds, Definitions, and Declarations on Matters of Faith and Morals*, 43rd ed., Latin-English ed., ed. Peter Hünermann et al. (San Francisco: Ignatius, 2012), Council of Trent, 14th Session (1551), ch. 8, no. 1691 (quoted on 59); see also Denzinger, *Enchiridion*, Council of Trent, 6th Session (1547), can. 32, no. 1582: "If anyone says that the good works of the justified man are the gifts of God in such a way that they are not also the good merits of the justified man himself; or that by the good works he performs through the grace of God and the merits of Jesus Christ (of whom he is a living member), the justified man does not truly merit an increase of grace, eternal life, and (provided he dies in the state of grace) the attainment of this eternal life, as well as an increase of glory, let him be anathema (cf. no. 1548, 1545–50)." For additional information, see Aquinas's treatment of these topics in the *Summa Theologica*, namely, on the cause of grace: i–ii, q. 112, p. 1140ff; and on merit: i–ii, q. 114, p. 1153ff.
68 For an overview on these topics, see Joseph Pohle, "Sanctifying Grace," in *The Catholic Encyclopedia*, vol. 6 (New York, NY: Robert Appleton Company, 1909), last accessed February 26, 2015. http://www.newadvent.org/cathen/06701a.htm; Joseph Pohle, "Justification," in *The Catholic Encyclopedia*, vol. 8 (New York, NY: Robert Appleton Company, 1910), last accessed February 26, 2015. http://www.newadvent.org/cathen/08573a.htm.
69 See Aquinas, *Summa Theologica*, i–ii, q. 111, a. 1, p. 1135ff.
70 See Aquinas, *Summa Theologica*, i, q. 43, a. 3; vol. 1, pp. 220–21: "The divine person [the Holy Spirit] is fittingly sent in the sense that He exists newly in any one; and He is given as possessed by anyone; and neither of these is otherwise than in by sanctifying grace."
71 See Aquinas, *Summa Theologica*, i–ii, q. 62, 851ff; i–ii, q. 63, a. 3, vol. 2, p. 856: "Now all virtues, intellectual and moral that are acquired by our actions arise from certain natural principles pre-existing in us, as above stated (a. 1; q. 51, a. 1): instead of which natural principles, God bestows on us the theological virtues, whereby we are directed to a supernatural end, as stated (q. 62, a. 1)."
72 See Aquinas, *Summa Theologica*, i–ii, q. 63, a. 4, esp. ad 1: "Infused and acquired virtues differ not only in relation to the ultimate end, but also in relation to their

to God, we have nothing of which to boast on our own.[73] According to Marmion, when a person understands grace thoroughly, he attributes his merits to the power of God working through him, for Christ is his all. "Believe me, my dear child, Our Lord wishes to be everything for you and in you," instructed Marmion to someone he was accompanying spiritually; "That is why He allows you to be so little in yourself. Try to assimilate St Paul's magnificent theology."[74] For Marmion, therefore, Saint Paul's theology was about the ways in which Christ wants to enliven the soul supernaturally, to divinize it.

So, who are we without God? With regard to merits, it is only necessary to recall a few basic points. While a Catholic cooperates in receiving grace, thereby glorifying God in his life, through what we call merits, those graces and merits are nonetheless not purely his own. Indeed, a Christian should attribute none of his merits merely to himself, even though they are a real part of his life.[75] In interpreting Saint Benedict's lines about proper attribution to God, Marmion reinforced these points:

> Among the instruments that the Holy Legislator puts into our hands there is one which expressly concerns this necessity of referring everything, in the work of our perfection, to Divine grace: "To attribute any good one sees in oneself to God, and not to oneself; as to the evil always to impute it to oneself and recognize it as one's own" [Rule of Saint Benedict, chap. 4, no. 42–43].

> The work ended, the good achieved, St Benedict further wishes that we should refer the glory to Him without Whom we can do nothing. Those who seek God, he writes in his Prologue, are not to be puffed up by their good observance; "Knowing that

---

proper objects."

73 See Marmion, *Monk*, 222: "And after God's mercy has endowed us with this Divine gift, we cannot use it without God: it is of faith, *de fide*, that we cannot have, by ourselves, in the order of grace, one good thought meritorious for heaven. . . . As we see, all good comes from God; and if it is true that the merits of our deeds are our own, they are so because God allows us to merit." Here Marmion footnoted the 16th chapter of the 6th session of the Council of Trent (1547), can. 32: "Nevertheless, a Christian should never rely on himself or glory in himself instead of in the Lord (cf. 1 Cor 1:31; 2 Cor 10:17), whose goodness toward all men is such that he wants his own gifts to be their merits" (Denzinger, *Enchiridion*, no. 1548).

74 Marmion, "Letter to an English superioress, no. 1, 19 April 1906," in *Letters*, 125.

75 Cf. Marmion, *Union*, 59: "That you may glorify Jesus acting in you and that you may not attribute to yourself the little good that you might think you do of yourself."

the good which is in them comes not from their own power but is wrought by the Lord, they magnify the Lord Who worketh in them": *operantem in se Dominum magnificat,* "saying with the Prophet, 'Not unto us, O Lord, not unto us, but unto Thy name give the glory' (Ps 113:9)" [cf. Rule of Saint Benedict, Prologue, no. 29–30].[76]

Therefore, a Christian accredits his merits and his gifts to God, while nonetheless acknowledging his real cooperation in bringing them into reality. Furthermore, a Christian does not deny the merits of Christ at work in him.

If a Christian were to attribute all of his or her merits to Christ, then the consequence of that attribution would be that he is nothing, according to merits. If a merit were a coin, one side would say that it belongs to God, and the flip side would say that it does not belong to me. A Christian can describe himself as nothing as a shorthand way of stating the obverse (flip side) of attributing his merits to God. On this point, Marmion wrote, "Let us beseech Him to show us, in the light of His grace, that He is all and that without Him we are nothing; one ray of Divine light can do more in this way than any reasoning."[77] Let us strive to understand the obscure reality the mystic comprehends so easily by his contact with God. You and I are nothing, not in an essential sense (as in lacking being), nor in a moral sense (as in lacking any inherent goodness). You and I are nothing because neither of us can merit eternal life from our unaided, natural actions, and we cannot boast vaingloriously of God's actions in each of us. Marmion reiterated these points without flagging, because they were of great significance to him. Given the centrality of these points to the thesis of this book, it is worth emphasizing them here as well:

> There are two Divine utterances — and these two utterances are the completing of one another — which make known to us the ways of Providence as regards ourselves and in the light of which we may comprehend the wherefore of the spirit of abandonment.
>
> Christ Jesus pronounced the first of these two utterances: "Without Me, you can do nothing": *Sine me, nihil potestis facere* (Jn 15:5). We have often meditated upon these words, but it is sovereignly useful to penetrate into them anew. All the reunited effort of

---

76 Marmion, *Monk,* 132–34; cf. Benedict of Nursia, *The Rule of Saint Benedict in English 1980: In Latin and English with Notes,* ed. Timothy Fry (Collegeville, MN: Liturgical Press, 1981), chap. 4, no. 42–43; prologue, nos. 29–30.
77 Marmion, *Monk,* 244.

nature cannot produce one supernatural act, one act which has any proportion with our end, which is the beatifying Vision of the Adorable Trinity.

But God, Who accomplishes all His works with infinite wisdom, has given us, in grace, the means of realizing within ourselves His Divine designs. Without grace, which comes from God only, we are incapable of doing anything whatsoever in order to reach our supernatural end; St Paul tells us that without grace we cannot have a good thought to be counted worthy of eternal beatitude: *Non quod sufficientes simus cogitare aliquid a nobis* QUASI EX NOBIS [Not that we are sufficient of ourselves to claim anything as coming from us (2 Cor 3:5)].[78]

So we find our true sufficiency in Christ's graces when we turn to him in our nothingness.[79]

We then, like Saint Peter, give glory to God for all of the good works that he does in us:

As each has received a gift, employ it for one another, as good stewards of God's varied grace: whoever speaks, as one who utters oracles of God; whoever renders service, as one who renders it by the strength which God supplies; in order that in everything God may be glorified through Jesus Christ. To him belong glory and dominion for ever and ever. Amen. (1 Pt 4:10–11)

Since God works supernatural merits through us, may God be praised.

REFLECTIONS ON A PROPER ATTRIBUTION TO EACH PERSON OF THE BLESSED TRINITY

While completely disproportionate to the Spirit's role in producing this economy of grace, the following small mention about attribution to the Holy Spirit does at least make this study properly comprehensive, to a certain degree. According to Marmion, the Spirit unites to those who remain in a spirit of annihilation:

He is the same identical Spirit which inspired Jesus in every act and thought; and it is by union with Him that the interior of Jesus Christ is formed in our hearts. He is the *Pater pauperum*, the

---

78 Marmion, *Monk*, 374.
79 Cf. Marmion, *Mysteries*, 455–56 (quoted in part in Appendix 1).

Father of the poor [from the sequence for Pentecost], and He does not disdain to unite Himself with those who remain in adoration and a spirit of annihilation in His presence. He is the Spirit of Holy Charity; and being the same in all unites us in holy love.[80]

Just as the Holy Spirit inspired Jesus, so too he inspires and works through those who do not offer any obstacles to his work in them. So, when we follow Christ "in His Being of grace,"[81] we attribute our graces to their proper Source (the Father), Cause (Christ Jesus), and Agent (the Holy Spirit).

To follow Christ properly, we must also pray for our graces. Let us conclude this section, then, with part of Marmion's description of his prayer after Holy Communion:

> "Heavenly Father, I adore Thee, I give Thee thanks, I unite myself to Thy divine Son and, with Him, I acknowledge that all I have, all that I am, comes from Thee...."
>
> Then I unite myself to the Word and I say to Him: "O eternal Word, of myself I know nothing, I am nothing but I know by faith what Thou knowest and I can do all things in Thee." Finally, I unite myself to the Holy Spirit: "O substantial Love of the Father and the Son, I unite myself to Thee; I want to love as Thou lovest. I am a worthless creature, but graciously permit me to unite myself to Thee with my whole heart and transport me to the bosom of God."[82]

In this prayer Marmion clearly employed "being nothing" as mystical shorthand, both to highlight the need to request graces and to attribute those graces properly to each Person of the Holy Trinity.

---

80 Marmion, "Letter to an English superioress, no. 3, 5 October 1906," in *Letters*, 128–29.
81 Marmion, *Soul*, 58.
82 Marmion, *Priest*, 376–77.

CHAPTER 2

The Spiritual Setting:
THE USAGE AND CONCEPT
HISTORY OF BEING NOTHING
AND RELATED TERMS

S INCE UNDER THE GIFT OF WISDOM WE FEEL—
indeed, suffer— our nothingness as a touch from God, we need a
way to vent this feeling.[1] Over the centuries, many of the greatest
mystics have expressed it by speaking and writing about their own nothingness. Yet as it stands that statement is about as specific as saying that
master sculptors have employed chisels. The spiritual masters have devel-
oped in their ways of responding to God's grace—in their toolbox, so to
speak—in varied and subtle ways, and this chapter tracks their progress.

In order to appreciate the ways in which Marmion's thoughts on humility
connected with those of the Catholic tradition, this chapter opens with a
few preliminary thoughts from Marmion on the topic. The second section
then reviews key authors in the Catholic tradition on the topic. It serves as
a content history for the phrase "being nothing," showing that mystics have
become more confident and refined in speaking in this way as dogmatic
thought gave them clearer license to do so. To be clear, though, this term
is not something inferred from speculative thought. Since it replaced older
expressions of the same sort, it was clearly a practical *desideratum* employed
to express the self-knowledge gained from experience.

Catholic mystics have also employed various other terms associated with
nothingness: to be worth nothing, to be unworthy, to want to possess nothing (except as God wills), to want nothing (except as God wills), to refuse

---

1   Cf. Aquinas, *Summa Theologica*, ii–ii, q. 45, a. 2; vol. 3, 1374–75: "Accordingly it
belongs to the wisdom that is an intellectual activity to pronounce right judgment about
Divine things after reason has made its inquiry, but it belongs to wisdom as a gift of
the Holy Ghost to judge aright about them on account of connaturality with them:
thus Dionysius says (Div. Nom. ii), 'that Hierotheus is perfect in Divine things for he
not only learns, but is patient of Divine things.' Now this sympathy or connaturality
for Divine things is the result of charity, which unites us to God, according to 1 Cor.
6:17: 'He who is joined to the Lord, is one spirit.'"

nothing (of proper requests), etc. It is helpful to understand these terms properly. Are some of them interchangeable? When distinct, are some of them able to be categorized together? Are they interrelated? These are the necessary questions analyzed in the opening of the second section. Think of this chapter as a primer on the various types of chisels of the trade; the next, as a primer on the techniques to apply with them. Since few mystics have defined their terms, Marmion's combination of dogmatic and spiritual theology clarifies these ways of speaking, their interrelation, and their effects in spirituality.

NOTHINGNESS: SOME PRELIMINARY THOUGHTS FROM BLESSED COLUMBA

Is there anything more elusive than true humility? It cannot be won or caught. Any sense of achieving it would destroy it. Yet it can sometimes be recognized, and false imitations of it can certainly be perceived. It can even be described, so we turn to the saints to teach us its practice. Two of the great teachers in this regard were Saint John Cassian and Saint Benedict. [2] Marmion followed the two of them in making humility central to the practical aspects of spirituality: "I simply make Our Lord, & St Paul, & St Benedict speak; & explain their doctrine." [3] Given Saint Benedict's importance to Marmion, let us first orient ourselves with Abbot Columba's interpretation of Saint Benedict, before going into a more complete usage and concept history of other authors cited by Marmion on this topic.

Marmion judged the seventh step of humility in the *Rule of Saint Benedict* to express the "summit" of the virtue. [4] It reads:

> The seventh step of humility is that a man not only admits with his tongue but is also convinced in his heart that he is inferior to all and of less value, humbling himself and saying with the Prophet: I am truly a worm, not a man, scorned by men and despised by the people (Ps 21[22]:7). I was exalted, then I was humbled and overwhelmed with confusion (Ps 87[88]:16). And again, it is a blessing that you have humbled me so that I can learn your commandments (Ps 118[119]:71, 73). [5]

2   Cf. Benedict of Nursia, *The Rule of St. Benedict*, chap. 7; John Cassian, *The Institutes*, vol. 58 of *The Works of the Fathers in Translation*, trans. Boniface Ramsey (New York, NY: Newman Press, 2000), bk. 4, chap. xxxix, no. 2.
3   Marmion, "To a bishop friend, no. 19, 6 December 1919," in *Letters*, 46.
4   Marmion, *Monk*, 234.
5   Benedict of Nursia, *The Rule of St. Benedict*, chap. 7, nos. 51–54.

Saint Benedict here presented two aspects of his humility: first, he employed a Biblical hyperbole about his value; and second, he judged himself inferior to others. Let us follow Marmion's ways of unpacking these ideas.

Nothingness: An Aid to Humility, With Regard to God

Let us first consider Marmion's interpretation of the seventh step of humility with regard to our value before God. "May God deign to allow us to rest a moment, at least in thought and desire, on the sublime summit towards which St Benedict has traced the path and marked the stages!" wrote Marmion. "Thus beholding our ideal, let us be convinced of the truth of our nothingness [*de notre néant*] and of the essential and constant need we have of help from above,"[6] he continued. Here Marmion directly connects his phrase of being nothing with Saint Benedict's phrase of being a worm. Is acknowledging ourselves as nothing equivalent to stating we are worms? Marmion's term was both the contemporary equivalent of Saint Benedict's term and a superior one. Although Saint Benedict's term expressed the same feeling in a similarly hyperbolic way, Marmion's term was more exact, for it corresponded with centuries' worth of theological reflections and the language of many new Doctors of the Church on the topic of grace. When being nothing is used to state the consequence of attributing all of our merits to God, it properly balances both the presence of many merits and the possession of interior humility about them. While we may not always employ the term with the most profound virtue of humility, it is none-theless the appropriate term. When used for the proper ends, it builds this virtue, and the third chapter will examine the ways building this virtue in this form helps our relationship with God. Not surprisingly, then, "being nothing" has superseded the Biblical hyperbole of being a worm. If Saint Benedict's seventh step of humility were the ideal, then the means toward seeking it would be, for Marmion, to acknowledge our nothingness.

It could even be debated that Saint Benedict had acknowledged his own nothingness in just this way, for he quoted the Vulgate about nothingness at the end of his sixth step of humility. Following more exact translations of the Hebrew, the English translation of the *Rule of Saint Benedict 1980* doesn't reflect this detail in Saint Benedict's biblical reference:

> The sixth step of humility is that a monk is content with the lowest and most menial treatment, and regards himself as a poor

---

6 Marmion, *Monk*, 234; Marmion, *Moine*, 310–11.

and worthless workman in whatever task he is given, saying to himself with the Prophet: "I am insignificant and ignorant, no better than a beast before you, yet I am with you always" [ad nihilum redactus sum et nescivi; ut iumentum factus sum apud te et ego semper tecum] (Ps 72[73]:22–23).

Here is a stricter translation of the same Latin words from the Vulgate-dependent Douay-Rheims version of the Bible, "I am brought to nothing, and I knew not. I am become as a beast before thee: and I am always with thee" (Ps 72:22–23).[7] Are his Biblical proof texts in the seventh step of humility just variations on this one in the sixth? That is a possibility. Is it part of a greater whole that also references the theology of grace? There is no direct connection here to the theology of grace, but Saint Benedict did previously provide some commentary on the interplay between grace and good works in his prologue:

> These people fear the Lord, and do not become elated over their good deeds; they judge it is the Lord's power, not their own, that brings about the good in them. They praise (Ps 14[15]:4) the Lord working in them, and say with the Prophet: Not to us Lord, not to us give the glory, but to your name alone (Ps 113[115:1]:9). In just this way Paul the Apostle refused to take credit for the power of his preaching. He declared: "By God's grace I am what I am" (1 Cor 15:10).[8]

There is here cause for conjecture that Saint Benedict may have been instructing his monks in accepting their nothingness as a way to glorify God for working within them. It is certainly easy to see the ways in which subsequent saints and authors have done so under the greater clarity of more reflection on the nature of merits.

Nothingness: An Aid to Humility, With Regard to Yourself

So, how should you interpret this term subjectively with regard to your relationship with yourself and with others? Let us explore some preliminary answers to these questions by reviewing a long but noteworthy summary of Marmion's ideas on the topic from *Christ the Ideal of the Priest*:

> Christian humility is, above all, an attitude of soul, not towards our fellow-men nor towards ourselves, but towards God. Certainly humility does involve a certain deference towards our neighbor

---

7 Ps 72:22–23 DRB.
8 Benedict of Nursia, prologue to *The Rule of St. Benedict*, nos. 29–31.

and even in certain cases submission, while in that intimate judgement which man makes of himself it will suggest maintaining a healthy modesty. But these are merely the consequences of a disposition which goes deeper. The fundamental attitude of the humble soul is the desire to abase [*s'abaisser*] itself before God and live always in accordance with the state of life which God has appointed for it: it is the desire always to think and act in accordance with what the Lord expects of it. Humility therefore presents the soul before God in its misery and in its nothingness [*en son néant*] just as it is. It may be defined thus: "the virtue which inclines man to accept the status which is proper to him in relation to the divinity." What are men here on earth? Beings on their way to eternity; they are merely passing through the world.

In the order of creation, and still more in the supernatural order, man possesses nothing which he has not received: *quid habes quod non accepisti* [what do you have that you have not received]. And the Apostle adds: "Why dost thou glory as if thou hadst not received it" (1 Cor 4:7). Humility does not consist in a theoretical acceptance of this dependence but rather in a voluntary proclamation of it by a practical submission of ourselves to God and to the whole divine order of things. In his attempt to live according to his proper status the humble man will repress all those inordinate desires which impel him to seek his own advantage outside the laws appointed by nature and by God.

Humility, as St Thomas says, is certainly a virtue of the will. But it is regulated by knowledge. *Normam habet in cognitione* [it has its norm in understanding — *Summa Theologica* ii–ii, q. 161, aa. 2 & 6]. What knowledge? The knowledge of the sovereignty of God on the one hand and of the nothingness of man [*du néant de l'homme*] on the other.[9]

With regard to your relationship with yourself, Marmion suggests a "healthy modesty . . . in that intimate judgement which man makes of himself."[10] He goes on to say, "Christian humility is, above all, an attitude of soul, [. . . not] towards ourselves."[11] Taken together, these comments stress the need to maintain a proper justice to yourself.[12] We each need to love our-

---

9   Marmion, *Priest*, 132–33; Marmion, *Prêtre*, 121–22.
10 Marmion, *Priest*, 132–33.
11 Ibid.
12 For the interplay between accepting our nothingness and justice, see Marmion, *Monk*, 226–27.

selves as children of God, practice self-care, and be merciful to ourselves, in just the same way we extend non-indulgent mercy to others. For example, let us refrain from asking ourselves how we may appear before God (as doing well or doing poorly). Since it is rather difficult to judge ourselves or to know God's detailed thoughts on the progress or regress of any of his adopted children, it seems wise to decline the urge to investigate this matter. God has a predilection for each of us. Let us trust the process and the Giver, offering ourselves non-indulgent mercy along the way.

All of our lives appear incomplete and imperfect before God, until we allow Christ to compensate for our incompleteness before the Father. To accept our nothingness is to begin to be grateful for the compensation Jesus ultimately makes on our behalf. Here is a practice that may help. After making your evening examination of conscience, make this traditional prayer for daily neglects: offer the Sacred Heart of Jesus to the Father for all of the sins you've committed this day and during all of your life, for the good you have done badly this day and during all of your life, and for the good you ought to have done this day and during all of your life, trusting the Father will accept Jesus's heart as reparation for your incomplete, imperfect day and life. To appreciate this prayer will help you to see Christ really is your All.

This disposition will have an impact on your sense of place in this world. Marmion wrote, "In his attempt to live according to his proper status the humble man will repress all those inordinate desires which impel him to seek his own advantage outside the laws appointed by nature and by God."[13] If you were to acknowledge God's work in your life as grace, then you would be keen to stay within the order of grace. You would seek your proper place, not presuming to seek more or less status than God wants for you. You would live according to who you are today, not according to who you should be today (or in the future), trusting Christ will triumph in your life. This practice is not to compromise with emptiness but to look for the opportunities already present and to come. It is to be grateful for the action of God in your life at each moment. And at each moment, to act with poise, for to trust the Holy Spirit will fill our feelings of nothingness with inspiration is to be in poise and to trust Christ will compensate for our incompleteness is to remain in poise. David, as slinger and faithful warrior, exhibited these traits; Michelangelo, as lover of grace and beauty,

---

13   Marmion, Priest, 132–33.

made them into a model; you, as one considering the power of God and the order of grace, can find this poise.

Too often we fail to stay within the order of grace. More specifically, we break with the grace of the present moment through acts of self-reliance, some oriented toward self-preservation, others oriented toward grasping at who we want to become. Oh how often do we shrink from the task at hand or go forward without God, messing up his plan. Since the real miracle is happening in the present moment, we must stay present. To do so is both fundamental for living a successful life and necessary for staying within the order of grace. [14]

The practical conclusion is that we must break with anything harmful in our past and with any excessive clinging to a specific form of the future. Perhaps a quick assessment of a deep act of forgiveness will throw this concept into relief. If you were to forgive in a way that wills the other person's good (perhaps from afar), then you would thereby help to heal the situation. If you were to forgive in a way that wills the other person's eternal happiness, even praying the other person may enjoy heaven more than your own future enjoyment of it, then that type of forgiveness would allow you to move forward into a new triumph of grace in your life. [15] By acknowledging the incompleteness the offense caused in your life and by giving it over to God, you alter your own notion of God's triumph in your life. Let us now return to Marmion's point: "The fundamental attitude of the humble soul is the desire to abase [*s'abaisser*] itself before God and live always in accordance with the state of life which God has appointed for it: it is the desire always to think and act in accordance with what the Lord expects of it." [16] God expects us to produce his glory according to his ways, for example by taking on his

---

14   Given the importance of staying present to the current moment, let us take a brief aside to attend to some secular advice on the topic from Patsy Rodenberg, extrapolated from her initial work in the theater: "In the thirty years since I first stumbled across these energies, I have taught them whenever and wherever I could. I have had the privilege to work with the most successful and famous performers on the planet, but I have also coached business people, teachers, physicians, police, politicians, even convicts. Whether the challenge was to close a sale, win a patient's trust, manage a classroom full of unruly teenagers, command the floor of the House of Commons, deal with hostile reporters, or survive in a maximum security prison, the clear winners are those with presence. In fact, you can't win anything without it; even if it only visits you for a moment, it is the moment that will change your life. Those branded as 'losers' have only lost their presence"; from Patsy Rodenberg, *Presence: How to Use Positive Energy for Success* (London, England: Penguin, 2009), xvi.

15   Cf. Fr. James Blount, "On the Flame of Love," last accessed January 2, 2020. https://www.youtube.com/watch?v=Cyqeg_NEx-o.

16   Marmion, *Priest*, 132–33; Marmion, *Prêtre*, 121–22.

"easy yoke" of forgiveness and humility. Let us never forget these words of Jesus, "Come to me, all who labor and are heavy laden, and I will give you rest. Take my yoke upon you, and learn from me; for I am gentle and lowly in heart, and you will find rest for your souls" (Mt 11:28 – 30).

It can be painful, at first, to accept ourselves and the order of the world in this way. God's Providence has allowed the evil that has happened — in the Bible, in our history books, in our news, and in our lives. Confronted with so much evil, we can feel insignificant. At times, our humanity struggles to bear the weight of evil, unless we renounce any excessive emotional response to it. At those moments when it most impacts our humanity, intellectual arguments do not satisfy. When confronted with someone in this state, I simply say, "I do not defend God for allowing it to happen, yet I know He wants to heal you of its effects."

As one who has at times intensely felt the presence and effects of evil, I offer you a prayer that has helped me; it is a short adaptation of a part of Francis MacNutt's cleansing prayer after healing ministry: "Lord, this suffering weighs heavily on my humanity — it feels more than I can bear — please bear it for me."[17]

Confronted with our own human weakness, we can feel pretty miserable, unless we allow God to transform this misery. "Humility therefore presents the soul before God in its misery and in its nothingness [en son néant] just as it is," continued Marmion.[18] We have the choice to become cynical and resentful or to trust that God is working a miracle of grace, a triumph of grace, in us. The former is not an easy yoke. The latter does not initially appear easy, but God can cut us free from the evil we allow to cling to us. As a good country billboard can remind you: God is with you. If needed, pray the following prayer: "Deliver me from unforgiveness and whatever causes a lack of peace in me." If necessary, schedule an appointment for spiritual healing with someone who offers that ministry in your diocese.[19] Trust that God's love is more profound than any sinfulness, present distress, or pain.

The true joy in life comes with being present to God and others here and now. Since grace can abound where sin occurs (cf. Rm 5:20), we can patiently and calmly hope in God during the real and seemingly precarious

---

17 Cf. Francis MacNutt and Christian Healing Ministries, "Prayer to be set free," last accessed July 24, 2021. https://www.christianhealingmin.org/index.php?option=com_content&view=article&id=647&Itemid=389.

18 Marmion, Priest, 132–33; Marmion, Prêtre, 121–22.

19 I explore this topic in greater depth in "Second Station," 101–14.

situations of our lives. In accepting God's compassion on us here and now, we acquire a grounded vulnerability full of compassion for ourselves, others, and the situation.[20] Voila? No, I doubt that I can say "see there" just yet.

This section simply sets the groundwork that humility does affect your relationship with yourself, in a profoundly liberating way. In the third chapter we will discuss in greater detail the ways to acquire interior peace and poise.

Of the four temperaments (i.e., basic personality types), this reflection is of greatest value to the choleric, i.e., to the person who habitually responds to stress by way of an (interior) anger oriented toward fixing the problem. Art and Lorainne Bennett offer the following advice to the choleric in their spiritual/psychological assessment of the four temperaments:

> He will need to develop compassion, humility, tenderness, and understanding in dealing with others. But it will be first necessary to convince the choleric that he needs the spiritual life, that he can trust a spiritual director, that he must humble himself before God and learn the virtue of obedience. He will learn to be more understanding and forgiving of his fellow man and will develop greater humility when he realizes that the natural gifts of his temperament are gifts from God and are not something he personally earned or deserved.[21]

While this advice applies most forcefully to me and my fellow cholerics, it is applicable to all.

We can all benefit from having greater humility. We fear humility only because we do not understand the ways in which it benefits us and the ways in which to do it beneficially. We don't diminish ourselves through this virtue; we gain God's liberation by way of it. Through humility, we gain interior freedom, a true confidence in God and ourselves, a grounded vulnerability, courage, and the ability to receive transformative graces in greatest measure.

Humility is the ground of truly confident action. By way of it, you can also find the right response to any situation, for you will value God, yourself, and others in a way that will enact, perhaps by way of help from others, a grace-filled resolution to any difficulty.

---

20   On developing a grounded vulnerability by accepting God's compassion more fully, see James Finley, "Spirituality and Healing: Transforming Trauma (#5), Tucson, AZ, June 20–22, 2014," last accessed August 13, 2020, https://www.youtube.com/watch?v=Kc2XVSpkoeA and www.contemplative-life.org.
21   Art Bennett and Laraine Bennett, *The Temperament God Gave You: The Classic Key to Knowing Yourself, Getting Along with Others, and Growing Closer to the Lord* (Manchester, NH: Sophia Institute Press, 2005), 32.

Nothingness: An Aid to Humility, With Regard to Others

If we are seriously to take Saint Benedict as a spiritual master, then we must grapple with the point of view that humility profoundly applies to our relationships with others. Saint Benedict wrote, "[He] admits with his tongue but is also convinced in his heart that he is inferior to all and of less value."[22] Can Marmion integrate Saint Benedict's point of view with a healthy acceptance of our merits and our objective value in relation to others? This entire work is dedicated to that question, but let us here offer some preliminary answers on the way by which accepting your nothingness may change your relationships with others in a profoundly positive way.

In our guiding quotation, Marmion wrote, "Christian humility is, above all, an attitude of soul, not towards our fellow-men."[23] This statement, taken in isolation, seems to be in tension with Saint Benedict's seventh step of humility (quoted above). Is humility a spiritual matter disconnected from our relationships with others? On the contrary, it is something spiritual that takes as a foundation a healthy psychological balance between our own needs and those legitimate needs of others. Of course, you should take care to avoid the extreme in which a person becomes overly focused upon pleasing others, perhaps even to the point of neglecting his needs or of losing himself. Neither Saint Benedict nor Marmion could be seen as endorsing such an extreme point of view with regard to our relationships with others. Indeed, the reflections in this work are only meant to help every lover of God, every lover of one's spouse and family, every lover of one's friends, neighbors, and coworkers to fulfill those loves, to strengthen those relationships within a healthy balance between serving one's own legitimate needs (personal, vocational, familial, and professional) and the legitimate needs of loved ones. Therein lies the correct understanding of Christian humility, which is never oriented toward unhealthy relationships with others.

Some people fear that the practice of Christian humility opens a person to being bullied. If you were one of them, then I hope this reflection liberates you to see the importance of advocating and working for the fulfillment of your authentic needs.[24] Let us not forget to love ourselves with God's love! There are many types of bullies — overtly aggressive, covertly aggressive,

22 Benedict of Nursia, The Rule of St. Benedict, chap. 7, nos. 51–54.
23 Marmion, Priest, 132–33.
24 If you need outside help with a bully, from friends or a counselor, you should not hesitate to get it. If you are in a healthy relationship, then you should be safe when advocating for your authentic needs.

passive aggressive, passive avoidant, etc. — all of whom can prompt a false humility that makes you feel like a loser. In the face of a bully, you would need to be most present to yourself, to God's graces, and to the circumstance in order to interact effectively with them. Above all, you may need the confidence in God discussed at the end of this work in order to have a deeper and more balanced confidence in yourself, leading to the grounded vulnerability that can withstand any challenge. Indeed, you would be least likely to be bullied if you were fully present to a circumstance in a balanced way, neither in an excessive way nor in a defective way, poised as someone protected from on high.[25]

How often do you seek God's help? Here is an idea: request the help of the Holy Spirit throughout the day by taking certain moments of the day as reminders to do so. When you answer a phone call or cross the threshold into a meeting, say "Come Holy Spirit" silently to God. These reminders will give you added courage and insights in your difficulties and also build a habit of prayer.

Let us now turn to the topic of submission within the context of Christian humility: "Certainly humility does involve a certain deference towards our neighbor and even in certain cases submission."[26] Every concept of humility, even a secular one, contains a proper deference to authority, elders, specialists, etc. A Christian can look to the examples of numerous spiritual masters in order to understand this idea in the context of the humility here discussed. Indeed, even a Christian highly confident in God's help would want to learn more about our spiritual masters' sense of "certain cases of submission" before adopting the type of humility here discussed. Blessed Columba used the word submission a second time in our guiding quotation: "Humility does not consist in a theoretical acceptance of this dependence but rather in a voluntary proclamation of it by a practical submission of ourselves to God and to the whole divine order of things."[27] Under most instances of the divine order of things, submission to the circumstances of Providence can align well with the psychological balance just discussed.

Occasionally, we experience difficulties within that same divine order of things. We refer to those difficulties as crosses, which all individuals must bear by the grace of God. It is at those moments we most feel our nothingness. It is at those moments we most need to pray, "Lord, I am nothing without

---

25   Cf. Rodenberg, *Presence*, 146–74.
26   Marmion, *Priest*, 132–33.
27   Ibid.

THE GRACE OF "NOTHINGNESS"

you, please do this through me." Marmion called our humility a "voluntary" act that takes the form of a "practical submission." These two thoughts are indispensable for interpreting the topic of submission. According to Saint John Chrysostom, the Father did not submit the Word to take flesh and to suffer an ignominious death; rather, the Word, in loving humility, chose (voluntarily) to take flesh and to do what was needed to redeem humanity (in practical submission to the divine plan), including "taking the form of a servant" and becoming "obedient unto death, even death on a cross" (Phil 2: 7 – 8). [28] Every Christian knows of the victories associated with Jesus's choices, but in times of trial it is especially worth also recalling those very choices Christ made out of love of each of us. Jesus voluntarily undertook acts of practical submission to a divine order that led, by way of the cross, to the redemption of sinners. Anytime you imitate Christ in doing the same, you are in effect indicating that you are "inferior to" and "of less value" than those for whom you suffer your cross. Read in this light, Saint Benedict's seventh step of humility begins to look a lot more like the disposition of a good parent who makes innumerable sacrifices for the good of a child, all done within a proper view of the whole and a proper psychological ordering of our own and others' needs. Besides, good parents already practice this virtue with each other, according to Saint Paul's teaching on mutual subjection in marriage: "Be subject to one another out of reverence for Christ" (Eph 5:21).

You can eventually arrive at seeing other people as similar instruments of God's grace. Adolphe Tanquerey, a mid-twentieth-century manualist of spiritual theology to whom the works of Marmion were not unknown, offered perhaps the best solution to the complexity of seeing yourself as the least of men: "To consider oneself in all sincerity as the lowest of men. This is a degree of humility rarely found. The saints attain it by saying to themselves that if others had received as many graces as they, they would have made much better use of these divine gifts." [29] Under such a view of your nothingness, you could eventually offer yourself as a victim to God's mercy for those who have, objectively speaking, fewer merits and gifts in their lives — i.e., if you crave Saint Thérèse's most efficient route to becoming a saint (see Appendix 2, to be discussed later). After having laid more

---

28 Cf. John Chrysostom, "Homily VII: On Philippians 2:5–11" in *Homilies of S. Chrysostom: Philippians, Colossians, Thessalonians* (Oxford: John Henry Parker, 1843), 75ff., esp. 77–82.
29 Adolphe Tanquerey, *The Spiritual Life: A Treatise on Ascetical and Mystical Theology*, trans. Herman Branderis, 2nd revised ed. (Tournai: Desclée De Brouwer, 1930), no. 1131.7.

groundwork for understanding submission in greater detail, we will return to this topic under the lens of the saints' words about coming to perfect joy.

Finally, when I speak of accepting our nothingness, some people look at me as if I've told the person next to them to "sell what you possess and give to the poor" (Mt 19:21). If you fear being asked more than you can bear, don't "be sorrowful"; Marmion's gentle approach personalizes these words of Jesus for you: "With God all things are possible" (Mt 19:21, 26).

NOTHINGNESS IN THE CATHOLIC TRADITION

In order later to go more deeply into Marmion's practical advice, we must both analyze these preliminary thoughts on our topic and compare them to some tried and true authors of the Catholic spiritual tradition.

In his work *The Three Ages of the Interior Life: Prelude of Eternal Life*, Reginald Garrigou-Lagrange analyzed this type of language in spiritual authors as a mystical and hyperbolic manner of speaking.[30] More specifically, Garrigou-Lagrange outlined five different ways in which spiritual authors treat of nothingness as hyperbolic shorthand:

> Likewise, the mystics speak briefly of the nothingness of the creature in order to express what theologians would state in the five following propositions: 1) the creature of itself is nothing, for it was created *ex nihilo*; 2) compared to God, the already existing creature is nothing, for there is no more perfection after creation, no more being than before, although there are now more beings; 3) by its essential defectibility the creature tends to nothingness and sin; 4) sin is less than nothingness itself, for it is not only the negation, but the privation of the good; it is a disorder and an offense against God; 5) the creature is nothing in our affection if we love it without subordinating it to God, for thus it turns us away from Him.[31]

Strikingly, Marmion's use of nothingness does not appear in this list. As we have seen, the awe owed to the Creator under the natural virtue of religion makes a person feel a sense of nothingness, but the mystical shorthand manner of "being nothing" here discussed requires a more comprehensive grounding in the Christian anthropology (grace). So, the first two of Garrigou-Lagrange's categories only express part of the answer, for neither

30 Cf. Reginald Garrigou-Lagrange, *The Three Ages of the Interior Life: Prelude of Eternal Life*, vol. 2, trans. M Timothea Doyle (1948; rpt. Rockford, IL: TAN, 1989), 13–20.
31 Ibid., 17.

thanksgiving for our creation nor a philosophical extrapolation on that point entirely encompasses our gratitude for grace. Garrigou-Lagrange's third and fourth categories refer to sin as nothingness. This interpretation is indeed part of the answer about our nothingness, for sin creates a real gap in human flourishing. Some Protestants could easily accept this natural aspect of our nothingness while negating the real intrinsic renewal brought by grace, and perhaps many Protestant spiritual authors have intended their use of the term in this limited, non-mystical way. Catholic authors, though, seem to imply much more in their mystical shorthand. With regard to Garrigou-Lagrange's fifth and final category, it pertains to the need to subordinate our tastes to God's ways so as to avoid obsessive attachments to creatures. The definition discerned from Marmion's writings is, there-fore, a sixth category, hereafter termed the evangelical category. While the Catholic mystical tradition has made use of the first five categories, there remain other Catholic uses of "being nothing" that can only be understood by adding this additional evangelical category.[32] Furthermore, this evan-

---

32   In failing to include this sixth category, Garrigou-Lagrange seems to put himself at odds with his colleague Juan Arintero's use of the term in: Juan Arint-ero, *Mystical Evolution in the Development and Vitality of the Church*, vol. II, trans. by Jordan Aumann (Saint Louis, MO: B. Herder, 1951; reprint: Rockford, IL: TAN, 1978), 50–52, 61–69; and also with Adolphe Tanquerey's use of it in: Adolphe Tanquerey, *Spiritual Life*, no. 839ff., 401–4, to name two of the leading manual-ists of spiritual theology of his time. It also seems that Garrigou-Lagrange's own use of the term elsewhere in his works is in tension with the limited nature of these five categories. In Reginald Garrigou-Lagrange, *The Three Ways of the Spiritual Life* (London: Burns, Oats & Washbourne, 1938), 37–38, he quotes the following private revelation from the 60th chapter of the *Dialogues* of Saint Catherine of Siena: "And do you know what shows the imperfection of their love? It is that, as soon as they are deprived of the consolations which they find in Me, their love fails and can no longer survive. It becomes weak and gradually cools towards Me when, in order to exercise them in virtue and to detach them from their imper-fection, I withdraw spiritual consolations from them and send them difficulties and afflictions. I act in this way in order to bring them to perfection, to teach them to know themselves, to realize that they are nothing and that of themselves they have no grace." Garrigou-Lagrange comments on this text thus: "This is the quasi-experimental knowledge of the distinction between nature and grace, quite different from that which we have through speculative theology. It is not difficult to understand in abstract the difference between the two orders; but to see it in concrete, and to perceive it almost continuously, supposes a spirit of faith which, in this degree, is found hardly in any but the Saints" (ibid., 38, n. 1). Further-more, in *The Three Ages of the Interior Life*, vol. 1, 105–6, Garrigou-Lagrange taught: "This quasi-experimental knowledge of God, of His goodness, will grow with the knowledge of our nothingness and wretchedness, according to the divine words spoken to St Catherine of Siena: 'I am who am; thou art she who is not.'" Also see

gelical category of being nothing sheds new light upon the ascetical uses of wanting nothing, having nothing, and feeling nothing that are included in Garrigou-Lagrange's final category. As Garrigou-Lagrange notes, Saint John of the Cross's focus on nothingness and Saint Francis of Assisi's focus on absolute poverty should be interpreted as hyperbolic language about detachment.[33] So, "to desire nothing, to ask for nothing, and to refuse [nothing]" are versions of ascetical nothingness.[34] Such language aims to shake people from their obsessive attachments so as to allow them to appreciate what God is giving them. The detachment from things, when willed by God and done in proper measure, is not done for its own sake. We do it for the higher goal of coming to detachment from self and attachment to God. Therefore, to want nothing (except what God wills) and to have nothing (except what God wills) must in some way serve to deepen the disposition of being nothing.

With this categorization in mind, it is now possible to examine some of the most relevant uses of the evangelical and ascetical categories of nothingness among the authors in the Catholic mystical tradition cited by Marmion.

Reginald Garrigou-Lagrange, *Christian Perfection and Contemplation: According to St. Thomas Aquinas and St. John of the Cross*, trans. M. Timothea Doyle (Saint Louis, MO: B. Herder, 1937), 404: "As St. Paul says, we bear an exceedingly precious treasure, grace and the Blessed Trinity, in a fragile vase; the greater also will be our appreciation of the value of the treasure, and the keener our aspiration to live intimately by it. This is taught by the passive purifications, a mystical state which, far from making the soul proud, humbles it profoundly. Without these purifications, it is scarcely possible to love to be nothing in order that God may be all; *amare nesciri et pro nihilo reputari* [To love to be unknown and to be reputed as nothing]." That Garrigou-Lagrange quotes that Latin dictum as if it were well known is of note. The phrase appears to come from Saint Philip Neri; see Giacomo Pietro Bacci, *Vita di S. Filippo Neri, Apostolo di Roma*, edition with added contributions from some companions (Rome: Tipografia Marini e Compagno, 1837), last accessed April 20, 2015. https://books.google.it/books/reader?id=kX0002h5FlMC&printsec=front-cover&output=reader&pg=GBS.PP7, Appendix of added contributions, 144 [e-page 140]: "Desiderava sopra tutto ne' Soggetti di Congregazione l'umiltà, il non volere apparire agli occhi degli uomini, l'odiare gli applause, e quell' *Amare nesciri, et pro nihilo reputari* [He was above all desiring that there be humility in the congregation, i.e., not to want to appear in the eyes of men, to hate applause, and *amare nesciri et pro nihilo reputari*.]" Therefore, in failing to include the sixth category recommended by this paper, Garrigou-Lagrange's categories for nothingness seem to be in tension with the spiritual theology of his time, his own spiritual theology, and, by his own account, the popular phraseology of his period.

33 Cf. Garrigou-Lagrange, *The Three Ages of the Interior Life*, 2:14–16.
34 Marmion cites these three points of view as typical of Saint Francis de Sales in Marmion, "Letter to Dom Gerald Van Caloen, Abbot of Olinda, no. 2, 10 May 1897," in *Letters*, 83.

THE GRACE OF "NOTHINGNESS"

In the Apostolic Period: 2 Corinthians 12:11b

Surprisingly, the history of the usage and concept of "being nothing" can be traced as far back as the apostolic period, for contemporary exegesis supports the theory that Saint Paul may have spoken about "being nothing" in the evangelical sense defined above. An exegete, upon seeing some exegesis follow dogmatic theology — even worse, spiritual theology — would be highly tempted to cry foul before even reviewing the work. The work must be anachronistic, he would fear. Yet could it be possible that we have only recently reached a new understanding of mystical speech that allows us to penetrate a text heretofore enigmatic? I'll leave it to you to decide whether it's a bit like painting a bowl of spaghetti into a depiction of the Last Supper — or a wind turbine into the background of American Gothic. The enigmatic text in question is 2 Corinthians 12:11b, "For I am not at all inferior to these superlative apostles, even though I am nothing [ουδεν γαρ υστερησα των υπερλιαν αποστολων ει και ουδεν ειμι — *ouden gar usteresa ton uperlian apostolon ei kai ouden eimi*]."[35] The meaning of these words has long been the subject of debate. Rudolf Bultmann best expresses the division among exegetes regarding it: "Is it sharpest irony —'though I am nothing in your eyes?' Or, is it the highest pathos of seriousness in the sense of [2 Cor] 12:5–10 (cf. 1 Cor 15:9f) —'though I credit myself with none of it, because the divine δυναμις [*dunamis*] accomplished it all?'"[36] However, to read the words as an evangelical form of the mystical shorthand term of nothingness allows both of Bultmann's suggestions to be true and does away with the debate altogether. What follows is a terse summary of some relevant scholarship on it.

This verse's strange hyperbole has proven itself to be quite perplexing to exegetes. Some exegetes offer only a quick account of Paul's non-inferiority with regard to his adversaries, without touching upon the difficulty of his self-admitted nothingness.[37] *Peake's Commentary on the Bible* most succinctly states this explanation of the text: "Though a 'nonentity' he [Paul] is on par with the super-apostolic legates from Jerusalem."[38] This approach, however, does not investigate the perplexity of why Paul ended his fool's speech

---

35 Eberhard Nestle and Erwin Nestle, *Novum Testamentum Graece*, 2 Cor 12:11b.
36 Rudolf Bultmann, *The Second Letter to the Corinthians*, trans. Roy Harrisville (Minneapolis, MN: Augsburg Publishing House, 1985), 231.
37 Cf. Arthur Peake, *Peake's Commentary on the Bible*, ed. Matthew Black (London: Thomas Nelson, 1962), 968; Margaret Macdonald, "2 Corinthians," in *The Oxford Bible Commentary*, ed. J. Barton and J. Muddiman (Oxford: Oxford University Press, 2001), 1149.
38 Peake, *Peake's Commentary on the Bible*, 968.

(cf. 2 Cor 11:1 – 12:13) in this manner. Since Paul had already gone to great pains to make a boastful rebuttal to these super-apostles in order to demonstrate his non-inferiority, why did he choose to end this argument by attributing to himself such an absolutely negative term?

There are numerous explanations. For one, Paul had found himself in the uncomfortable position of needing to expound some of his merits, address some of his limitations (e.g., of speech, as in 2 Cor 11:6), and clarify some of his actions, i.e., of not having taken money from the Corinthians for his ministry (cf. 2 Cor 11:7). As he was of blameless lineage (cf. 2 Cor 11:22) and charged with a certain ministry (cf. 2 Cor 11:23), he based his defense on two key points: 1) the love with which he had offered his ministry, as exhibited by the self-abnegation and sufferings he had undergone for it (cf. 2 Cor 11:23 – 29); and 2) his high standing as a mystic (cf. 2 Cor 12:1 – 10). When read in conjunction with his explanation in 2 Corinthians 11:14 that visions can be misleading, the latter argument served less as a mark of distinction than as a leveling affront against rival visionaries. Hence, Paul was not presenting himself as a nonentity, and so our exegesis would be incomplete were it to avoid commentary on why he called himself nothing.

The *New Jerome Biblical Commentary* and the *Eerdmans Commentary* hold that Paul was merely responding in ironic fashion to a detractive use of nothingness lobbed at him by his adversaries.[39] The *New Jerome Biblical Commentary* succinctly sums up this view, noting: "His opponents may have described Paul as a complete nonentity (cf. 2 Cor 10:10b)."[40] Yet it seems absurd to posit such an absolute detraction against the founder of the Church in Corinth and the Apostle of the Gentiles. How could men with such absolute disrespect for the founder of that local church — not to mention the rest of his prerogatives — have won over part of that church? No one allows a founder to be called "nothing," no matter what his faults are, and it is highly improbable that encroachers savvy enough to win over some of the community would have tried such an absolute vilification.

Of those who admit a spiritual interpretation for Paul's nothingness, there are two camps. Some argue for a spiritual interpretation solely from

---

39 J. Murphy-O'Connor, "The First and Second Letters to the Corinthians," in *New Jerome Biblical Commentary*, ed. R. Brown (Englewood Cliffs, NJ: Prentice Hall, 1990), 828; J. Barclay, "2 Corinthians," in *Eerdmans Commentary on the Bible*, ed. J. D. Dunn (Grand Rapids, MI: William B. Eerdmans, 2003), 1371. The *Eerdmans Commentary* does not directly attribute the detraction to Paul's opponents, but I have categorized them together since both exegetes assume that Paul was responding to such a detractive mentality.
40 J. Murphy-O'Connor, *New Jerome Biblical Commentary*, 828.

preexisting Pauline and Christian concepts. Others employ a philological argument, noting that Paul was both using the Socratic midwifing technique and referencing "the Delphic teaching that human beings are nothing in comparison with the divine power."[41]

In the first group are Meyer and Barnett. Meyer holds that this verse is a litotes that demonstrates the same humility found in 1 Corinthians 15:8 – 10, in which Paul notes that he is the least of the apostles and states: "But by the grace of God I am what I am, and his grace toward me was not in vain."[42] Barnett's argument includes the context of 2 Corinthians 12:12 to add greater weight to this type of argument:

> This qualification [of Paul's nothingness] flows into the next verse, where its real significance is seen. In fact, the "signs of the apostle" mark him out as an apostle, making him in fact superior to those he calls "superlative" apostles. Thus the disclaimer is a veiled claim in the form of litotes (understatement); in saying that he is nothing, at the same time he is saying that he is everything. Nonetheless, he upholds the canons of Christian humility (cf. 10:1), and as he proceeds to infer, it is God, not he, who validates his ministry because God is the source of what he does.[43]

Both exegetes hold that Paul's rhetorical response was more than a stylistic choice and that a spiritual interpretation for Paul's nothingness is most in line with the rest of the Pauline corpus. Some exegetes, however, may fear this interpretation as an anachronistic theological reading of the text.

As for those who align with Betz's philological argument,[44] they are Furnish in the Anchor Bible[45] and Thrall in her commentary.[46] Thrall offers that Paul had found some common ground with Greek culture in both the Socratic midwifing technique and in the Delphic teachings about attribution to divine power. She writes:

---

41 Victor Paul Furnish, "II Corinthians," in The Anchor Bible, vol. 32a (Garden City, NY: Doubleday, 1985), 552 – 53.
42 Heinrich Meyer, Critical and Exegetical Commentary on the New Testament: Corinthians, vol. 2, trans. W. A. Dickson and W. Stewart (Edinburgh: T. & T. Clark, 1879), 483.
43 Paul Barnett, The Second Epistle to the Corinthians (Grand Rapids, MI: William B. Eerdmans, 1997), 579.
44 Unfortunately, I am unable to access Betz's work, which was written in German, and so his work comes to me secondhand.
45 Cf. Furnish, The Anchor Bible, 552 – 53.
46 Cf. Margaret Thrall, A Critical and Exegetical Commentary on the Second Epistle to the Corinthians, vol. 2 of The International Critical Commentary (Edinburgh: T & T Clark, 2000), 833 – 37.

The ουδενια [oudenia] becomes a philosophical principle, and ignorance, correspondingly, is shown to be genuine wisdom, by contrast
with the alleged wisdom of the rhetoricians. The Socratic ουδενια,
moreover, is to be linked with the ancient Delphic teaching on self-
knowledge, which enables man to recognize his own "nothingness"
in face of the power of the divine. The tradition, it appears, was
also familiar to hellenistic Judaism, since Philo makes use of it.
Hence, it is possible that it was known to Paul. [47]

In the light of Thrall's research, we can lay aside any concerns about the
previously described interpretation being anachronistic. Indeed, the remain-
der of Thrall's research further supports the suitability of the previously
described line of thought: "If it is to this type of thought, then, that he
is in part indebted, it would seem that the irony has disappeared. He is
speaking seriously, for the philosophic and Delphic concept of human
'nothingness' has some affinity with his own sense that he was 'nothing'
apart from Christ."[48]

Yet, just as Socrates' irony both caught his opponents and demonstrated
his own dominance, so too, she argues, Paul may have used the term in
two ways:

> Consequently, if Paul's acknowledgement of his "nothingness" has
> something of the background claimed for it by Betz, his assertion
> ουδεν ειμι [ouden eimi] may likewise be ambivalent in its import.
> It is wholly serious, in that, apart from the power of Christ, he
> knows himself to be really "nothing." But at the same time, in
> relation to his opponents, he speaks ironically and with polemical
> intent. His concession is "mock-modest." It is shown to be such
> by his insistence that he is the equal of the rival missionaries.
> Since neither they themselves nor the Corinthians considered they
> were "nothing," Paul does not seriously, in relation to these people,
> mean it of himself. He affects to do so in order to compel the
> Corinthians to realize the strength of his own apostolic claims.[49]

Does Thrall here offer two contrasting interpretations? The first is that Paul
uses the term nothingness to render all to Christ, apart from whom he
would be nothing (cf. Jn 15:5); the second is that Paul does not hold this
term to be true intrinsically and thus uses his insight mockingly against his

---

47 Thrall, A Critical and Exegetical Commentary, 836.
48 Ibid., 836–37.
49 Ibid., 837.

opponents without holding it to be true. She emphasizes the reality of the former — "He knows himself to be really 'nothing'" — and she qualifies the latter — "Paul does not seriously, in relation to these people, mean it of himself."[50] These two viewpoints, however, would not be incompatible if the term were understood as the evangelical form of the mystical shorthand term of nothingness, for that approach both admits the presence of many merits and attributes them to God. Thrall does not explicitly offer this synthesis, but her work easily opens itself to that interpretation. Indeed, if she were to read this text with a hermeneutic of faith, accepting intrinsic justification and mystical living, then she could easily read this text without finding in it any paradox. Under that reading, the text, in fact, becomes a boasting in the Lord, "Let him who boasts, boast of the Lord. For it is not the man who commends himself that is accepted, but the man whom the Lord commends" (2 Cor 10:17–18).

In the Patristic Period

The Greek-English Lexicon of the New Testament and Other Early Christian Literature reports ουδεν [ouden, "nothing"] was not used self-referentially in this period.[51]

During and After the Debate about Semipelagianism

Christian authors began more commonly to speak of "being nothing" around the time of the Semipelagian controversy in the early fifth century. This controversy revolved around the level of free will permitted to Christians in cooperating with grace. The heresy asserted that nature in some way would have a claim on grace or could assist it.[52] Given that a disposition of nothingness is in clear opposition to the self-reliance of Semipelagianism, I here provide the text that provoked this controversy:

> Therefore, the aforesaid teacher of the Gentiles, although testifying that he has received the rank of an apostle by the grace of God when he says: "By the grace of God I am what I am" (1 Cor 15:10a), nonetheless also declares that he has responded to divine grace

---

50 Thrall, A Critical and Exegetical Commentary, 837.
51 Walter Bauer, "oudeis, oudemia, ouden, 2.b." in A Greek-English Lexicon of the New Testament and Other Early Christian Literature, trans. W. Arndt and F. W. Gingrich, 2nd ed. (Chicago, IL: University of Chicago Press, 1979), 592.
52 For an overview, see Joseph Pohle, "Semipelagianism," in The Catholic Encyclopedia, vol. 13 (New York, NY: Robert Appleton Company, 1912), last accessed February 28, 2015. http://www.newadvent.org/cathen/13703a.htm.

when he says: "His grace in me was not in vain, but I have labored more abundantly than all of them — yet not I, but the grace of God with me" (1 Cor 15:10b). When he says: "I have labored," he is indicating the effort of his own will. When he says: "Yet not I, but the grace of God," he is pointing to the power of the divine protection. When he says: "With me," he is declaring that it has worked together not with a lazy or careless person but with one who labors and toils.[53]

The former part rejects the works righteousness of pure Pelagianism. The latter part, especially in the last sentence, represents a false attempt to allow free will a greater role than it has in the process. Under the Semipelagian mindset, grace would come to the aid of self-reliance in order to produce merits. The opposing and orthodox view is as follows: first, that grace must begin, maintain, and complete every meritorious work, thereby involving God in every step; and second, that free will must cooperate with God's grace while retaining the freedom to reject it. Free will, in other words, cannot merit grace, and actions undertaken by self-reliance are presumptuous about whether they would receive grace to carry them out. While the Semipelagian heresy was condemned shortly after its inception, in practice it remains alive today. It remains in the practical self-reliance of the vast majority of Christians and in the failure to credit God for His part in our merits. Many Christians simply try to make themselves holy, even as they often pray for help in their plans for this process. The opposite and correct approach is to discern God's work in your life and to cooperate in implementing those graces.

SAINT AUGUSTINE. Saint Augustine (354–430), the eventual victor in this debate about grace, hinted at a mystical interpretation of John 15:5 in saying, "Whether then it be little or much, without Him it is impracticable; for without Him nothing can be done."[54] But these words seem little more than an emphatic rhetorical effect upon the verse itself. While Saint Augustine was trying here to stress the need for grace, he came short of saying man is "nothing" in the way expressed in what we have labeled the evangelical shorthand term of nothingness. Similarly, he never used such a term in his

---

53   John Cassian, *The Conferences*, vol. 57 of *The Works of the Fathers in Translation*, trans. Boniface Ramsey (New York, NY: Newman Press, 1997), conf. 13, chap. xiii, no. 2.
54   Augustine of Hippo, "Tractate 81 (John 15:4–7)," vol. 7 of *Nicene and Post-Nicene Fathers, First Series, Tractates on John*, trans. John Gibb, ed. Philip Schaff (Buffalo, NY: Christian Literature Publishing Co., 1888), rev. and ed. for New Advent by Kevin Knight, last accessed August 13, 2014. http://www.newadvent.org/fathers/1701081.htm, LXXXI, no. 3. See Marmion's application of it in Marmion, *Mysteries*, 455 (Appendix 1).

most psychologically attentive work, The Confessions.[55] There is a passage to consider in the City of God:

> Their holy words and works and way of life, which somehow broke the opposition of the hardest hearts and filled them with the peace of righteousness, won for them an immense glory in the Church of Christ. They took no complacency in this, as though it were the purpose of their virtue, but, on the contrary, referred their glory to the glory of God, by whose grace they were able to do what they did. And, with the flame of grace in their own souls, they fired those for whom they worked with the flame of the love of the same God who made the Apostles what they were.
>
> For their Master had taught them not to pursue virtue for the sake of human glory: "Take heed that you do not justice before men to be seen by them: otherwise, you shall not have a reward of your Father who is in heaven" (Mt 6:1). On the other hand, He did not want them so to misunderstand these words as to fear to please men and so, by concealing their virtue, to help them less. Hence, He pointed out to them the motive they should have in making themselves known to the world. "So let your light shine before men," He told them, "that they may see your good works and glorify your Father who is in heaven" (Mt 5:16). Not, notice, "that you may be seen by them," not, that is, with the intention that they may be converted to you — since you yourselves are nothing [quia non per vos aliquid estis] — but "that they may glorify your Father who is in heaven," so that, by being converted to Him, they become as you are.[56]

This passage includes all of the aspects of an evangelical use of nothingness; it refers to the workings of grace, attributes our goodness to God, and uses a term similar to "nothingness" in a hyperbolic way. It may well be the first move toward a mystical, hyperbolic use of "nothingness," but it is not quite an evangelical usage of the "being nothing" as we have defined it here. An astute reader of the original Latin will notice Augustine does not use *nihil*, meaning "nothing"; he uses *aliquid*, expressing not evangelical nothingness

---

55 Augustine of Hippo, Confessions, trans. J. G. Pilkington (Garden City, NY: International Collectors Library, 1900), last accessed August 29, 2014. https://archive.org/details/confessionsofstaooaugu.

56 Augustine of Hippo, The City of God: Books I–VII, vol. 6 of Fathers of the Church: A New Translation: Writings of Saint Augustine, trans. Demetrius Zema and Gerald Walsh (Washington, DC: Catholic University of America Press, 1950), 275–76; Augustini De Civitate Dei (NP: Publisher Unknown, Date Unknown), bks. v, xiv, last accessed October 17, 2014. http://www.thelatinlibrary.com/augustine/civ5.shtml.

but a pejorative rebuke. A more precise translation would read "not that you are anyone"; a more liberal translation could be "since you are not someone of significance."

Intriguingly, Armand Maurer argues that Saint Augustine was the initiator of the mystical shorthand term of nothingness.[57] According to Maurer, Saint Augustine attempted to construct a literal interpretation of the creation account in Genesis by way of a hypothesis of seminal principles (i.e., that everything was created in seed form from the outset). This point of view led Augustine, according to Maurer, to borrow and employ what we have called the evangelical sense of nothingness in a new setting. Unfortunately, this theory of Maurer's could not be substantiated in Saint Augustine's treatises on Genesis.[58] At best, it remains an open question whether Saint Augustine intended to use the mystical shorthand term of nothingness. Even if he were not the originator of a mystical use of this term, his works on grace during the Semipelagian controversy may have inspired such an interpretation of John 15:5.

SAINTS JOHN CASSIAN AND BENEDICT. In the West, Saint John Cassian (360–435) and Saint Benedict (480–543) contributed to the understanding of humility with their similar versions of the ladder of humility, already reviewed in part above. Yet Saint Cassian's influence was not entirely positive, as he gave voice to Semipelagianism. Although this influence was a decidedly negative one, his efforts still brought to light the need for the Church to consider the relationship between grace and free will.

ST BARSINUPHIUS OF GAZA AND VENERABLE JOHN OF MEROSALA. Somewhat later, in the Christian East, in a tradition unknown in the West for centuries (and probably unknown to Marmion as well), the

---

57 Cf. Armand Maurer, *Medieval Philosophy. A History of Philosophy*, vol. 2, ed. Etienne Gilson (New York: Random House, 1962), 15–16: "The gardener plants and waters his garden, but in reality he does nothing; it is God who gives the increase. For St. Augustine, this Pauline dictum holds good not only in the order of grace but also in nature. Parents, for example, who beget a child are nothing; God forms the infant. The mother who nourishes her child does not count for anything; God gives the increase. God is working continually in nature, activating seminal principles to develop the visible forms we see around us. . . . Augustine's constant tendency is to minimize as far as possible the efficacy of creatures in order the more to exalt the power and creative activity of God. . . . The doctrine of seminal principles shows the same concern to insure the supremacy and power of God and to emphasize the frailty and nothingness of creatures."
58 Cf. Augustine of Hippo, *Saint Augustine on Genesis: Two Books on Genesis against the Manichees and On the Literal Interpretation of Genesis: An Unfinished Book*, trans. Roland J. Teske, vol. 84 of *The Fathers of the Church: A New Translation* (Washington, DC: Catholic University of America Press, 1991).

letters of Barsinuphius (†563) and John of Merosala may have contained the first uses of the mystical shorthand term of nothingness:

> I am nothing; and even if I were [something], I would not be mocking you [by sending you to the holy and Great Old Man, Abba Barsanuphius, to answer your questions about humility]. For if I had sent you to him and you had not obtained a response, then it would have been mockery. Therefore, it is to your benefit that there are two people praying for you; for two people are more than one. It appears that even the Lord does the same; for he says: "My Father is greater than I" (Jn 14:28), whereas he, too, was able to perform the works of his Father. This is why he says: "Whatever the Son sees the Father doing, he, too, does likewise" (cf. Jn 5:19). Indeed, not once but many times would he send his disciples to the Father, saying, "If you ask anything of my Father in my name, he will give it to you" (Jn 16:23); and again: "I will ask the Father" (Jn 14:16); and again "I do nothing on my own; but the Father who dwells in me does his works" (cf. Jn 14:10).[59]

It is notable that this use of the evangelical sense of nothingness is suffused with quotes about Jesus attributing his power to the Father in a context separate from the Vulgate.

THE SECOND COUNCIL OF ORANGE. Semipelagianism was condemned at the Second Council of Orange in 529, a condemnation confirmed by then-Pope Boniface II. The story of the contemporary reception of the condemnation of Semipelagianism, a heresy that is pervasive in our time, is quite illuminating about the state of spiritual theology today — in particular in some Benedictine formation. Indeed, this point in our historical review is something of a breaking point between two contemporary interpretations of theology. One mentality tends to skip forward at this point to the twentieth century, minimizing a millennium's worth of developments in spiritual theology, most especially those provided by the scholastic period. The other mentality sees the following developments in spiritual theology as relevant breakthroughs in our understanding and practice of the faith, provided by tried-and-true sources.

Here is some anecdotal evidence of this break. Some of today's older

---

59 Barsinuphius and John, *Letters*, vol. 2, vol. 114 of *Fathers of the Church*, trans. John Chryssavgis (Washington, DC: CUA Press, 2007), letter 783; see also, letters 404, 467, 497, 567, 613, 763.

monks at Saint Louis Abbey recall the times around the Second Vatican Council in which their formators stressed, almost daily, the 22nd canon of the Second Council of Orange. These monks can still remember the number and content of this canon into their ninth decade of life:

> Those things that are proper to man. No one has anything of his own except lying and sin. But if a man has anything of truth and justice, it is from that fountain for which we should thirst in this desert, so that, as though refreshed by some of its drops, we may not falter along the way. [60]

To have stressed it so frequently, their formators held this content to be a vital antidote to common spiritual pitfalls. These same formators drew much from Marmion in their lessons to the young monks of those days. When those monks went off to the seminary, in the time just after the Second Vatican Council, they learned much of the *nouvelle theologie*, they became excited about reading the Bible, and they took up the call to return to the sources of their charism — for Benedictines, the desert fathers and Saint Cassian. (*Nota bene*: these monastic sources occur in the time before or during the Semipelagian heresy.) With enthusiasm these monks explored novel ways of thought and the new openings provided by the Council as their primary theological interests. In a time when Thomism became passé, neither Marmion nor the 22nd canon of the Second Council of Orange received a thought in the Benedictine formation of the next generations here. This situation was not unique to Saint Louis Abbey: when I visited Marmion's abbey, Maredsous, they joked that the real miracle of Marmion's beatification was not that someone was healed at his intercession but that there was still someone on earth looking to give him the opportunity!

Perhaps since the *nouvelle theologie* did not emphasize intrinsic justification, the topic of grace became less emphasized in the preaching and teaching of those decades in which the *nouvelle theologie* influenced the Church. No one outright negated that God works to heal, transform, and perfect us; they just explored other areas of theological interest. No one ever denied the validity of the mystical saints or Doctors of the Church on prayer; they just researched their own tradition. As we move forward from this break, let us recall that many of the authors that follow here are Doctors of the Church who are recommended to everyone.

---

60   Denzinger, *Enchiridion*, Second Council of Orange (529), can. 22, no. 392.

In the Middle Ages

Some people think monks and nuns pine for a time when monasticism and Catholicism were dominant, perhaps because we wear clothes from the past. While there may be a false romanticism of this sort among a few of our number, the reason for this timeline is to show there are yet better times ahead, in terms of spiritual theology. It is, though, valuable to follow the progression of ideas during this period, so as to understand those that follow.

SAINT BERNARD. Saint Bernard (1090–1153) preached: "If ignorant about ourselves, how can we be humble, thinking ourselves to be something when we are really nothing?"[61] For this faithful son of Saint Benedict, such ideas recurred several times throughout his works.[62] Of most value to this quick study are two selections. The first comes from one of his sermons on the Song of Songs:

> Even the Pharisee gives thanks, although his justice merits no praise from God. And if, as the Gospel points out, his act of thanksgiving does not increase his grace, why is this so? Because the pieties that our mouths proclaim will not justify the pride of our heart in the sight of him who is repelled by the arrogant. "God is not mocked, O Pharisee. What do you have that was not given to you?" "Nothing," he says, "and therefore I offer thanks to the giver." But if there is really nothing, then you had no antecedent merit to warrant your reception of the things of which you boast. And if you admit this, then in the first place it is futile to give yourself airs at the expense of the publican who does not possess as much as you because he has not received as much. Secondly, make sure you realize that God's gifts are entirely his own; if you attribute to yourself some of the glory and honor that are his, you may deservedly be convicted of fraud, of attempting to defraud God. If you brazenly boast of gifts as though they were your own, I should prefer to believe you are deceived, not that you wish to defraud. It is an error I should hope to correct. But when you make thanksgiving, you manifest that you regard nothing as your own, you wisely acknowledge that your merits are really God's gifts. When you despise others, however, you betray the inner

---

61 Bernard of Clairvaux, "Knowledge and ignorance of God and of self," in *Commentary on the Song of Songs*, arranged by Darrel Wright, last accessed August 14, 2014. https://ia600500.us.archive.org/20/items/StBernardsCommentaryOnTheSongOfSongs/StBernardOnTheSongOfSongsall.pdf, sermon 37, part iii, no. 5.
62 Cf. Bernard of Clairvaux, *Commentary on the Song of Songs*, sermon 3, part 3; sermon 17, part 20; sermon 21, parts 2, 7; sermon 25, part 7.

reality of your condition, you are speaking from a double heart, with one lending your tongue to a lie, with the other usurping the honor due to truth. Never would you judge the publican more despicable than yourself if you did not consider that you are more honorable than he.[63]

Given Saint Bernard's rebuke of this Christian Pharisee, we must refrain from acting in a proud and hypocritical manner, otherwise our knowledge of our nothingness is worthless.

Next, Saint Bernard stressed in his fourth sermon for Advent that to learn the truth is but a step toward living it:

When our Savior comes, he will transform the body of our humiliation, conforming it to the body of his glory only if our heart has first been transformed and conformed to the humiliation of his heart. That is why he told us, learn of me, for I am meek and humble of heart (cf. Mt 11:29). Consider well these words, for humility is twofold: one of thinking; the other of feeling — here called "the heart." By the former we realize that we are nothing, and this we learn from ourselves and from our weakness; by the latter we spurn worldly glory, and this we learn from him who emptied himself, taking the form of a servant (Phil 2:7). When they sought him for a kingdom, he fled (cf. Jn 6:15), but when they sought him for the great test and shameful suffering of the cross, he willingly offered himself (cf. Jn 18:4).[64]

Saint Bernard here calls those who follow this spirituality to a profound oblation. At the very least, let us take away his distinction that unless this knowledge were to progress into a disposition of humility and respect for others as non-inferiors (morally speaking), it would be of little service to the person. Saint Bernard here unmasked how easy it is to hide behind the knowledge of theology while neglecting to live its practical demands. Given Saint Bernard's influence, his teaching would have broadcast this approach to humility.

VENI SANCTE SPIRITUS. Among the laity, the spiritual term of nothingness would probably have made its first popular appearance in

---

63 Bernard of Clairvaux, "Our thanksgiving and God's glory," in *Commentary on the Song of Songs*, sermon 13, part 2.
64 Bernard of Clairvaux, *Sermons for Advent and the Christmas Season*, trans. Irene Edmonds et al. (Kalamazoo, MI: Cistercian Publications, 2007), "On the Lord's Advent," Sermon 4, no. 4, 29.

the thirteenth century in the text of the sequence *Veni Sancte Spiritus* [Come, Holy Spirit], a hymn of Gregorian chant associated with Pentecost that is attributed either to Pope Innocent III or Stephen Langton.[65] The pertinent part of the "golden sequence," as it is also known, runs "*Sine tuo numine, nihil est in homine, nihil est innoxium* [without thy Divinity, there is nothing in man, nothing is harmless]."[66] Given the context of calling for the presence and aid of the Holy Spirit, this line is properly interpreted as fitting the evangelical category rather than one of the categories pertaining to *creatio ex nihilo*. Marmion, who was always attentive to the meaning of the proper chants for the great liturgical feasts, cited this portion of the sequence as an exemplar of the disposition of humility that is necessary, along with prayer, for receiving greater gifts from the Holy Spirit.[67] What a liturgical insight this is! An astounding point follows from Marmion's especially advantaged interpretation of this line of the *Veni Sancte Spiritus*: the Church has been trying for centuries to form every member of the Roman Rite in this disposition in order to remove any obstacles to the gifts of the Holy Spirit within every individual.

BLESSED ANGELA OF FOLIGNO. The Middle Ages were a time in which scholastics, mendicants, and visionaries came to the forefront of ecclesiastical life. With regard to our topic, the language used by the visionaries of this time usually benefitted, at least indirectly, from scholastic reflections on the data of faith brought to their regions by the mendicants. These visionaries discussed their own nothingness more confidently, both because of their experiences and because of the language and spiritual guidance available to them. I find Marmion's use of medieval mystics to be well-curated, helpful, and relevant. Nonetheless, if it feels a bit like I'm remarking on every red barn on a long road trip, just skip ahead to Saint Thérèse. In the meantime, Blessed Angela of Foligno (1248 – 1309) is the first medieval visionary I will here review.

While visions are not the measure of the spiritual life (which is measured by charity and openness to the gifts of the Holy Spirit), it is nonetheless worth noting the effects produced by one of Blessed Angela's visions:

---

65 Cf. Hugh Henry, "Veni Sancte Spiritus et Emitte Coelitus," in *The Catholic Encyclopedia*, vol. 15 (New York, NY: Robert Appleton Company, 1912), last accessed August 29, 2014. http://www.newadvent.org/cathen/15342a.htm.

66 Church Music Association of America, *Parish Book of Chant: Expanded Second Edition* (N.p.: Church Music Association of America, 2012), last accessed August 2014. http://media.musicasacra.com/books/pbc_2nd.pdf, 143–45 (e-pages 164–66).

67 Cf. Marmion, *Mysteries*, 391–92.

And immediately the eyes of my soul were opened and I beheld the plenitude of God, whereby I did comprehend the whole world, both here and beyond the sea, and the abyss and all things else; and therein did I behold naught save the divine power in a manner assuredly indescribable, so that through excess of marveling the soul cried with a loud voice, saying, "This whole world is full of God!" Wherefore did I now comprehend that the world is but a small thing; I saw, moreover, that the power of God was above all things, and that the whole world was filled with it.

Then [He said to] me, "I have shown [you] something of My power," the which I did so well understand that it enabled me better to understand all other things. He said also, "I have made [you] to see something of My power; behold now and see [My] humility." Then was I given so deep an insight into the humility of God towards man and all other things that when my soul remembered His unspeakable power and comprehended His deep humility, it marveled greatly and did esteem itself to be nothing at all, for in itself it beheld nothing save pride. [68]

With regard to this topic, Blessed Angela of Foligno's major contribution, as that of most visionaries, is a frank avowal of her nothingness. Also in the Book of Divine Consolation, she wrote: "Faith is born of humility, for knowing itself to be nothing, and lacking in all divine things, it [believes] what is told [to] it according [to] our faith. Perceiving through its humility, moreover, that it [has] no power of itself and is not able by its own power to achieve aught, it [puts] its hope in God."[69] Then, in her testament and last admonition she instructed her followers thus: "Be [you] so humble that [you] do perpetually esteem yourselves as nothing."[70] Blessed Angela of Foligno not only acknowledged her nothingness, she also exhorted and taught others to do the same, linking growth in faith to it.

SAINT CATHERINE OF SIENA. The next visionary, often quoted by Marmion and greatly appreciated by those who know her well, is Saint Catherine of Siena (1347–1380), a Doctor of the Church. At the outset of her life as a visionary, she received the following message in her first

---

68   Angela of Foligno, Book of Divine Consolation, trans. Mark Steegman (London: Chatto and Windus, 1909), last accessed August 15, 2014. http://archive.org/stream/divineconsolatioooangeuoft#page/n5/mode/2up, treatise III, third vision, p. 172 [e-page 218]. I have updated some of the language.
69   Ibid., 113 [e-page 158]. I have updated some of the language.
70   Ibid., 259 [e-page 305]. I have updated some of the language.

vision, according to the biography written of her by the illustrious Saint Raymond of Capua:

> The holy virgin told her confessors, of whom, though unworthy, I was one, that at the beginning of her visions, that is to say when the Lord Jesus Christ first began to appear to her, he once came to her while she was praying and said, "Do you know, daughter, who you are, and who I am? If you know these two things, you will be blessed. You are she who is not; where[as] I am He who is. Have this knowledge in your soul and the Enemy will never deceive you and you will escape all his wiles; you will never disobey my commandments and will acquire all grace, trust, and light."[71]

This evangelical sense of her nothingness afterwards became fundamental for her. Raymond writes that at the time of her death, she offered the same spiritual advice to her followers:

> Her first and fundamental principle was that people who wish to begin to serve God must rid their hearts of all that kind of love into which the senses enter, not only for people but for any kind of creature whatsoever, and that they must seek for God the Creator single-mindedly and wholeheartedly. The heart, she said, cannot be entirely given to God unless it is delivered from all other affections and is simple and open and free from double-mindedness. She also said that from her childhood days her one aim had been to labour towards this end. She said, further, that she had realized that the soul cannot reach this perfect state, when it can give its heart to God completely, unless it prays; and she showed that prayer must necessarily be founded upon humility, and not derive from any belief in his own virtue on the part of the person praying, who on the contrary should always recognize that of himself he is nothing.[72]

This inclusion from her life as a visionary demonstrates that Saint Catherine found it paramount to combine an evangelical disposition of nothingness with the ascetical nothingness of holding to nothing that would distract her from God. Indeed, her acceptance of her own nothingness rendered her ascetical life significantly more facile, for she was thereby filled with gratitude to the point of wanting only God:

---

71 Raymond of Capua, The Life of St. Catherine of Siena, trans. George Lamb (New York, NY: P. J. Kennedy & Sons, 1960), 79.
72 Ibid., 330.

For what wound of pride can enter into a soul that knows itself to be nothing? Who can glory in anything he does, when he knows that he himself has not done it, or imagine himself to be superior to others if in his heart of hearts he knows himself not to be? How can a man despise or envy others who despises himself as nothing, how glory in worldly wealth, when he despises his own glory? Incarnate Wisdom said, "If I glorify myself, my glory is nothing" (Jn 8:54). Further, how will he dare to call things of the world his own when he knows that he himself is not his own property but belongs to Him who made him? This being so, what soul will take delight in the pleasures of the senses when it knows that it is daily fettering itself to non-being thereby? And lastly, who will be indolent when he knows that his being is not his own but something to be begged from Another? From these considerations, thus briefly stated, you will realize, reader, that all vices are driven out by those three words, "You are not."[73]

While previously her appreciation of her nothingness could have been described as a shield against attack, here she described it as an antidote to improper desires.

She appreciated her nothingness at yet a deeper level: since God had created her, He had already fallen in love with her and, in a sense, espoused her despite her eventual fall into sinfulness/nothingness.[74] She expresses this fact in her fourth prayer in this way: "I have sinned, O Lord, have mercy on me. O what an admirable thing it is that you created your creature despite [recognizing] before your creature were even to have had life . . . that she should have to commit sin and not follow your Truth."[75] Due to her confidence in God's creative love for her, she could overcome her sense of her nothingness by using it as a type of "springboard," as Murray puts it,[76] for praising God for having chosen to create her and love her. This springboard effect is present in her twentieth prayer:

73 Raymond of Capua, *The Life of St. Catherine of Siena*, 81.
74 Paul Murray, "Saint Catherine of Siena" (lecture, Pontifical University of Saint Thomas in Urbe, Rome, 2013); and Paul Murray, "Thomas Aquinas at Prayer" (lecture, Pontifical University of Saint Thomas in Urbe, Rome, 2014).
75 Catherine of Siena, "Orazione VII" in *Le Orazioni* (N.p.: Centro Internazionli di Studi Cateriniani, Date Unknown), last accessed February 13, 2015. http://www.centro-studicateriniani.it/download/Le%20Orazioni.pdf. My translation.
76 Paul Murray, "Saint Catherine of Siena" (lecture, Pontifical University of Saint Thomas in Urbe, Rome, 2013).

I have sinned, O Lord, have mercy on me.

You, Eternal Deity, You are life, I am death; You are wisdom, I
am stupidity; You, light, I, darkness; You, infinitude and I, finite;
You, unwavering rectitude, I, miserable tortuosity; You, the doctor and I, the infirm. And who could come to you, O Most High,
Eternal Deity, to thank you for the innumerable gifts that you
have given to us? You, Yourself, will come with a light that You
will offer to her who wants to receive it and with Your rope you
will fasten [to Yourself] her who allows herself to be united [to
You] by not making any resistance to Your will.[77]

If occasionally we find ourselves feeling down about ourselves due to
a sense of our nothingness, let us recall this confidence of Saint Catherine,
by which she used her deepening self-knowledge to praise the Source of
all perfection. Saint Catherine's various forms of confidence and gratitude
indeed allow us to anticipate significant effects of the disposition of nothingness: the obverse of the disposition of nothingness is to understand
that every aspect of each life is a grace. Since a truly humble soul receives
grace in fullest measure, to accept your nothingness does not lead to your
annihilation; rather, it leads you to receiving gifts in fuller measure and
to appreciating them and the Perfect Giver.

BLESSED BLOSIUS. Immediately prior to the Council of Trent and
somewhat contemporaneously with it lived Blessed Blosius (i.e., Louis de
Blois, 1506–1566), a Benedictine abbot and spiritual writer. Of Blosius's
many instructions about nothingness, two of his comments about prayer
will be of best service to this study, opening up new aspects of it.

Of the benefits of aridity in prayer he wrote:

It is a common error to imagine all is lost when we are deprived
of sensible consolation, and to fancy ourselves once more holy
and acceptable to God when it returns; but, as already said, in
this we are deceived. Oftentimes God is the most nearly present
by grace where He is felt the least, and often dryness of heart is
better for a man than the most copious abundance of sweetness.
For in dryness and barrenness a man more clearly realizes that of
himself he can do nothing.[78]

---

77 Catherine of Siena, "Orazione XX" in Le Orazioni, 25. My translation.
78 Blosius, A Book of Spiritual Instruction [Institutio spiritualis], trans. Bertrand Wilberforce,
ed. a Benedictine of Stanbrook (London: Art and Book, 1900; reprinted and revised,
London: Burns and Oats, 1955), chap. vii, 43.

In short, to persevere through aridity builds our virtues and allows progress on the true measure of our lives, charity. Aridity is simply an aspect of the spiritual life, just as trials are. "Count it all joy, my brethren, when you meet various trials," wrote Saint James, "for you know that the testing of your faith produces steadfastness. And let steadfastness have its full effect, that you may be perfect and complete, lacking in nothing" (1:2–4). As we pass through times of trial, let us recall that we will eventually become mature and complete. To help us pass through these trials, Blosius advised beginners to aspire to a sense of nothingness and intermediates to apply the types of asceticism connected to it.[79]

Since persevering through aridity also prepares us later to receive greater gifts in fuller measure, we turn now to Blosius's comments about union with God:

> For when, through love, the soul goes beyond all work of the intellect and all images in the mind, and is rapt above itself (a favour God only can bestow), utterly leaving itself, it flows into God: then is God its peace and fulness. In this peace of mind the soul can rightly sing: "In pace, in idipsum, dormiam et requiescam — In peace, in the self-same, I will sleep and I will rest" [Ps 4:9].
>
> The loving soul, as I have said, flows out of itself, and completely swoons away; and as if brought to nothing, it sinks down into the abyss of divine love, where, dead to itself, it lives in God, knowing nothing, feeling nothing, save only the love that it experiences.
>
> It loses itself in the infinite solitude and darkness of the Godhead; but so to lose itself is rather to find itself.
>
> Then, putting off whatever is human and putting on what is divine, it is, as it were, transformed and changed into God, as iron placed in fire receives the form of fire, and is changed into fire. Just as the iron thus glowing with fire does not cease to be iron, so the soul, as it were, deified, does not change its nature and still remains itself.[80]

---

79 Cf. ibid., 128: "Aspirations for the Purgative Way: O Good Jesus, good Jesus, good Jesus! O my hope, my refuge, my salvation, have mercy on me. Have mercy, have mercy, have mercy! I am poor and needy: I am nothing: I can do nothing. . . ."; 130–31: "Aspirations of union . . . Remove, in thy mercy, I beseech thee, all hindrances, and make me one spirit with thee, for the glory of thy name. Hear me, O Lord; hear me; hear my prayer, not to gratify my will, but for thy own good pleasure. Teach me, I beseech thee; enlighten, direct, and help me in all things, that I may do nothing, speak nothing, think nothing, will nothing, except what will be pleasing in thine eyes."
80 Blosius, *A Book of Spiritual Instruction* [*Institutio spiritualis*], chap. xii, part 2, no. 1, pp. 84–85.

This description of contemplative union occurs in stillness, raised above knowledge and feeling . . . It has nothing to do with visions. We shall later see that Marmion held this type of experience of union with God to be the normal expression of it.

You may be wondering, "Does 'being nothing' drop away once I have reached union with God?" To that I must respond: What?! No self-naughting?! More importantly, in his account of the effects of mystical union, Blessed Blosius emphatically reinforces the path of nothingness throughout the spiritual journey, thereby rejecting the notion that it drops away:

> For God's sake they willingly submit themselves to other men,
> they gladly obey all for God, with all their heart they choose the
> lowest place. They are not puffed up on account of the many
> excellent gifts which they have received, since they plunge most
> deeply into their own nothingness. They think nothing whatever
> of themselves, knowing well that it is God who works all the good
> they do. Constantly do they remain fixed in true humility and
> filial fear, and acknowledge that they are unprofitable servants. [81]

These effects of union with God are useful to recall the next time you encounter a saintly imposter — a sly seducer who sweet-talks his prey into pseudo-spiritual snares. Such a charlatan could never take the route of nothingness, not in act, nor sustain it as a maneuver for his benefit. Of course, he could temporarily say he is nothing, but his actions will speak louder than his words in the end: "Whatever a man sows, that he will also reap. For he who sows to his own flesh will from the flesh reap corruption; but he who sows to the Spirit will from the Spirit reap eternal life" (Gal 6:7b–8).

It is also the case that those with their screws strewn all over the floor could follow this spirituality without it thereby crediting their crazy points of view. That this spirituality can help us to understand some hints at holiness does not guarantee it for its followers.

After the Protestant Controversies on Grace

With the rise of the Protestant controversies over grace, intrinsic justification, and merits, attention to this issue became more dogmatic. This dogmatic trend reached a critical point at the Council of Trent (1545–1563), which had the following to say on the matter:

---

81 Ibid., chap. xii, part 4, no. 2, point c, p. 97.

However, this satisfaction that we make for our sins is not ours in such a way that it be not through Christ Jesus. For, while we can do nothing of ourselves as of ourselves, we can do everything with the cooperation of him who strengthens us [cf. Phil 4:13]. Thus man has nothing wherein to glory, but all our glorying is in Christ [cf. 1 Cor 1:31; 2 Cor 10:17; Gal 6:14], in whom we live [cf. Acts 17:28], in whom we merit, in whom we make satisfaction, bringing forth worthy fruits of penance [cf. Lk 3:8; Mt 3:8]. These fruits have their efficacy from him, by him they are offered to the Father, and through him they are accepted by the Father. [canons 13–15][82]

The three Doctors of the Church reviewed in the following sections — Saint Teresa of Avila, Saint John of the Cross, and Saint Francis de Sales — were all deeply touched by the tensions in Christianity during their lives. Their writings have a distinctively Catholic use of the mystical term of nothingness that could not be mistaken as merely giving thanks to the Creator for creation. Marmion held each of these Doctors in great esteem. He called the two Carmelites "the best writers on the life of prayer."[83] Even though Marmion did not personally follow Saint John of the Cross on some of his teachings regarding prayer,[84] he did nonetheless allow for others to do so: "Now we must never forget that everyone has his own personality. There are no two of you exactly the same. And so it is for prayer: there are no two souls who have quite the same way of praying or talking with God."[85] As for Saint Francis de Sales, the holy bishop's influence upon Marmion was greater than that of either of the Carmelites, for, according to biographer Mark Tierney, Saint Francis de Sales's influence upon Marmion ranked behind only the notable influences of the Word of God, the Rule of Saint Benedict, and the theology of Saint Thomas Aquinas.[86] While Saint Francis de Sales had already been named a Doctor

---

82 Denzinger, *Enchiridion*, Council of Trent, 14th Session (1551), ch. 8, no. 1691. For Marmion's recognition and application of this definition, see Marmion, "Letter to a Dominican sister of Dublin, 27 February 1916," in *Letters*, 202.
83 Marmion, "Conference, Maredret, May 9th, 1911," quoted in Philipon, *Spiritual Doctrine*, 163–64.
84 Cf. Columba Marmion, "Letter to Mother Marie-Joseph van Aerden, 25 September 1918," in *Correspondance: 1881–1923* (Paris: Francois-Xavier de Guibert, 2008), 938 (hereafter *Correspondance*).
85 Marmion, "Conference, Maredret, May 9th, 1911," quoted in Philipon, *Spiritual Doctrine*, 164.
86 Cf. Tierney, *Blessed Columba Marmion*, 148–49.

of the Church before Marmion began to write, Marmion's appreciation of the two Carmelites came well before they were later recommended for universal attention in this way.

SAINT TERESA OF AVILA. Saint Teresa of Avila's (1515–1582) works are classics, invaluable for understanding the grades of prayer. Most dabblers in spiritual reading have read her works and can probably recall in them several expressions of hyperbolic humility, such as "I am imperfection incarnate."[87] In this cause to establish firmly this spirituality, her witness to the interplay between nothingness and contemplative prayer is noteworthy. At the beginning of Chapter 15 of The Book of Her Life, in which she treated of the prayer of quiet, she joked about how a novice at this prayer attempted to prolong it by her own efforts: "The poor little thing doesn't understand that since by its own efforts it can do nothing to draw that good to itself, so much less will it be able to keep it for longer than the Lord desires."[88] At the end of the chapter, she taught that growth in true humility is the sign of an authentic visit from the Lord:

> When the prayer comes from God's spirit, there is no need to go dredging up things in order to derive some humility and shame because the Lord Himself gives this prayer in a manner very different from that which we gain through our nice reasonings. For such humility is nothing in comparison with the true humility the Lord with His light here teaches and which causes embarrassment that undoes one. It is well known that God gives a knowledge that makes us realize we have no good of ourselves; and the greater the favors, the greater is this knowledge.[89]

This authoritative insight about the sense of nothingness the Lord infuses during his visits should help any dabbler in this topic to pay closer attention to his prayer and its effects. To this witness, we can add a further reflection from The Interior Castle:

> Once I was pondering why our Lord was so fond of this virtue of humility, and this thought came to me — in my opinion not as

---

87 For example, Teresa of Avila, The Book of Her Life, vol. 1 of The Collected Works, trans. Kieran Kavanaugh and Otilio Rodriguez, 2nd ed. (Washington, DC: ICS Publications, 1987), 261–62.
88 Teresa of Avila, The Book of Her Life, ch. 15, no. 1, p. 139.
89 Teresa of Avila, The Book of Her Life, 146. For Marmion's reception of this point, see Marmion, Monk, 244: "Let us beseech [God] to show us . . . that without Him we are nothing; one ray of Divine light can do more in this way than any reasoning."

a result of reflection but suddenly: It is because God is supreme Truth; and to be humble is to walk in truth, for it is a very deep truth that of ourselves we have nothing good but only misery and nothingness. Whoever does not understand this walks in falsehood. The more anyone understands it the more he pleases the supreme Truth because he is walking in truth. Please God, Sisters, we will be granted the favor never to leave this path of self-knowledge, amen.[90]

So, this Doctor of the Church held accepting our nothingness as a mark of mystical orthodoxy and orthopraxy.

SAINT JOHN OF THE CROSS. When those attentive to spiritual theology think of the term "nothing," their thoughts must eventually turn to Saint John of the Cross (1542–1591). In his famous "path of nothing" on his own graphic design for the *Ascent of Mount Carmel*, he instructed others to search for neither the goods of heaven nor the goods of earth: "not possessions, not glory, not joy, not knowledge, not consolation, and not rest"; up the center of the diagram is repeated one word: "nothing"; on the summit stands a phrase: "and even on the Mount, nothing."[91] This is hyperbolic language about detachment and asceticism, but it also expresses the necessity to die to sin in order to live with God (cf. Rom 6:10). Both aspects are common to Marmion and Saint John of the Cross.[92] While it is beneficial to have and hold to nothing that would distract us from loving God for himself, rather than for his gifts, such an outlook is only undertaken within the overall scheme of enjoying whatever gifts, either natural or supernatural, that our good God offers for our happiness and perfection.[93] Given our attachment to those gifts, we need Saint John of the Cross's insistent teaching to help detach us from fixating on them. Furthermore, the ascetical category of nothingness is in a sense derivative from the more basic evangelical category, for ascetical practices must serve

---

90 Teresa of Avila, "Sixth dwelling place" in *The Interior Castle*, vol. 2 of *The Collected Works*, trans. Kieran Kavanaugh and Otilio Rodriguez (Washington, DC: ICS Publications, 1980), 420–21.
91 John of the Cross, *Ascent of Mount Carmel*, in *Collected Works*, trans. Kieran Kavanaugh and Otilio Rodriguez (Washington, DC: ICS Publications, 1991), 110–11.
92 See Philipon, *Spiritual Doctrine*, 104: "The *agendo contra* of St. Ignatius and the 'path of nothingness' of St. John of the Cross are merely different ways of expressing the same necessity for death to self, which is an indispensable condition for a new life in Christ. As a true disciple of St. Paul, Dom Marmion takes, as the basis of his whole doctrine, absolute death to sin and a vigorous war against all the vicious tendencies of our nature."
93 Cf. John of the Cross, *Dark Night of the Soul*, in *Collected Works*, bk. 2, chap. 9, no. 1.

to increase humility and charity.[94] Indeed, this truth was acknowledged by Saint John of the Cross and therefore served as the foundation for his ascetical teaching: "The humble are those who hide in their own nothingness and know how to abandon themselves to God."[95]

Linked to the *Ascent of Mount Carmel* is Saint John of the Cross's *Dark Night of the Soul*. It specifically outlines the seasons of aridity we will encounter on "the ascent that is really a descent" into humility.[96] The first season of aridity is the dark night of sense, and it overlaps with the detachment from worldly rewards just mentioned. The second season of aridity is called the dark night of the spirit. Through it, God purifies any remaining misaligned aspects of our relationship with him, including any remaining self-reliance. It has a significant passive element in which we merely suffer the loss of God's consoling presence and gifts until we are freed from our love disorder with God. The following words from one of Marmion's letters of spiritual direction are an echo of this Carmelite's teaching on this dark night: "The very nature of the trial through which you are passing is the terrible uncertainty it leaves in the soul as to her state. She seems to herself to have lost faith and love, for she feels nothing. It is pure naked faith. This longing for God is a most powerful and constant prayer."[97] At this point, we must introduce a new aspect of ascetical nothingness: to feel nothing. While this experience may sound cruel, it is, in fact, the purification from a disordered desire to want to win God as a trophy.[98] Indeed, only when we consider ourselves as unworthy of divine visitations are we purified of this temptation.[99] In this passive purification, there is no sense of progress, for God leads each person along an obscure path. So, if one element of the process is to surrender entirely to the Lord, then accepting our inability to progress without God's help is among the most efficient ways through it.

SAINT FRANCIS DE SALES. Saint Francis de Sales's (1567–1622) gentle and pastoral explanations are a helpful counterbalance to Saint John of the Cross's zealous but severe language. In Saint Francis de Sales's chapter

---

94 Oblative ascetical practices, suffered or undertaken to help others, may also flow from a deep expression of humility.

95 John of the Cross, *Sayings of Light and Love*, in *Collected Works*, no. 163.

96 Paul Murray, "John of the Cross" (lecture, Pontifical University of Saint Thomas in Urbe, Rome, 2014); see also John of the Cross, *Dark Night*, bk. 2, chap. 18, no. 2.

97 Marmion, "Letter to a young girl, 31 December 1919," in *Letters*, 179.

98 Cf. Alex Kurian, *Ascent to Nothingness: The Ascent to God according to John of the Cross* (London: St. Paul's, 2000), 34–35.

99 Cf. Marmion, *Monk*, 154–55.

on interior humility, he encouraged the soul under his care to rejoice as Mary did in the Magnificat (cf. Lk 1:46–55) about her gifts by which she magnifies the Lord.[100] The holy bishop's only concern was that we should maintain discretion about our humility:

> We often say that we are nothing, that we are misery itself and nothing but refuse, but we should be very annoyed were we taken at our word and have this said of us by others; on the contrary we pretend to run away and hide ourselves only that others may run after us and find us; we make a show of wishing to be the last and so take the lowest place at table but only that we may be asked to go higher. True humility is not ostentatious and speaks few words of humility, desiring not only to hide the other virtues but itself above all, and, were it lawful to lie, or give scandal, it would make a show of arrogance and pride to cloak itself and remain completely hidden and unknown. In my opinion, Philothea, you should refrain from expressions of humility or use them when they really express your interior dispositions. Never lower your eyes without humbling your heart or make a show of wishing to be last unless it is sincere; this is such a universal rule that there must be no exceptions. . . . A truly humble man would prefer another to call him a useless wretch than to say it of himself; at least he does not deny it, but freely admits it, only too glad that others should think the same as himself.[101]

In other words, it is one thing to understand our nothingness, another to appreciate its benefits, and yet another to realize how to conceal it in order to maintain those benefits. If we are to become grateful by this practice, it best expresses itself in equanimity and interior peace within a typical life.

The final step is to know when to reveal that humility so as to share its benefits: "When charity demands, we must freely and gently instruct our neighbor in what is necessary, not only for his instruction but for his encouragement; for humility, while it conceals and hides virtues to preserve them, will manifest them at the bidding of charity, to increase, develop, and preserve them."[102] While the practice of interior humility preserves the virtue and its effects, charity is always principal. A charitable discussion of humility does not extinguish humility; it spreads it. In all things, we must

100 Francis de Sales, *Introduction to the Devout Life*, trans. Michael Day (London: Burns & Oats, 1956), 103.
101 Francis de Sales, *Introduction to the Devout Life*, 103–4.
102 Ibid., 105.

glorify God, either by lifting our souls to him or by becoming a means of edifying others. At no point should a Christian, by duty an evangelizer, lose sight of this most fundamental line of prayer: "Our Father who art in heaven, Hallowed be thy Name!" (Mt 6:9 – 13).

In Modernity

Some of the closest influences upon Marmion, namely from the French school of spirituality, and some of the most practical and sublime insights, namely from Saint Thérèse of Lisieux, have yet to be presented in this historical review. In fact, the preceding sections have merely prepared us to review both the modern period and then Marmion's own contributions to an evolving field of thought.

THE FRENCH SCHOOL. On the occasion of Columba Marmion's beatification, Archbishop Connell of Dublin offered a homily on Marmion's spirituality at S. Agatha Dei Gothi in Rome, the church in which Marmion had been ordained.[103] He proposed Marmion had fallen under the influence of the French school of spirituality while still a diocesan priest in Ireland, due to the significant influence of Father Gowan, a French Vincentian serving there. To prove the connection, the archbishop noted that Marmion's Christ-centered approach was typical of the French school[104]— but there is another spiritual characteristic of that school, namely self-abnegation/self-annihilation.[105] When considering this other characteristic, we can see Marmion's focus on nothingness was one point he had in common with Pierre de Bérulle (1575 – 1622), the initiator of the French school.[106] In some

---

103   Desmond Connell, Homily at the beatification of Columba Marmion (Homily, S. Agatha Dei Gothi, 4 September, 2000, English), last accessed August 16, 2014. http://www.marmion.be/marm3108.html.

104   Cf. ibid.: "From Gowan's personal direction, and his guidance in reading, Marmion would first have met a French tradition. Later he absorbed the thinking of what is called the French School: the line of Bérulle, Condren, Olier. The chosen themes, and even the order in which they appear in his work, are unmistakable: the person of Christ, the Incarnate Word, present through the mysteries of his life on earth in the life of the Church and through the mediation of the Church in the lives of the faithful."

105   Jordan Aumann, Christian Spirituality in the Catholic Tradition (London: Sheed & Ward, 1985), 218 – 28, e.g., 220: "Several events in the life of Bérulle weaned him from the abstract school and emphasis on self-abnegation; he turned to a spiritual doctrine based on the positive commitment of adherence to Christ."

106   Cf. Gionta, Le Virtù Teologali, 24 – 25: "There are other points of contact between the two authors [Bérulle and Marmion]. One can here mention the invitation to accept one's nothingness before the divine majesty." My translation. For more on Marmion's relation to the French school, see Gionta, Le Virtù Teologali, 24 – 31, 331.

regards, then, Marmion's focus upon nothingness was typical of his spiritual milieu. To participate in Christ's mysteries (or, to "imitate the Divine Word in His 'states'"[107]) certainly came to the forefront in Marmion's works, as it did in the French school of spirituality, but he nonetheless insisted in his works upon accepting our nothingness as a major way to open ourselves to grace. In other words, amid his meditations on the exterior aspects of the faith, he included reflections on the interior life as well. In this regard, he exhibited both of these characteristics of the French school. While many today who are liturgically minded often recall the exterior aspects of Marmion's spirituality, the interior aspects of his spirituality should not be minimized. In fact, Marmion gets the balance between these two elements correct.

SAINT THÉRÈSE OF LISIEUX. Saint Thérèse of Lisieux's (1873–1897) little way of spiritual childhood is both the culminating point of this concept history and also the bridge to the next section about the proper way in which to live out our nothingness. This great Doctor of the Church has transformed Catholic spirituality, and nowhere is it more evident, with regard to this theme, than in her offering of herself to God as a victim to his merciful love (see Appendix 2). In that prayer, she stated several intentions: to love God and make him loved, to offer the merits of Christ and the saints — not her own — to God, to go to God "with empty hands," paying no attention either to her weaknesses or merits and trusting only in God's love for her, and yet, to offer herself as a victim to God's merciful love for the redemption of the world.[108] These intentions, and Saint Thérèse's spirituality in general, are a profound and unique meditation on how to live our nothingness, for to go to God "with empty hands" is simply a beautiful rephrasing of the concept of "being nothing."

Her entire teaching on spiritual childhood is connected to the theme of "being nothing." While this theme appeared most explicitly and succinctly in her letters and last conversations (which were probably unavailable to Marmion), the content discussed so briefly in them was already apparent to him in her published autobiography. In this excerpt from one of her letters, her appreciation of the disposition of nothingness is clear: "Ah! how

---

107   Marmion, *Mysteries*, 52.
108   Cf. Thérèse of Lisieux, "Prayer 6," in *Archives du Carmel de Lisieux*, last accessed August 16, 2014. http://www.archives-carmel-lisieux.fr/english/carmel/index.php/pri-6. See also Conrad de Meester, *With Empty Hands: The Message of Saint Thérèse of Lisieux* (London: Burns and Oats, 2002). This section is also indebted to the ability to find the following quotes easily in the systematic approach of François Jamart, *Complete Spiritual Doctrine of St. Thérèse of Lisieux*, trans. Walter van de Putte (New York, NY: Alba House, 1961).

little known are the goodness, the merciful love of Jesus, Brother! . . . It is true, to enjoy these treasures one must humble oneself, recognize one's nothingness, and that is what many souls do not want to do."[109] Certainly, a child is not nothing in a philosophical sense, but a child trusts entirely in God and his or her parents because he knows how small and powerless he is. Saint Thérèse's genius was, in part, to restate the dense and complicated theological term of nothingness in common language even children could understand. Treatises on nothingness cannot compare with a sentence such as this: "Perfection seems simple to me, I see it is sufficient to recognize one's nothingness and to abandon oneself as a child into God's arms."[110] This statement makes nothingness both intelligible and attractive, and that effect frequently appears in the Little Flower's work.

Furthermore, it is from her very nothingness that her great hope emerged: "What pleases Him is that He sees me loving my littleness and my poverty, the blind hope that I have in His mercy."[111] Since she did not have any confidence in her merits, she placed her confidence in Christ. In this regard, she wrote, "Marie, if you are nothing, you must not forget that Jesus is All, so you must lose your little nothingness in His infinite All and think only of this uniquely lovable All."[112] In other words, to accept our nothingness creates a void in the soul that allows a transformative power to fill it. Were we to take another path than this type of childlike confidence, we would risk trying to buy sanctity through our merits. In a passage undoubtedly known by Marmion, she reflected:

> He made me understand my own glory would not be evident to
> the eyes of mortals, that it would consist in becoming a great saint!

---

109 Thérèse of Lisieux, "Letter 261, to Fr. Bellière, 26 July 1897," in *Archives du Carmel de Lisieux*, last accessed August 29, 2014. http://www.archives-carmel-lisieux.fr/english/carmel/index.php/lt-261-a-266/1172-lt-261-a-labbe-belliere; see also Jamart, *Complete Spiritual Doctrine of St. Thérèse of Lisieux*, 31.

110 Thérèse of Lisieux, "Letter 226, to Fr. Roulland, 9 May 1897," in *Archives du Carmel de Lisieux*, last accessed August 29, 2014. http://www.archives-carmel-lisieux.fr/english/carmel/index.php/lt-221-a-230/1128-lt-226-au-p-roulland; see also Jamart, *Complete Spiritual Doctrine of St. Thérèse of Lisieux*, 118.

111 Thérèse of Lisieux, "Letter 197, to Sister Marie of the Sacred Heart, 17 September 1896," in *Archives du Carmel de Lisieux*, last accessed August 29, 2014. http://www.archives-carmel-lisieux.fr/english/carmel/index.php/lt-191-a-200/1079-lt-197-a-soeur-marie-du-sacre-coeur; see also Jamart, *Complete Spiritual Doctrine of St. Thérèse of Lisieux*, 32.

112 Thérèse of Lisieux, "Letter 109, to Marie Guérin, 27–29 July 1890," in *Archives du Carmel de Lisieux*, last accessed August 29, 2014. http://www.archives-carmel-lisieux.fr/english/carmel/index.php/lt-101-a-110/945-lt-109-a-marie-guerin; see also Jamart, *Complete Spiritual Doctrine of St. Thérèse of Lisieux*, 33.

> This desire could certainly appear daring if one were to consider how weak and imperfect I was, and how, after seven years in the religious life, I still am weak and imperfect. I always feel, however, the same bold confidence of becoming a great saint because I don't count on my merits since I have none, but I trust in Him who is Virtue and Holiness. God alone, content with my weak efforts, will raise me to Himself and make me a saint, clothing me in His infinite merits.[113]

Saint Thérèse, therefore, made nothingness the central disposition for the pursuit of union with God, albeit in an entirely novel way. Moreover, her unique and simplified approach to this topic probably provided the spiritual framework for Marmion's focus on humility and confidence.[114]

Finally, the influence of Saint Thérèse's little way overflowed into many different practical aspects of the spiritual life, and nowhere is this more evident than in her novel approach to asceticism. She grounded her asceticism so thoroughly in humility that she valued herself as unworthy to ask for suffering or to undertake atypical ascetical practices. She trusted God would provide her the sacrifices and the graces necessary to offer them:

> I didn't expect to suffer like this; I'm suffering like a little child. I would never want to ask God for greater sufferings. If He increases them, I will bear them with pleasure and with joy because they will be coming from Him. But I'm too little to have any strength through myself. If I were to ask for sufferings, these would be mine, and I would have to bear them alone, and I've never been able to do anything alone.[115]

For example, in speaking of heavy penances, she said, "We must be very restrained on this point, for often nature is involved in this matter more than anything else."[116] By nature, she means selfishness. The book of her

113 Thérèse of Lisieux, "Manuscript A," in *Archives du Carmel de Lisieux*, last accessed August 29, 2014. http://www.archives-carmel-lisieux.fr/english/carmel/index.php/31-40/32, 32; see also Jamart, *Complete Spiritual Doctrine of St. Thérèse of Lisieux*, 51–52.

114 For an example of Marmion's approach, to be discussed later, see Marmion, *Mysteries*, 455ff. (Appendix 1). On this point Gionta also connects Marmion to Saint Thérèse of Lisieux; see Gionta, *Le Virtù Teologali*, 226.

115 Thérèse of Lisieux, last conversations, yellow notebook, August 11, no. 3, in *Archives du Carmel de Lisieux*, last accessed February 28, 2015. http://www.archives-carmel-lisieux.fr/english/carmel/index.php/carnet-jaune/2320-carnet-jaune-aout; see also Jamart, *Complete Spiritual Doctrine of St. Thérèse of Lisieux*, 201.

116 Thérèse of Lisieux, last conversations, yellow notebook, August 3rd, no. 5, in *Archives du Carmel de Lisieux*, last accessed February 28, 2015. http://www.archives-carmel-lisieux.

last conversations, *Novissma Verba*, also records another illuminating statement from her on this subject:

> In the life of Blessed Henry Suso there is a very striking passage with regard to corporal penances. He had employed the most frightful penances, which had well-nigh ruined his health, when an angel appeared to him and told him to stop, adding: "You are not to fight any longer as a simple soldier; from this moment I shall arm you as a knight." And he made the saint understand the superiority of the spiritual conflict over the mortifications of the flesh. "Very well, my little mother. God has not willed me to fight as a simple soldier. He has armed me as a knight, and I have engaged in the war against myself in the spiritual domain, by abnegation and little hidden sacrifices. I have found peace and humility in that hidden conflict where nature finds nothing for herself."[117]

Let us allow Blessed Marie Eugene of the Child Jesus, a leading twentieth-century commentator on Carmelite spirituality (1894–1967), to express these insights with greater precision. He argued that while our ascetical and spiritual lives should be adapted to our weakness and progressively grow toward greater heights, to ground our asceticism in our weakness does not negate the absolute character of our desires.[118] Asceticism is, after all, at the service of growing in virtue, most especially, according to Marmion, the virtue of humility.[119] In commenting upon Saint Thérèse of Lisieux's novel approach to asceticism, Marie Eugene wrote:

> In order to combat a generalized pride, Saint Thérèse constructs a spirituality of humility, her "way of spiritual childhood." To remain a child, to cultivate carefully in oneself the awareness of one's littleness and trusting weakness, to rejoice in one's poverty, to display it gladly before God as an appeal to His mercy; such, in her opinion, is the most proper attitude to attract God's glance and the plenitude of His transforming and consuming love. Really to acquire this attitude and to keep it, demands a complete immolation.[120]

---

fr/english/carmel/index.php/carnet-jaune/2320-carnet-jaune-aout; Thérèse of Lisieux, *Novissima Verba: The Last Conversations of St Thérèse of the Child Jesus* (London: Burns Oates & Washbourne, 1929), 103; see also Jamart, *Complete Spiritual Doctrine of St. Thérèse of Lisieux*, 126.

117 Thérèse of Lisieux, *Novissima Verba*, 103–4.
118 Cf. Marie Eugene, *I Want to See God: A Practical Synthesis of Carmelite Spirituality*, vol. 1, trans. M. Verda Clare (Chicago, IL: FIDES Publishers, 1953), 80–96.
119 Cf. Marmion, *Monk*, 186–87, 218.
120 Marie Eugene, *I Want to See God*, 93.

In fact, God transformed her interior asceticism into a great overall oblation.

When Marmion taught about the spiritual life and asceticism, he simply focused upon humility and trust in God. In words highly reminiscent of Saint Thérèse, he taught, "We ought not to strive to dazzle God by our perfection, but rather to draw down His mercy by the confession of our weakness."[121] Indeed, he taught we advance by accepting mercy more fully into our lives:

> Be a monument of His mercy for all eternity. The greater the wretchedness and the unworthiness, the greater and more adorable His mercy: *Abyssus abyssum invocat* [abyss calls upon abyss]: the abyss of our wretchedness invokes the abyss of his mercy. It is an immense consolation for me to see that you are travelling by this road which is so sure, which leads to such heights, and which glorifies the precious blood of Jesus Christ and the mercy of God. It is the way I have chosen too. Help me by your prayers.[122]

The way of nothingness is, then, the way of opening ourselves to the mercy of God. We become more grateful, too, when we receive mercy in greater measure.

Until we view the entire process, asceticism included, under the liberating mercy of God, we are prone to build monuments to ourselves. Ruth Burrows sums up this temptation against spiritual childhood in the phrase to make ourselves "beautiful for God."[123] Since our anxiety about measuring up to some standard produces self-reliance, we strive to make ourselves beautiful for God according to it. With the disposition of nothingness, however, there is no external, worldly measure. We merely ask for mercy from God in ever more liberating ways. Or, perhaps, we recognize that we drastically fail to measure up to Christ, our unattainable model of perfection. This failure leads us to beg for more mercy.

In keeping with Marmion's liturgical interests and in accord with Saint Thérèse "little way," I speculate he probably viewed the ascetical process within the context of this prayer:

> Deliver us, we beseech Thee, O Lord, from all evils, past, present, and to come; and by the intercession of the blessed and glorious ever Virgin Mary, Mother of God, and of the holy Apostles, Peter and Paul, and of Andrew, and of all the Saints, mercifully grant

---

121 Marmion, *Monk*, 216.
122 Marmion, *Priest*, 363–64.
123 Cf. Ruth Burrows, *Guidelines for Mystical Prayer*, 7th ed. (London: Bloomsbury, 2007), 136–37; cf. 128.

THE GRACE OF "NOTHINGNESS"

> peace in our days, that through the assistance of Thy mercy we
> may be always free from sin, and secure from all disturbance.[124]

While no one would deny the necessity of this prayer, which Marmion made
during the very fraction of the Eucharist, many people fail to allow this
prayer to have its full effect on a practical, subjective level. While Semipe-
lagians do not deny the necessity of grace, they do construct obstacles to
it. Those who obstruct the power of this august prayer are trying either to
elevate or to liberate themselves — all in cooperation with God's grace, in
their minds — rather than make themselves "monuments to God's mercy."[125] To follow spiritual childhood or to accept to be a monument to God's
mercy is to reverse completely the mentality of spiritual accomplishment.
A Semipelagian simply refuses to be sanctified deeply because he is always
trying to sanctify (or perfect) himself. Rather than accept his nothingness,
he uses self-reliance to break free from it. In doing so, he refuses the liberation of allowing God to sanctify him at ever-deeper levels.

To accept our nothingness is the way to allow God to bring about a
truly liberating asceticism. Only in going to God "with empty hands," constantly begging for mercy, do we allow God to take the initiative according
to his providential plan. Only those who are content to remain small in
their own minds become monuments to God's mercy. To them is granted
the ability to have a deep gratitude for every sacrament, every moment
of silence, every encounter with another image of God, every consolation,
every cross, every act of purification, every accomplishment, and every act
of oblation on behalf of others. The real crux of the matter is to allow God
to be in total control. "Blessed are the poor in spirit," preached Jesus, "for
theirs is the kingdom of heaven" (Mt 5:3). Blessed indeed are those who
actually trust in Christ to accomplish the kingdom of heaven (including the
beginnings of union with God here below) in them through the practice
of poverty of spirit.

Due to the significance of these assertions about a Thérèsian influence
upon Marmion and how salient these insights are for a proper acceptance
of our nothingness, it is worth validating them briefly. The best way to
gauge Saint Thérèse's influence on Marmion is by his own contribution
to her cause for canonization, which he made by way of a response to the

---

124 "Libera Nos" in *The Daily Missal and Liturgical Manual* (1962), ed. *Summorum Pontificum* (London: Baronius Press, 2008), 954–55.
125 Cf. Marmion, *Priest*, 363.

Roman pontiff's request for his assessment of her. [126] Marmion's official assessment of her was:

> It seems that in this age when few feel called to go to God by the career of the sublime austerities of former times, God wills to show us that love can supply for everything, and that this way of love is the easiest and shortest way of perfection.
>
> Sister Thérèse of the Holy Child Jesus, Carmelite of the Carmel of Lisieux, appears to us to be a shining confirmation of this truth. She said of herself that in Christ's Mystical Body she desired to be the heart and to do all through love. And this love, mother of every virtue, was expressed in her by that perfect fidelity to all her duties, by that absolute abandon to God's good pleasure, by that boundless confidence in the goodness and love of her Heavenly Father, which are the perfect expression of the Spirit of Adoption. [127]

Of greatest note is Marmion's juxtaposition of this easiest and most direct way to perfection with the great austerities of former times. When it comes to growing in humility and charity, greater asceticism does not always lead to more virtue. In surveying the options available to him, Marmion chose Saint Thérèse's approach.

Since Marmion was among the first spiritual authors to incorporate Saint Thérèse's spiritual insights into a systematic and well-defined spirituality, perhaps he was indirectly influential upon making the spirituality of this eventual Doctor of the Church more widely and quickly received. If to accept our nothingness helps us to move more efficiently through the nights of sense and spirit, then spiritual childhood's unique way of being nothing provides the route by which to live out Saint John of the Cross's ascetical and experiential nothings. Read in the light of Saint Thérèse's life and teaching, Saint John of the Cross's writings appear more descriptive of what can occur to an oblative soul than prescriptive about the steps we need to take.

With this background on the Catholic tradition in mind, we are now prepared to receive Marmion's practical advice on the spiritual life.

---

126   Cf. Marmion, *Union*, 20–21.
127   Marmion, *Union*, 21.

CHAPTER 3

Applying Marmion's Spirituality to Your Life

W E TURN NOW TO INVESTIGATE THE ROLE THIS
spirituality can play in preparing us to receive union with
God, God willing. By union with God, this work accepts the
common definition of a life that is lived in grace and enlivened by the gifts
of the Holy Spirit in which we experience an intimate connection with God.

Marmion's spirituality integrates God's actions with our reception of them.
Section one reviews the objective side of the process, God's actions for us;
section two, the subjective side, our response to God's actions; section three,
the results that follow from the combination of the two. The second section
highlights the reciprocal interplay between our exterior and interior responses
to God. By the exterior response, this work refers to the general ways by which
we conform to God: intellectually, to what we can know about God and His
plan; sacramentally, to the acceptance of God's plan as it comes to fruition in
the means given by God for its realization; and behaviorally, to the everyday
ramifications of God's plan for our actions. By the interior response, this work
refers to the ways by which we progress in our friendship with God through
greater attentiveness to him, humility, interior purification, confidence, and
stages of prayer. Putting it all together, while living the normal aspects of
exterior conformity to a standard Catholic life, we deepen our response to
God's plan by removing our interior obstacles to the graces offered by it. In
particular, this work examines a fine point of our interior response to God.

THE OBJECTIVE DIVINE PLAN:
THE SETTING FOR A SPIRITUAL THEOLOGY

If God were not already offering friendship to you, then it would be
foolish to pursue such a friendship. Indeed, to accept our nothingness
apart from God's plan for our salvation and sanctification could result in a
disastrous nihilism. It is necessary, then, to situate Marmion's advice within
the fullness of the divine plan — to the extent that it has been revealed to
and understood by us.

The Interplay between the Objective and Subjective Aspects in Marmion's Spirituality

The following passage demonstrates many of Marmion's major themes relative to the divine plan for us and offers us a structure by which to survey his understanding of God's side of our relationship with him:

> We have many times spoken of the magnificence of the Divine Plan. God wills to make us children by making us partakers of the very filiation of his Son Jesus, and thus cause us to draw eternal beatitude at the very fountainhead of the Divinity (cf. Eph 1:5). The Masterpiece of the eternal thoughts which is Christ, the wonderful mysteries of the Incarnation, the Passion, the Resurrection and the Triumph of Jesus, the institution of the Church and the Sacraments, grace, the virtues, the gifts of the Holy Spirit, all this marvelous supernatural order has come forth from this movement of the Heart of God so as to make us His children: *Ut adoptionem filiorum reciperemus* [so that we might receive adoption as sons] (Gal 4:5). It is an admirable order, a work of power, of wisdom and love of which the spectacle ravished St Paul.
>
> When our souls contemplate these divine perfections and works, not according to a philosophy that would make of it an abstract, cold and dry study, but in prayer, and when God touches us with His light, all terrestrial superiorities are effaced, all created perfections appear as nothingness, all human greatness fades away like smoke. Before this omniscient, this sovereign wisdom, this absolute power, this august sanctity, this justice into which not the least movement of passion enters; before this boundless goodness, this inexhaustible tenderness and mercy, the soul cries out: "Who is like to Thee, O my God? *Quis sicut Dominus Deus noster, qui in altis habitat?*" (Ps 112:5). And how profound are Thy thoughts! An intense reverence seizes us to the very depths of our souls, and we are lost in our nothingness: what are we, what are the celestial spirits, what are the human multitudes, in the face of this wisdom, this power, this eternity, this holiness? *Omnes gentes quasi non sunt* [recte: sint] *sic sunt coram eo* [All the nations are as nothing before him] (Is 40:17).
>
> But let us be careful to remark, for this again is very important, that this sense of reverence in the soul, while yet being very intense and real, is not distinct from those of confidence and love. Humility does not contradict any of the aspects of the truth, God is to be contemplated in all His perfections and in all His works; He is at once Lord and Father; we are at once creatures and adopted children; and

it is from this total contemplation in the Almighty Power of the sovereign Lord and the Supreme Goodness of a Father full of tenderness that reverence towards God, the root of humility, ought to arise.[1]

From the outset, this passage displayed Marmion's theology as thoroughly grounded in the gratuitous divine plan for each person. This passage calls to mind the following central themes in Marmion's theology: the holiness of the Blessed Trinity,[2] the Father's overflowing plan for each person's holiness,[3] that Jesus is the revealed way to holiness[4] (i.e., that Jesus is both the model of[5] and means to[6] holiness), and that the Holy Spirit has given the gift of holiness to the members of the Church.[7]

One phrase in particular speaks to Marmion's overall approach to spirituality: he called Christ "the Masterpiece of the eternal thoughts" prior to listing various aspects of the mission of the Word Incarnate. Indeed, for Marmion, Christ Jesus is the Masterpiece of the divine plan and the center of his spirituality. Philipon sums up Marmion's Christo-centrism in this way: "Other spiritual authors may surpass him in the depth of their analysis and descriptions of the phases of the mystical life; none has equaled him in the force of his Christo-centrism."[8] Given the centrality of the Savior of mankind in the divine plan — both for our salvation and for our coming to union with God — this focus is most fitting. Marmion often summed up this focus by saying Christ is our all,[9] such as he did in the following phrase written to his sister Rosie (Mother Peter) Marmion: "In conclusion, my dear sister, do not forget that Jesus Christ is all, and that we are agreeable to the Father in the measure in which we are united to Him."[10] More specifically, only through Christ do we come to liberation from our disintegrated lives full of attachments in order to live a peaceful and grateful friendship with God. It was in this sense that Jesus is God's masterpiece in Marmion's eyes.

1   Marmion, *Monk*, 224–25.
2   Cf. Marmion, *Soul*, 23–28.
3   Cf. ibid., 23–28; see also Marmion, *Mysteries*, 442–45.
4   Cf. Marmion, *Union*, 31–33; Marmion, *Mysteries*, 16–20.
5   Cf. Marmion, *Soul*, 42–57; Marmion, *Mysteries*, 14–15, 31; Marmion, *Monk*, 15–17, 107, 428; Marmion, *Priest*, 41.
6   Cf. Marmion, *Soul*, 58ff.; Marmion, *Mysteries*, 99–100, 456; Marmion, *Monk*, 31; Marmion, *Priest*, 40–53, esp. 40–41.
7   Cf. Marmion, *Soul*, 109, 114–127; Marmion, *Priest*, 298–99.
8   Philipon, *Spiritual Doctrine*, 98–99; also see Gionta, *Le Virtù Teologali*, 23–24.
9   Cf. Marmion, *Soul*, 24–25, 44; Marmion, *Union*, 31, 33.
10 Marmion, "Letter to his sister Rosie, 17 October 1891," in *Correspondance*, 55. My translation.

In the above passage about a "total contemplation,"[11] Marmion also mentioned the unifying theme of his spirituality, namely divine adoption: "God wills to make us children by making us partakers of the very filiation of his Son Jesus, and thus cause us to draw eternal beatitude at the very fountainhead of the Divinity (cf. Eph 1:5)."[12] This theme unified Marmion's spirituality because his reflections on the spiritual life depend upon the spiritual fruition brought to us by divine adoption. That choice is not novel. All classic Catholic spiritualities depend upon this theme at least implicitly, since the divine plan for our sanctification reached a new stage in the divine adoption offered by Christ. Yet Marmion distinguished himself by returning explicitly and often to this central point. "All of [Marmion's] preaching," reflected Thibaut, "centered upon this dogma of the divine Paternity and of our adoption in Jesus Christ."[13] Since arguments for divine adoption occupied the latter sections of the first chapter published by Marmion,[14] this theme was axiomatic for him. He could not speak of the unswerving divine plan for our sanctification without speaking of God's revealed means for fulfilling it. The key by which to read this foundational chapter — indeed, all of Marmion's spirituality — is in its first paragraph in which Marmion quotes Ephesians 1:5 – 6: "He destined us in love to be his sons through Jesus Christ, according to the purpose of his will, to the praise of his glorious grace which he freely bestowed on us in the Beloved."[15] Indeed, Thibaut called Ephesians 1:5 the "fundamental theme" of Marmion's spirituality.[16]

Included in divine adoption are the indispensable roles of the gifts of baptism and of the sacramental life. Marmion demonstrated the significance of these divinely ordained means of sanctification in these words:

> It must be repeated, because experience shows how in the long run, even with souls who seek God, the practical estimation of these means of salvation sometimes leaves much to be desired. The sacraments are, with the doctrine given by the Church, the official channels authentically created by Christ to make us attain to His Father. It is to wrong Him not to appreciate their value, their riches,

---

11 Marmion, Monk, 224 – 25.
12 Marmion, Monk, 224; for a detailed assessment of this theme, see Gionta, Le Virtù Teologali, 101 – 53.
13 R. Thibaut, L'Idée Maîtresse de la Doctrine de Dom Marmion (Namur: Maredsous, 1947), 22. My translation.
14 Cf. Marmion, Soul, 30ff.
15 Cf. ibid., 21.
16 R. Thibaut, L'Idée Maîtresse de la Doctrine de Dom Marmion, 20.

their fruitfulness, while He is glorified when we draw from these treasures acquired by His merits: we thus acknowledge that we hold all from Him, and that renders Him very pleasing homage.[17]

Through the sacraments, we are incorporated into Christ so as to become not just supernaturalized coworkers but deified sons and daughters full of the divine life. We become sons and daughters who receive the grace to act in supernatural ways and the privilege, if retained, of being heirs of eternal life. The supernatural aspect of divine adoption must be stressed: "There is not an atom of this holiness in creation," warned Marmion. "It proceeds from God by a supremely free act of His Almighty Will, and that is why it is supernatural."[18] In other words, we must respect the divinely ordained means for the distribution of grace, even if God can give grace outside of his revealed means for doing so.

That Marmion's meditations humbled him, as is demonstrated in the passage about "total contemplation,"[19] is one of the links between his meditations on the divine economy and those on the interior life. Yet his sense of his own nothingness was not merely the result of study, for it occurred, according to him, "when God touches us with His light."[20] So his humble feelings were not "distinct from those of confidence and love."[21] For Marmion, therefore, there existed an interplay between the exterior and interior aspects of his spirituality. Together they formed a unified approach to God in which neither side detracted from the other. Marmion indeed had "total contemplation."[22] In fact, he explicitly stated that we must have both "a precise idea of what holiness is" while also maintaining "a view of the whole [of the Christian life]."[23] While the rest of this chapter is dedicated to developing a precise idea of the role of the disposition of nothingness in our interior response to God, this section has maintained a view of a fully integrated Catholic approach.

The Thrice-Holy God: The Objective Source of Marmion's Confidence in God

One aspect of the divine plan merits additional emphasis: God wills our holiness. Why do we seek union with God? We do so because he invited us to it,

---

17   Marmion, *Soul*, 84.
18   Ibid., 38.
19   Marmion, *Monk*, 224–25 (quoted above).
20   Ibid., 224–25.
21   Ibid.
22   Ibid.
23   Marmion, *Soul*, 22.

because he is leading us to it. The Second Vatican Council helpfully proclaimed it in the language of the "universal call to holiness."[24] Marmion argued that God desires each person to become a saint, and his argument centered upon the thrice-holy God's constant work to effect holiness in each person:

> The first reason we have for aiming at perfection is that it is God's will: "This is the will of God, your sanctification" (1 Thess 4:3). God wishes us not only to be saved but to become holy. And why is God decided on this? Because He Himself is holy: "I am the Lord your God: be holy because I am holy" (Lev 11:44; 19:2). God is holiness itself; we are his creatures; he desires that the creature shall reflect His image. Indeed, He wishes us as His children to be perfect: "You . . . are to be perfect, even as your Heavenly Father is perfect." That is a precept, a command, of Jesus.
>
> God finds His glory in our holiness. Never forget this truth: that each degree of holiness to which we shall have come, each sacrifice we have made in order to acquire it, each gleam of virtue that adorns our soul, will be a glory for our Father forever.[25]

So, there are two reasons for which we should have confidence in God's constant desire for our holiness: 1) Jesus Christ has incorporated us into the communion of love of the Trinity, and 2) our holiness glorifies God.[26] In the Triune God's exclusive love for you and me, he exclusively and incessantly seeks this end for each of us. Indeed, the Trinity wants to grow our holiness in order to incorporate us more fully into God's eternal communion of love.

That God constantly works to effect good is not a new idea. For example, the prophet Jeremiah related this message from God about it: "I will make with them an everlasting covenant, that I will not turn away from doing good to them" (Jer 32:40). Over time, we have gained a greater understanding of the type of good that God wants to effect in us, namely holiness.

Perhaps the words "holiness" and "saintliness" have lost their edge today? Marmion argued from the metaphysical point of view, explaining it as "the manifestation of [God's] glory" in each person.[27] That is certainly at the root of the matter, but perhaps it would be more useful to restate this abstract concept. In some way, God wants us to shine, for in shining we glorify him. Yet he wants us to shine in a way that actually glorifies him, not necessarily

---

24 Cf. *Lumen Gentium* in *The Documents of Vatican II: With Notes and Index* (Vatican City: Libreria Editrice Vaticana / Saint Pauls, 2009), 52ff.

25 Marmion, *Mysteries*, 442–43; also see Marmion, *Soul*, 26ff.

26 Also see Marmion, *Soul*, 39.

27 Marmion, *Soul*, 27.

in worldly ways. More specifically, he wants us to shine in ways in which others can recognize Christ in us. Perhaps contemporary theologians can here update Marmion's theology. In the time following the charismatic renewal, I would here present this shining in a broader pneumatological point of view, though I will later reinforce the classic distinction between ordinary and extraordinary gifts. Allow me to speculate that the Paraclete's constant desire to help us probably entails, first and foremost, whatever is most conducive to greater union with us, such as making us whole and purifying our hearts; but it can also entail making us aflame with his love and his gifts. While charisms and charismatic gifts are meant only for the upbuilding of the Church, not of one's union with God, they nonetheless glorify God. To become brilliant for God's glory, therefore, can entail releasing the charismatic gifts in our lives, even if they are not, strictly speaking, aids for our own holiness. Let us never underestimate any of God's gifts, for our graces, charisms, and intimate stages of prayer all manifest God's glory, each according to God's purpose for them. Today we need them all.

Regardless of the expressions used to explain sanctification, God constantly wills it (cf. 1 Thess 4:3b). Since God's desire is always in action, he is not merely hoping for our holiness or cheering for it. He is, like an artist on fire with inspiration, obsessing about it.

Let us bring this "first principle" of the science of saints[28] into contact with the theme of this work. The task of accepting our nothingness, if undertaken properly, does not result in a void. Rather, it opens us to the greatest gift of union with God. Indeed, we know by science that an absolute vacuum, empty even of energy or virtual particles, is impossible, since the law of the conservation of energy holds that something will always fill it.[29] Let us allow this fact from creation to build our confidence that a proper spiritual life will not produce an inner vacuum. Does God not want to fill any unobstructed space in our souls? "He who descended is he who also ascended far above all the heavens, that he might fill all things" (Eph 4:10).

Only sin and error bring about a potentially lasting emptiness in the spiritual life, to the extent that they block God's action. Since we obstruct God, perhaps most frequently in interior sins, we must, in a sense, remove our self-created obstacles to God.[30] While the process of removing obstacles

---

28 Cf. Marmion, *Soul*, 26.
29 See Henning Genz, *Nothingness: The Science of Empty Space*, trans. Karin Heusch (Cambridge, MA: Perseus, 1999), 94–95, 189–92, 204–5, 207–8, 307, 315.
30 Cf. Marmion, *Soul*, 272–73, 365, 368.

can produce feelings of emptiness, those feelings merely mourn the loss of our egoism, and they recede as God fills the gap. Marmion knew this well:

> As you know, I can feel what a void this loss has made in your poor heart. It must bleed for a time; but God Himself wishes to fill up the gap. It is by successive detachments that He ends by becoming our All; and at times this separation from all human solace is almost like death. I have gone through it; and know that poor human weakness could not bear it, were it to last. But little by little God becomes our All, and in Him we find again what we seem to have lost.

> For souls like yours, God wants to be All, "*Deus meus et omnia* [My God and my All]" (Saint Francis of Assisi); but as long as they could lean on any human aid, how legitimate and holy soever it might be, He could not be their All. This is the perfection of the virtue of poverty; it is perfect hope: to have lost all created joy, and lean on God alone.[31]

Since God wants to become our All, he will recompense us for the emptiness we feel in the process of allowing him to empty us of our selfishness. This principle of God's constant desire for our holiness reminds us to trust the God who brings good from evil. The God praised in the Exultet of Easter controls this process. We rejoice in the "happy fault, that merited to possess such and so great a Redeemer."[32] How, then, can we later doubt our Redeemer's constant desire to sanctify us?

THE SUBJECTIVE RESPONSE:
A CATHOLIC'S THREE-FOLD RESPONSIBILITY

With regard to what a believer must do in order to cooperate with the divine plan, Marmion offered much advice. Unfortunately, he did not often group his recommendations into compact summaries or an organized approach. The chapters of the second half of *Christ the Life of the Soul* offer us a catalogue of diverse topics, for example: faith in Jesus Christ, baptism, death to sin, the sacrament of penance, truth in charity, supernatural growth in Christ, the Eucharistic Sacrifice, the Bread of Life, the Voice of the Spouse, prayer, "love one another," the Mother of the Word

---

31 Marmion, "Letter to an English superioress, no. 17, 26 May 1908," in *Letters*, 143–44; see also Gionta, *Le Virtù Teologali*, 315.
32 "Exultet," in *The Daily Missal and Liturgical Manual* (1962), 596ff., esp. 599.

Incarnate, and the heavenly heritage.[33] The later chapters of *Christ the Ideal of the Monk* offer us another diverse catalogue: our faith, monastic profession, the "instruments of good works," compunction of heart, self-renunciation, poverty, humility, the good of obedience, the Divine Office, monastic prayer, the spirit of abandonment to God's will, good zeal, and the peace of Christ.[34] Indeed it could be difficult, when commenting on Marmion's wide-ranging assortment of topics, to avoid collecting merely a miscellany of valuable, yet standard, themes in Catholic spirituality. While all of Marmion's topics are worthy of deep consideration, this study will try to restrict itself to the most relevant aspects of Marmion's teaching about the ways in which a spiritual man or woman, already formed in many of these topics, can come to union with God. Thankfully, Marmion did offer a simple, unifying vision of a spiritual person's subjective response to God's plan in a passage of spiritual accompaniment Thibaut called "a summary of [Marmion's] admirable doctrine":[35]

> A tending towards God in Himself with a sense of confusion at our unworthiness and confidence in His goodness and in the Precious Blood of Jesus Christ are the three notes of real union with God. Do not fear. This way is sure. Nothing glorifies God so much as the triumph of his grace in a soul that acknowledges her misery, her weakness, her unworthiness, and that hopes for all from his power and His goodness. This is the "praise of the glory of His grace" of which Saint Paul speaks.[36]

Adapted slightly, this passage offers the following advice: first, tend toward God in himself; second, acknowledge your unworthiness, or nothingness; and third, have confidence in God. The following survey of Marmion's advice follows this structure.

To Tend toward God in Himself

The Shema (cf. Deut 6:4–9) and Jesus's teaching on the greatest commandment (cf. Mt 22:36–30) have long offered believers general commands about loving God above all creatures. Yet, given what Marmion wrote of sanctification, the responsibility to tend toward God in himself is more specific. In a way reminiscent of Saint Benedict's principle of "truly [seeking]

33 Marmion, *Soul*, 15.
34 Marmion, *Monk*, x.
35 Marmion, *Union*, 197.
36 Ibid.

God,"[37] Marmion had "attaining to God" specifically in mind (in as much as God wants and allows us to grow close to Him in an intimate relationship):

> It is therefore extremely important, as St Paul says, to run in the race, "not as at an uncertainty," as one beating the air (1 Cor 9:26), but so as to obtain a prize: *sic currite ut comprehendatis* [so run that you may obtain it] (1 Cor 9:24); to know as perfectly as possible the Divine idea of holiness; to examine with the greatest care, so as to adapt ourselves to it, the plan traced out by God Himself, whereby we may attain to Him: it is only at this price that our salvation and sanctification can be realized.[38]

Therefore, in order to tend to God in himself, you must accept union with God as the purpose for your life.[39] This turning to God is an act of love: "While faith unifies inasmuch as it considers and judges everything departing from God," says Gionta in his research on Marmion, "charity does so inasmuch as it orients everything to God; the first in fact consists more or less in 'seeing,' the second, in 'tending.'"[40] This love of God brings with it the exterior conformity of yourself to the goal. To turn to God in this way, you need to accept sacramental growth in the divine life as the scope for your life,[41] and you need to accept intellectual and behavioral conformity to Christ as the practical program for your life.[42] Accordingly, you need to conform your life to this end both by availing yourself of the gifts of divine adoption revealed for this purpose and by conforming practically to this end — indeed, to the life of Jesus Christ — in the concrete decisions of your vocation.

To this overview of our exterior response to God, it is advantageous in this context to add a few targeted reflections. Given that the bulk of this work focuses upon a little-known interior aspect of the spiritual life, it would be most efficient at this point to preempt some potential misconceptions that could arise about the reciprocal interplay between our exterior and interior responses. So, here follow three brief comments on the sacraments, on active asceticism, and on serving our neighbor.

---

37 Benedict of Nursia, *The Rule of Saint Benedict*, chap. 58, no. 7.
38 Marmion, *Soul*, 22.
39 On Marmion's point of view on seeking God, see Marmion, *Monk*, 1–18; on Marmion's understanding that union with God begins in this life, see Marmion, *Monk*, 104 (quoted on 143).
40 Gionta, *Le Virtù Teologali*, 286–87. My translation.
41 Cf. Marmion, *Soul*, 146–48, 161–64, 261ff., 273–74; Marmion, *Monk*, 100; Marmion, *Mysteries*, 60–63, 454; Marmion, *Union*, 38–39; Marmion, *Priest*, 54ff., 219–22.
42 Cf. Marmion, *Soul*, 132; Marmion, *Mysteries*, 434–37.

ON THE ROLE OF THE SACRAMENTS. In the New Testament's dispensation of the divine economy, the sacraments have an unsurpassed value. Indeed, the liturgies of the Church are the highest forms of our exterior response to God, for we offer them to the Father through Jesus Christ by means of the Holy Spirit. Thus, Marmion extolls the value of the Mass in this way:

> It is indeed through Jesus Christ, the Man-God, His beloved Son immolated upon the altar, that all glory and honour are rendered to the Father: "*Per ipsum et cum ipso et in ipso Deo Patri omnipotenti . . . omnis honor et gloria* [By Him, and with Him, and in Him, is to Thee, God, the Father almighty . . . all honor and glory]" (Ordinary of the Mass). In all religion there is no action that gives so much peace to the soul convinced of its nothingness, yet longing to render God a homage not unworthy of His Divine greatness. All the united homage of creation and the world of the elect do not give the eternal Father such glory as He receives from the offering of His Son. It needs faith to understand the value of the Mass — that faith which is like a participation of the knowledge God has of Himself and of Divine things. In the light of faith, we can regard the altar as the Heavenly Father does. What does He see upon the altar? He sees "the Son of His love, *Filius dilectione suae*" (Col 1:13), the Son in Whom He is well pleased, present in all truth and reality, *vere et realiter*, and renewing the sacrifice of the cross. God measures all things by the glory He receives from them; and in this sacrifice, as on Calvary, infinite glory is rendered to Him by His Well-Beloved Son. God cannot find more perfect homage than that. It contains and surpasses all. [43]

Since we offer nothing of merit on our own, we cannot construct a worthy way to honor God. Consequently, it is only through God's divinely revealed liturgies that we properly praise, honor, and worship Him. To participate in the sacraments and to offer (even if only spiritually) the Holy Mass are, therefore, central to our exterior response to God.

Similarly, the sacraments are vital to our spiritual life, for they are the divinely revealed means by which we have communion with God and receive God's graces. But we do not automatically receive all of the graces offered by the sacraments — therein lies the problem. Marmion was deeply aware both of the graces objectively offered by the sacraments and of the need to unlock our subjective reception of them:

---

43 Marmion, *Soul*, 251; for the translation of *per ipsum* . . . , see: "The Ordinary of the Mass" in *The Daily Missal and Liturgical Manual* (1962), no. 24, 950–51.

THE GRACE OF "NOTHINGNESS"

I see clearly that this is the great fountain of grace: Jesus brings with him the Holy Spirit and all sorts of graces and favors. I see clearly that if I were able to make of my life a preparation and a continual thanksgiving for the Holy Mass, I would receive the most precious graces during the Holy Sacrifice, since all my small actions, my aspirations, and my renouncements offered during the day in view of Holy Communion would be the virtual intention for the moment of communicating the next day. And what then would the involuntary distractions matter?

I was also struck by the thought that the Father gives us all things and that Jesus Christ gives us them in Holy Communion — the surest pledge of all of which we ask. With regard to his side, there isn't even the least doubt about whether he would be disposed to grant them to us: "With him have we not been given every gift?" (Romans 8:32). If I were to receive little, the fault, therefore, would be mine. When God is slow to give to me some grace, the angels adore in silent admiration the reasons that are the cause of it. May I join with them, therefore, in reverence![44]

Here Marmion noted that any imperfections in his relationship with God were his fault, due to his interior obstacles to the graces offered in Holy Communion. (He did not need to lament avoiding the sacraments.) Strikingly, he used his imperfect union with God as a motive to humble himself in order to improve his *"dispositio unionis* [disposition for union]."[45] Even more impressively, he found in his interior shortcomings a reason to adore Divine Providence. In this regard, he was like Saint Catherine of Siena, who praised God for his "unwavering rectitude" when she felt her "miserable tortuosity."[46] Is it not when we feel tortured interiorly that we feel both the temptation to discouragement and the related temptation of wanting a coping mechanism? There can be a time and a place for coping mechanisms, but to turn our attention to God in these moments is of overriding importance.

This passage also demonstrates that Blessed Columba's interior response was intrinsically linked to an already present trust in the gifts associated with divine adoption. To focus on his interior response to the sacraments

44 Marmion, Personal Notes, "Fête du Sacré-Coeur, 1888," quoted in Raymond Thibaut, *Dom Columba Marmion: Un Maître de la Vie Spirituelle*, new edition, 50e mille ed. (Namur: Maredsous, 1953), 72. My translation. See also: Marmion, Soul, 254, 272–73, 301.
45 Marmion, Soul, 273; see also Gionta, *Le Virtù Teologali*, 333–34.
46 Catherine of Siena, "Orazione XX" in *Le Orazioni* (N.p.: Centro Internazionli di Studi Cateriniani, Date Unknown), last accessed February 13, 2015. http://www.centro-studicateriniani.it/download/Le%20Orazioni.pdf. (See p. 56.)

was, then, the practical corollary to his trust in God's constant desire for his holiness. Since we have objectively powerful encounters with Jesus in the sacraments and in the Divine Office, [47] plus encounters with the Holy Spirit throughout the day (especially in *lectio divina* and our mental prayer), [48] to profit only a little from them should produce greater humility in us. In Blessed Columba's mind, humble resignation to the Divine plan — or abandonment to Divine Providence — was humility in practice. [49] For him, such resignation applied as much to the acceptance of our slow progress in the spiritual life as to anything else. [50] As we will see, Blessed Columba's humble acceptance of his flawed self-reliance eventually opened him to the constancy necessary to overcome his interior obstacles. His humble acceptance of his failures opened him to receive more fully Christ's graces. If we did not awake as saints this morning, then we too need to work on opening ourselves to the immense graces offered in the sacraments.

ON THE ROLE OF ACTIVE ASCETICISM. To conform behaviorally to God's plan we must open ourselves to the power of God at work in us, that is, to grace, to the gifts of the Holy Spirit, and to God's Uncreated Love-Gift. [51] Asceticism encompasses the actions and choices, active and passive, associated with making the power of God more operative in our lives.

"What are passive choices?" you may ask. Well, those are the ways by which God, through the circumstances of life, liberates us, eventually by

---

47   For Marmion on the Divine Office, see R. Thibaut, *L'Idée Maîtresse de la Doctrine de Dom Marmion*, 195.

48   For a treatment on Marmion's contemplative prayer, see Philipon, *Spiritual Doctrine*, 162–65.

49   Cf. Marmion, *Monk*, 372ff. Thibaut, *Dom Columba Marmion*, 66 cites Marmion's notes from April 1888 on this point: "For example, when I pray to obtain humility, I must not complain that my prayer lacks a response, but I must be humbly resigned to God's mysterious choice to defer the gift; resolved, moreover, if it is His will, to continue to request it respectfully for a hundred years, since it is His own good pleasure." My translation.

50   See Gionta, *Le Virtù Teologali*, 251; for more from Gionta on abandonment in Marmion, see ibid., 324ff.

51   John Paul II, *Dominum et Vivificantem: On the Holy Spirit in the Life of the Church and the World*, May 18, 1986, last accessed July 3, 2021. Vatican.va, 10: "At the same time, the Holy Spirit, being consubstantial with the Father and the Son in divinity, is love and uncreated gift from which derives as from its source (*fons vivus*) all giving of gifts vis-a-vis creatures (created gift): the gift of existence to all things through creation; the gift of grace to human beings through the whole economy of salvation. As the Apostle Paul writes: 'God's love has been poured into our hearts through the Holy Spirit which has been given to us' (Rm 5:5)."

our free choice, from our heart's lower desires so as to show us a deeper yearning within us. For example, when parents become empty-nesters, they must eventually embrace the changed circumstances in their lives and find new meaning in them. The same occurs when a person retires and finds his or her true value in who he or she is, not what he or she does. Of course, life can bring about other existential crises, such as through the loss of a loved one, an illness, a crisis in the family, an injustice, or the loss of a job, and the masters speak of dark nights of the soul as well. At the appropriate time, usually when we see our props failing, we need to release them, even sometimes reject them, in preference for something deeper, such as authentically walking with God. If God is calling us to himself, then we cannot coyly pretend to seek both him and our idols. Passive asceticism, then, is the real "letting go and letting God" in our lives, often when we find it difficult. God will not accept being treated as a domesticated deity for our own ends.

What, then, are active choices? Under the traditional understanding of asceticism, we seek the liberation inherent in virtues, cut away the bondages associated with vices, and place a series of limitations on ourselves (e.g., fasts) in order to direct our passions and/or faculties to their proper ends.[52] On the practical level, this means choices such as making gooey butter cake just one finger tall, not two, because it is the same experience and one is healthier. These measuring fingers are, of course, horizontal fingers, such as when you say, "Just pour me another two fingers of scotch."

Together these two types of asceticism bring us to interior freedom. Without undertaking an asceticism of some kind, we would never remove any of our obstacles to union with God. Asceticism is, therefore, the "*unum necessarium* [the one thing necessary]," at least in the view of Juan Arintero, who also believed in God's objective desire for union with each of us.[53]

We need to expand our view of asceticism to have it encompass all of our distorted desires. Today we speak in terms of overcoming the compulsions and addictions that bind us, that seize our attention, that restrict our freedom, that limit our ability to love. These addictions, which we all have, include the actions we either undertake or avoid under compulsion or obsession in order to feel secure (or important, however you define it). Coming at it from another direction and including obsessive mindsets in the category of asceticism, if a sense of purposelessness hits a Christian or a sense of dissatisfaction at the lack of something overwhelms a Christian,

---

52 Cf. Marmion, *Monk*, 172ff.
53 Arintero, *Mystical Evolution*, 406.

then that special something may be limiting that child of God's search for meaning to too narrow a spectrum of it. In order to heal all of these struggles, we need to undertake the best processes available, such as those offered by Dr Gerald May, M. D., to heal any of our distorted desires.[54]

While spiritual men and women have by definition passed from the first stage of purifying themselves of their gravest obsessive attachments, this work must continue in each soul until the passions and faculties of the soul are put into rather right order. That said, the process by which you purify your ongoing attachments, most especially to yourself, changes as you progress. Indeed, this spirituality can bring about such a change, for through it you can allow passive asceticism, by which you accept to suffer exteriorly imposed deprivations, to play a greater role. Given that our passive asceticism overlaps closely with our interior response to God, the interplay between passive and active asceticism will be discussed at greater length later. At present it is enough to note that Marmion embraced the active form of asceticism:

> The reason of the primary necessity for penance is to re-establish order in us and restore to reason, itself being subject to God, the dominion over the inferior powers, so as to allow the will to yield entirely to God. That is life. Never forget this: Christianity demands mortification first of all so as to immolate in us that which is opposed to life. The Christian labors, by self-renunciation, to root out from the soul all element of spiritual death, so that the Divine life may increase in it with more liberty, ease, and fulness.[55]

Just above this quotation, Marmion relates active asceticism to Saint Paul's words, "If you live according to the flesh you will die, but if by the Spirit you put to death the deeds of the body you will live" (Rom 8:13) and

---

54 For an excellent treatment of the psychological and spiritual processes associated with healing addiction, see: Gerald G. May, *Addiction and Grace: Love and Spirituality in the Healing of Addictions* (New York: HarperCollins, 1988). May argues that we are all addicts and offers excellent counsel on responding to our addictions. See especially chapters 1–2, 5–7, pp. 3ff., 10, 13, 28ff., 36, 40, 94f, 141ff., 149ff. Here are two separate quotes relating to asceticism that are worth putting next to each other: "The only reason we could have for 'choosing' against true compassion and charity is that we are addicted to something else" (40); and "The excruciating reality is that truly free, loving choices cannot be easy. In fact, one might timorously propose that the most free and loving choices are those that call forth the relinquishing of what one holds most dear. It is another meaning of the cross. The joy and beauty of freedom and love must be bought with pain. We might wish God had created things otherwise, so that an easier life could be possible, but a careful look at our own history will prove such a wish empty" (117).

55 Marmion, *Soul*, 193; see also Marmion, "Self-Renunciation," in *Monk*.

THE GRACE OF "NOTHINGNESS"

Jesus's words, "He who loves his life loses it, and he who hates his life in this world will keep it for eternal life" (Jn 12:25). So, Marmion valued asceticism as a way to open ourselves to grace and God and through God to real life, indeed a divinized life.

ON THE ROLE OF CHARITY. Let us underline the active and charitable aspects of this program. Certainly, Marmion's practical response to God always included an element of charitable action.[56] While Marmion indeed focused much upon prayer,[57] thus making charity to God primary, he insisted we must love both God and neighbor. Of greatest note, he wanted his friend to love her neighbors in a human way — with affection.[58] Furthermore, while his focus on nothingness led to a peaceful abandonment to the will of God,[59] he was in no way a quietist. Rather, he was a man of zeal who preached the practice of good zeal[60] and the fulfillment of our duties: "We must not think that humility paralyses the spirit of initiative or devotion to duty. On the contrary, it is a source of moral strength. When the humble soul acknowledges its weakness and poverty, this does not mean that it gives up the fight, but rather that it finds in God and in the accomplishment of his will a powerful restorative for its energy."[61] A note about Marmion's courage may establish this point most easily: when German troops were approaching his abbey during the First World War, he, upon taking advice from religious and ecclesiastical leaders, personally smuggled some of his monks through the lines and eventually to safety in Ireland by posing as a cattle herder, thereby giving the entire community a greater chance at survival.[62] It would be a mistake, then, to read his focus upon nothingness as an excuse for a lack of action or love![63] Marmion's spirituality presupposes the desire to follow God's will and the promptings of the Holy Spirit in every situation, and this may be done in every vocation. To accomplish these exterior responses to God's love in our normal life is to tend toward God in our actions.

---

56 Cf. Marmion, Soul, 323ff.; Marmion, Monk, 397ff.; Marmion, Union, 121ff.; Marmion, Priest, 321ff.; for a detailed account of charity in Marmion, see Gionta, Le Virtù Teologali, 255–322, esp. 308ff., on charity to our neighbors.
57 Cf. Marmion, Monk, 243–49, 300–371.
58 Cf. Marmion, Union, 124–26.
59 Cf. ibid., 11–12, 15; Marmion, Monk, 372ff.
60 Cf. Marmion, Monk, 397ff.
61 Marmion, Priest, 134.
62 Cf. Tierney, Blessed Columba Marmion, 160–61.
63 Cf. Marmion, Soul, 331–32.

To Acknowledge Our Unworthiness/Nothingness[64]

If we were to survey Christians on the street about the worst category of vice, we would likely find many replying that pride is both the greatest sin and the root of the others. Many people, however, do not thoroughly understand pride, beyond associating it with some vague definition of defiant self-will. Marmion held a more precise view of it: "Now, the greatest obstacle is pride, because it is a fundamental obstacle, radically opposed to Divine union itself, and consequently to the grace whereof God alone is the source and without which we can do nothing."[65] What may be surprising to many people is that pride manifests itself often in us by way of self-reliance:

> There is, concerning your spiritual life, one truth which I want
> to impress on your soul. All our efforts are only of any avail in
> as far as Jesus Christ acts in us and helps us . . . (cf. John 15:5–7).
> Indeed, Saint Paul tells us that "God has given us His Son Jesus to
> be our Wisdom, our Justice, our Sanctification, our Redemption"
> (1 Cor 1:30). You have still too much confidence in your own
> activity, and consequently, you do not lean enough upon Him,
> you do not put yourself enough in His hands.[66]

---

64 A word must be said about the varying expressions for humility. In the above "summary of [Marmion's] admirable doctrine," around which I have organized this section, Marmion's counsel stated that we need: "A tending towards God in Himself with a sense of confusion at our unworthiness and confidence in His goodness. . . . Nothing glorifies God so much as the triumph of his grace in a soul that acknowledges her misery, her weakness, her unworthiness, and that hopes for all from his power and His goodness" (Marmion, *Union*, 197). While our unworthiness is not always a metonym for our nothingness, it can, when taken in the light of the "unworthy servants" of Luke 17:10, correspond to the refusal to attribute our merits to ourselves and be used as a stylistic alternative to "being nothing." To rely always on God and to refer all to him are the ways in which to express this unworthiness positively, since one who refers all of one's merits to God is one who already wants to rely on his grace for everything. In its negative form, then, Marmion's counsel about unworthiness aimed to heal the tendencies to appropriate God's graces to ourselves and to rely solely on ourselves to succeed. Undoubtedly, these two tendencies interrelate, but the root cause of them, at which Marmion aimed this counsel, was self-reliance. In this context, then, unworthiness and nothingness are so close as to be interchangeable, and the passages of this section show them to be equivalent. The virtue is what counts; the terms used to express it are of secondary importance. Unfortunately, in order to process this concept deeply, we will encounter this lexicon more than a few times — yet hopefully no more times than are needed.

65 Marmion, *Monk*, 215.

66 Marmion, *Union*, 34; Columba Marmion, *L'Union a Dieu: D'apres les Lettres de Direction de Dom Columba Marmion*, selected and annotated by Raymond Thibaut (Paris: Desclée, De Brouwer, 1934), 46 (hereafter *L'Union*).

So, we are finally prepared to address the fundamental problem of attempting to respond to Jesus's example and standards without having first availed ourselves of the divine assistance necessary to do so.[67]

Marmion further discussed this problem of self-reliance and the proper way by which to yield ourselves to God's action:

> One must not, before beginning any action, give in to nature, but first unite one's self to Our Lord. Before taking up an occupation, kneel down at Christ's feet and say to Him: "My Jesus, I leave there my natural activity, I want to do this thing solely for You, and I unite myself to You." And if during the occupation, you feel that you are letting yourself be carried away by nature, go back to Our Lord. It must not be A— [name of the religious] who is acting, for that would be good for nothing; but it must be Jesus who acts through A—, then it will be excellent.
>
> There are some people who have a great deal of activity; they pray, mortify themselves, and give themselves up to good works; they advance but rather limpingly, because their activity is partly human. There are others whom God has taken in hand, and they advance very quickly, because He Himself acts in them. But before reaching this second state, there is much to suffer, for God must first make the soul feel that she is nothing and can do nothing; she must needs be able to say in all sincerity, "I am brought to nothing, and I knew not. I am become as a beast before Thee" (Psalm 72:22–23).[68]

To fail to turn to God for help before each undertaking, then, is the fundamental obstacle for those non-beginners who are searching to make the next step in their spiritual lives.

In a related way, those struggling with self-reliance can also struggle with attributing God's graces to themselves. In attributing God's actions to

---

67 See Marmion, *Monk*, 211: "We all have obstacles within us that hinder God's action: sin, the roots of sin, perverse tendencies not fought against; for 'what fellowship hath light, with darkness?' (2 Cor 6:14). These obstacles are overcome by souls who renounce everything — created things, and themselves — who increase their capacity for what is divine, by detachment from all that is not God. They look only to God for all they need; they are humble in themselves, they rely only upon God; God fills these *pauperes spiritu* (people who are poor in spirit) with good things. As to the others, they bear within them a tendency particularly qualified to form an obstacle to God; this tendency is pride. Pride is radically opposed to the Divine communications; God cannot give Himself to these self-satisfied *divites spiritu* (people who are wealthy in spirit). This is a fact often to be met with."
68 Marmon, *Union*, 35.

ourselves, we produce a distorted sense of self-worth; this distorted sense of self-worth produces a sense of entitlement; from this sense of entitlement, we seek to possess some desired object. When we fail to obtain our desired object, we often judge ourselves harshly by the world's standards and lose the peace that leads to union with God. In a subtle reorienting of the Christian path, we develop, perhaps unconsciously, new motives for our external conformity to Christ's actions. In this reorienting process, we thwart the action of grace in our lives even more, and after long periods of forestalling grace, we become enmeshed in an ever-deeper self-reliance that eventually leads to bitter, discouraging feelings.

In order to help his friend to avoid these pitfalls and to avoid "[advancing] but rather limpingly,"[69] Marmion recommended she should accept her nothingness. This recommendation, in his opinion, would help her to "advance very quickly,"[70] for therein she would turn more easily and more often to God for help. Yet to turn this recommendation into a transforming experience, she needed to make of it a deep disposition, and Blessed Columba warned her that to do so would entail a great deal of personal sacrifice: "But before reaching this second state, there is much to suffer."[71] What exactly did she need to suffer? First, she needed to develop both a deeper self-knowledge about the ways in which she was diverting into the trap of self-reliance and a greater constancy against the temptations that had provoked those falls. Second, she needed to undertake active ascesis to root out the attachments identified by her attentiveness to these traps. To be specific, she needed to root out the great prizes of which she had felt deserving or of which she had hoped to become deserving. (Is it ever enough?) Third, she needed to accept that God needed to complete the process in his own ways: "For God must first make the soul feel that she is nothing and can do nothing."[72] While the practice can begin as an active one, in which you try your best to deflate your inflated self-worth and remove the sense of entitlement and possessiveness that follow from it, you cannot complete this transformation on your own. This disposition can only be achieved in its fullest sense after you have suffered passive purifications brought by God (to be discussed later). To want to go through this process is, however, already a great step, for this desire, according to Marmion, allows the rest

69 Ibid.
70 Ibid.
71 Ibid.
72 Ibid.

of the process to occur.[73] To accept your nothingness, then, is a key aspect of Marmion's program for the interior life.

Yet humility must become a disposition, otherwise the great difficulty of self-reliance would remain. Marmion wrote, "I feel more and more drawn to live in a state of habitual adoration and annihilation before Jesus in my heart. I tell you this for yourself, because I feel Our Lord will lead you also by that path."[74] So, it is already a great step to move from acknowledging your nothingness to having a conviction of it:

> It is a great thing to be conscious of our weakness and of the necessity of asking Our Lord's help. He said: "Without me you can do nothing" (Jn 15:5). You knew this already, but now it has become a deep conviction. Our miseries are our title to God's mercy. St Paul was conscious of his weakness, but instead of being discouraged he said: "Gladly will I glory in my infirmities, that the power of Christ may dwell in me" (2 Cor 12:9). When one has been in the habit unconsciously of leaning on one's own strength, and this fails, it requires a certain time to get accustomed to leaning on God alone. This is the state you are in. You have made much progress in recent months, but you have not yet learned to put your trust in God alone. In your spiritual life, avoid examining yourself too much. It is enough that God knows you. Lose yourself in him, and you will find yourself in him. It is far more advantageous for you to look at God than to look at yourself. Your union with God who is immutable will give you the stability, the steady line of conduct which you seem to lack more or less at present. . . . [75]

Marmion indeed here underlined the importance of moving from merely understanding these principles to making them, by way of repetition, into a habitual part of his life.

We also see here that the deep conviction of our nothingness was not the final step for Marmion. While Marmion held the disposition of nothingness as fundamental, he also held that its benefits are not entirely fulfilled until you and I take the next step, to be discussed shortly, of placing our trust in God. To the extent that accepting our nothingness is a solution, it

---

73   See Marmion, "Letter to an unknown correspondent, 11 September 1897," in *Letters*, 79 (the relevant part is quoted later in this section); this letter is also quoted in Marmion, *Priest*, 362; Thibaut, *Dom Columba Marmion*, 95.

74   Marmion, "Letter to an English superioress, no. 7, 1 January 1907," in *Letters*, 133.

75   Marmion, "Letter to one of his nieces, a nun, no. 2, 26 March 1913," in *Letters*, 192–93.

resembles the progress made by hitting rock bottom in our addiction. In our addiction to self, we must hit rock bottom, our nothingness, in order to make deep progress by the help of God. Thankfully, every humbling episode of our lives can, like a painful hangover, help us to detach us from excessive desires and open us a little more to union with God, if we choose to learn the lesson of it all. We must learn to submit to God's plans for our happiness, rather than struggle to go against them, and we must also accept the reality of our weakness in order to allow God to take over. In response to these principles, you may object, arguing God would not lead you in this way. To such an objection, I would retort that God's fidelity to the old covenant allowed him to make use of the Babylonian exile in order to train his beloved people to love him properly (cf. Deut 30:1–20).

For us, these experiences of "exile" are the various crises we face whenever we are asked by God to relinquish control of our beloved spiritual idols. For example, if a novice were building a monument to himself through asceticism or sanctimonious acts, then God would need to topple his approach in order to build a proper one. If a spiritual man or woman were building a career for himself or herself through merely temporary acts of humility or service, then God would need to alter that course. Saint John of the Cross explained that the trials and temptations associated with these crises are necessary passive purifications.[76] These passive purifications are occasions in which external circumstances force us to confront our idols, especially those so entangled with our self-love that we alone would never be able to free ourselves from them. To understand better the difficulty here addressed, let us turn to the wisdom of the desert. Saint Cassian noted that vainglory is difficult to repeal: "The elders well describe the nature of this malady as similar to an onion or to those bulbs that, when one skin is peeled off, are seen to have another, and as often as they are stripped they are found to be covered."[77] How true that can be! With regard to this study, the author of *The Imitation of Christ* pinpointed the possible depth of this challenge with great accuracy: "Can nothing boast of its nothingness? This would be the height of vanity!"[78] This superb phrase notes you must reach a true transformation of heart that gives free reign to the Holy Spirit, otherwise you may never leave the beginning stages of a complex journey toward interior freedom.

---

76 Cf. John of the Cross, *Dark Night*, bk. 1, chap. 7, no. 5.
77 Cf. John Cassian, *Institutes*, bk. 11, chap. v.
78 Thomas à Kempis. *The Imitation of Christ*, trans. Leo Sherley-Price (London: Penguin Books, 1952), 146.

For God to break the false motives associated with vainglory, he must employ strong antidotes. Indeed, he must bring a person to naught, to a real acceptance of his or her nothingness, in order to prompt true progress — in his scheme, by his grace. Such detachments occur solely by suffering purifications brought by God, otherwise known as dark nights. Eventually, these purifications help you to accept yourself as a beloved child of God, someone full of glory and destined to glory, independent of any measure of your importance.

To accept your nothingness allows these dark nights, for it is the way to allow the necessary passive purifications to begin and pass most efficiently. Since a prayer for greater humility is always oriented toward the person's fullest flourishing by grace, God answers it. Also, when you pray for progress in accepting your nothingness, God accepts your invitation to spiritually "annihilate" you — in the sense of breaking you down in order to build you back up. Indeed, Saint John of the Cross implies that you should desire (and, therefore, pray for) these passive purifications and humiliations, since they are integral to getting beyond your limited efforts at coming to union with God. [79] In recognizing the need to purify some motives and in stepping back from some aspects of active asceticism to do so, you can actually request to enter the passive purification of a dark night. Once begun, the night is passed more efficiently by the disposition of nothingness as well, for through this practice you can reorient quickly to accepting the process of removing your obstacles to God through humility and grace. These nights can disorient and can indeed bring about a much more profound sense of your weakness and nothingness than could any meditation. If you were, however, already convinced of the need to accept your nothingness, then you could more efficiently learn the lessons of those painful moments. So, you may find comfort in your humiliations, for, paradoxically, you are never so close to coming to union with God than when you feel your weakness, failure, etc.

THE ASCETICISM OF SPIRITUAL CHILDHOOD. Many people have been puzzled by how Saint Thérèse's rather passive approach to asceticism can be a "complete immolation." [80] Hopefully this explanation of passive

---

79 Cf. John of the Cross, *Ascent of Mount Carmel*, bk. 1, chap. 4: "The necessity to pass through this dark night . . . to attain divine union with God . . ."; John of the Cross, *Dark Night*, bk. 1, chap. 7, no. 5: "No matter how earnestly beginners in all their actions and passions practice mortification of self, they will never be able to do so entirely — far from it — until God accomplishes it in them passively by means of the purgation of this night."

80 Marie Eugene, *I Want to See God*, 93.

purifications will clarify the demanding aspects of her little way. To remain small and to ask God to bring about what is required for your deepest growth is not, when properly and generously undertaken, an easy path. "If you abandon yourself without reserve to His Wisdom and Love," taught Marmion on this subject, "he will send you many mortifications far better than any you could choose for yourself."[81] Here Marmion is in complete agreement with Saint Thérèse's approach to asceticism and oblation.

To confide in God to bring about your deepest purifications does not, however, completely mitigate the role of doing penance in small ways with discretion. "We shall only arrive at that holy freedom at the price of a struggle ceaselessly renewed and faithfully sustained. We, too, must suffer so as to enter into glory,"[82] taught Blessed Columba. Once you have made union with God the reason for your purifications and have accepted the need for a humble path toward your goal, then you can return with zeal to your active asceticism — provided it is a proper asceticism and not something meant to try to appease a supposedly angry God the way the flagellants tried during the Black Death. To remove whatever obstacle lies within your purview should, though, as it was for Saint Benedict and Marmion, always be regulated by the pursuit of humility.[83] Whenever asceticism becomes about some goal outside of the production of God's glory and growth in humility — above all, when it is about the practice itself — then it becomes about building up your ego. Either something is an authentic gift offered by God or it is a distraction from a far better gift. To move toward the greater gifts, you may need to focus upon the fullness God intends for you in life. In moving toward that fullness, you can seek greater gifts by saying to yourself, "This lower good is not right for me now, for it doesn't best glorify God in my body or life" (cf. 1 Cor 6:20). Since changing the lens of analysis alters the deliberation, to do so can break the power an obsessive attachment holds over you.

---

81   Marmion, *Union*, 58; Gionta also connects Marmion's approach to asceticism with Saint Thérèse, *Le Virtù Teologali*, 261.

82   Marmion, *Mysteries*, 345.

83   Cf. Benedict of Nursia, *The Rule of Saint Benedict*, chap. 7, no. 55; see Marmion, *Monk*, 218: "Hence we easily understand why St. Benedict, who assigns us no other end than 'to find God,' founds our spiritual life upon humility. He had himself reached too near to God to be ignorant that humility alone draws down grace, and that without grace we can do nothing. All the asceticism of St. Benedict consists in making the soul humble, then in making it live in obedience (which is the practical expression of humility): this will be for it the secret of intimate union with God." Cf. Thomas Aquinas, *Summa Theologica*, ii–ii, q. 161, a. 5, ad 2. Also see Marmion, *Monk*, 186–87; Thibaut, *Dom Columba Marmion*, 58–59; and Gionta, *Le Virtù Teologali*, 261.

We who are nothing without the Spirit of Christ should want to be considered as nothing, possess nothing, control nothing, wish for nothing, know nothing, and attach ourselves to nothing, except as God wills it.[84] Outside of God's graced plan for each person, there is only vanity; everything, however, within God's plan is a treasured expression of divine perfection. As we detach from the self, we detach from the temptations to make and remake our own plans to acquire emptiness. When we are no longer self-reliant for making our happiness, we find our happiness in God, the perfect Giver who knows exactly how to give us good gifts.

When we are no longer self-reliant, we also become open to the gifts of others. Indeed, we only solve the puzzle of life when we piece together each other's graces and needs, for God has put the answer within the community as a whole. Pastor Michael Mather found this out in his ministry in a low-income urban community in Indiana. According to him, "The biggest spiritual problem in South Bend is that the poor don't believe they have any gifts, and the rich don't believe they have any needs."[85] The false measures of the world produce these mentalities. Our confusion about ourselves produces the inability to see the other person as a shining example of God's gifts and of our need for him or her. We should overcome these challenges by honoring each other through an incarnational spirituality, seeing Christ in each other and searching to bring each other's gifts to life.

MARMION'S COUNSEL ON ACCEPTING YOUR NOTHINGNESS: Three Stations. In speaking of Marmion's desire for humility, Thibaut noted, "Uncontent merely to learn the subject of this very necessary virtue, Dom Marmion [searched] to permeate his life with it."[86] How did he do so? How did he counsel others to do so? Marmion meditated daily on three "stations," namely about what we were, what we are, and what we could become, and he counseled someone he accompanied spiritually to do the same.[87] In the first station, Marmion examined his sinfulness, itself a kind of nothingness as the deprivation of the good. The middle station was, in fact, Marmion's daily meditation on his nothingness, and as such it is the key for interpreting his approach to humility. In the final station he examined

---

84 Cf. Marmion, Monk, 199; Marmion, Union, 56.
85 Michael Mather, Having Nothing, Possessing Everything: Finding Abundant Communities in Unexpected Places (Grand Rapids: William B. Eerdmans, 2018), 31.
86 Thibaut, Dom Columba Marmion, 95. My translation.
87 Cf. Marmion, "Letter to an unknown correspondent, 11 September 1897," in Letters, 79–80; also quoted in Marmion, Priest, 362–63; Thibaut, Dom Columba Marmion, 95.

what he could become, using it as an opportunity to reflect on the ways by which he could fall by presumption into sin. At first glance, this scheme is a little negative. Indeed, we may not retain it as part of what we take away from Blessed Columba's practices, but we can examine powerfully positive lessons under this scheme. The first station leads to an examination of mercy; the second offers advice on the spiritual inner healing possible for traumas and the overcoming of faintheartedness; the third offers some points on overcoming presumption.

First Station: Consider What You Were. Marmion expressed his first daily station in this way: "Consider what you were. If one has once sinned mortally in one's life, one has merited to be cursed for all Eternity by Him Who is Infinite truth and Infinite goodness."[88] Can we not all recall at least one moment — if not many moments — in which our sinful ways prompted us to suffer our shortcomings? Even someone far removed from a tearful act of contrition knows that the self-knowledge acquired during such a conversion can endure. Marmion's description of such moments of penitence runs thus: "What happens at all those moments of grace when, in the light which God gives us, we catch a glimpse of the abyss of our sins, our miseries, our nothingness, is that, seeing ourselves so defiled, we say to Christ as Saint Peter did: 'Depart from me, O Lord, for I am a sinner' (Luke 5:8). . . . I, myself, am too unworthy to dwell so near to you."[89] If we were ever easily to understand nothingness as a term for mystical experience, it is at these moments in which God shakes a person's sinful life to its core.

Even when Christ has forgiven and, in a sense, forgotten those sins, we must remember all that Jesus has done for us in this regard, albeit in a way purified of an ongoing sense of guilt or shame. Marmion offers Mary Magdalene as an exemplar for doing so:

> We do not have the purity of the Virgin Mary, but let us at least ask for the humility of Magdalene, for a contrite and penitent love. O Christ Jesus, I am not worthy that you should enter and live within me: my heart will not be for you a habitation of purity; misery dwells there. But this misery I recognize, I avow. Come and empty me of it, O you who are mercy itself; come and deliver me, O you who are all-powerful! "Come to us and save us, Lord God almighty" (Responsory for Vespers)! A prayer of that kind, joined with the

---

88 Marmion, "Letter to an unknown correspondent, 11 September 1897," in *Letters*, 79.
89 Marmion, *Mysteries*, 250 – 51.

spirit of penitence, attracts Christ, because a humility which abases
oneself in one's nothingness renders thereby, in itself, a homage
to the goodness and the power of Jesus: "If anyone comes to me,
I shall not cast that person out" (Jn 6:37).[90]

Given its phrasing about recognizing our misery in a post-conversion
moment of reflection, I imagine Marmion saying this prayer during his
daily consideration of this first station.

We must establish the need for liberation more fully by recognizing
two uncomfortable truths: our dissatisfaction with ourselves and the real
liberation experienced by the saints. Before doing so, let us note that some
people ignore their dissatisfaction by smugly comparing themselves to their
former selves or to worse sinners. Do you know the self-righteous musings
that can bubble to the surface while shopping at a big-box retailer? Let us
recall that to be obsessed with your own virtue is the distortion of the Pharisee in Jesus's parable of the Pharisee and the Publican (cf. Luke 18:9 – 14).
Yet the more we attend to Jesus's and the saints' examples and teaching, the
more we will want healing, culminating in the fulfillment of the fruits of
the Spirit (cf. Gal 5:22 – 23). By the way, with regard to our false impressions
about ourselves, psychology can help a person to uncover and treat a core
negative belief about himself or herself, and spiritual healing can join that
work to bring about liberation.

Judged on a human or worldly level, each person has often limited his
or her own flourishing in a number of ways. It seems quite common for
people to come to a certain sense of dissatisfaction about this fact. Rather
than going from strength to strength, many of us muddle on, sometimes
in the midst of the ongoing, undesirable effects of our past sins. Everyone
too has periods of lost time and periods of half-fulfilled resolutions. A
spiritual striver is probably often confronted more with a mounting sense
of imperfection than a sense of strength, for his or her ever-deepening
self-knowledge reveals new layers of impurity. When God draws close and
illumines our souls, we see the muck. Indeed, we can encounter thousands
of reasons for discouragement in various ways.

To feel some particular spiritual weight is an opportunity to turn that
aspect of your fallen-ness over to God or to seek some healing for it. While
God does sometimes touch a person's conscience in acute ways, He does not
overwhelm a person in this way. The overwhelming aspect derives instead

---

90 Ibid., 126.

from your bitter self-assessments or fears. If you take yourself too seriously, you fail to see the objective and exclusive love God has for you. In emphasizing that God can mercifully turn our weaknesses into divine strengths, Marmion taught just the opposite of these harsh self-assessments. For example, he wrote, "To realize our weakness and wretchedness knowing, however, that by the very fact of admitting them, we participate in the strength of Christ Himself, this is great wisdom and a great source of joy and confidence."[91]

In fact, the childlike can find humor in each of his foibles, for any acknowledged foible can bring him a step closer to accepting divine power in all its glory. Marmion knew it:

> St Paul gloried in the fact that all he had was from Jesus Christ, that while immensely rich in Him, of himself he had nothing but weakness, infirmity, and wretchedness. He felt that there were two men in him, the one poor and wretched, the other resplendent with the merits of Christ. So, when he comes to himself after his sublime ecstasy, he cries: "For such a one — caught up to the third heaven — I will glory, but for myself I will glory in nothing but in my infirmities." And he adds these astounding words: "Gladly therefore will I glory in my infirmities" (2 Cor 12:9a). And why? "That the power of Christ may dwell in me" (2 Cor 12:9b). We have our moments of temptation and discouragement. How miserable we feel at these times! We feel that we are worth nothing, that we can do nothing. Let us remind ourselves then, with St Paul, that we are infinitely rich in Jesus Christ.[92]

So, we are the closest to receiving the plenitude of grace when we acknowledge our nothingness. "It is God's will," writes Marmion, "to be glorified by the union of our weakness with the power of Christ."[93] Blessed Columba made this theme the topic of his final conference before his death. In his last lesson he wrote, "It is our wretchedness and our weakness which win us the strength of God."[94] This perspective should give us confidence. From this point of view,

91 Marmion, "Conference, Maredret, December 1922," quoted in Philipon, *Spiritual Doctrine*, 120. Also see Marmion, "Letter to an English superioress, no. 5, 29 November 1906," in *Letters*, 131–32; Marmion, "Letter to his sister Rosie, no. 4, 29 December 1922," in *Letters*, 65: "When I make my Stations daily, & contemplate God the Infinite, the All Powerful, crushed by weakness, and trembling in Gethsemani, I see instead of taking on Himself a glorified body, He assumed 'a body like unto that of us sinners' (Rom 8:3), in order to render our weakness divine in Him." Also see Gionta, *Le Virtù Teologali*, 242ff.
92 Marmion, "Retreat, Maredret 1898," quoted in Philipon, *Spiritual Doctrine*, 118.
93 Marmion, "Conference, Maredret, July 21st, 1916," quoted in Philipon, 118.
94 Marmion, "Conference, Maredret, December 1922," quoted in Philipon, 120.

we can say with the Psalmist, "My flesh and my heart may fail, but God is the strength of my heart and my portion forever" (Ps 73:26).

Saint Thérèse of Lisieux taught a similar confidence. Her teaching about accepting our imperfections was likely the basis for Marmion's reflections. While Marmion would not have known about the following content, contained in one of Thérèse's last letters, it sums up her overall approach to the topic, otherwise known by him:

> Beloved little Sister, let us never speak what appears great in the eyes of creatures. Solomon, the wisest king who ever was on earth, having considered the different works that occupy men under the sun, painting, sculpture, all the arts, understood that all these things were subject to envy, he cried out that they were only vanity and affliction of spirit! . . .
>
> The only thing that is not envied is the last place; there is, then, only this last place which is not vanity and affliction of spirit . . . .
>
> However, "The way of man is not within his power," and we surprise ourselves at times by desiring what sparkles. So let us line up humbly among the imperfect, let us esteem ourselves as little souls whom God must sustain at each moment. When He sees we are very much convinced of our nothingness, He extends His hand to us. If we still wish to attempt doing something great even under the pretext of zeal, Good Jesus leaves us all alone. "But when I said: 'My foot has stumbled,' your mercy, Lord, strengthened me!" (Ps 93). YES, it suffices to humble oneself, to bear with one's imperfections. That is real sanctity! Let us take each other by the hand, dear little sister, and let us run to the last place . . . no one will come to dispute with us over it.[95]

It is when we fail to measure up either to someone else's measure or to our own measure that we have affliction of spirit and need this healing. For example, we envy others when we feel we do not measure up to them, and we certainly receive their envy whenever we are vainglorious about some gift. The answer is to take no account of yourself, and this is exactly the example of Saint Thérèse: "I try to be no longer occupied with myself in anything, and I abandon myself to what Jesus sees fit to do in my soul, for I have not chosen an austere life to expiate my faults but those

---

95 Thérèse of Lisieux, "Letter 243, to Sister Geneviève, 7 June 1897," in *Archives du Carmel de Lisieux*, last accessed October 17, 2014. http://www.archives-carmel-lisieux.fr/english/carmel/index.php/lt-241-a-250/1150-lt-243-a-soeur-genevieve; see also Jamart, *Complete Spiritual Doctrine of St. Thérèse of Lisieux*, 35.

of others."[96] This self-forgetfulness and the corresponding abandonment to divine Providence are two of the greatest practical effects achieved by this spirituality.[97]

Second Station: Consider Who You Are.

> Second station: what we are. It is of faith that we are incapable of a good thought without God, "without me you can do nothing" (Jn 15:5); that is, we cannot make one step towards God without Him. Then our daily infidelities, our sins, our ingratitude, our best actions are very miserable indeed.[98]

For Marmion, our topic required daily attention. To reflect daily on our nothingness, however, could also bring risks for those who are not properly prepared for this practice, most especially for anyone who does not link it with the confidence mentioned in the following section. This risk prompts the consideration of whether the practice could of itself produce inappropriate sadness, acedia, or depression in any way. Is it meant to make you feel like trash? Absolutely not! If anything, it is meant to make you feel gifted and safe in your giftedness, recognizing God has an unlimited compassion for you. It is oriented toward the "perfect love [that] casts out fear" (1 Jn 4:18). So, this section aims to quell such concerns, especially with regard to whether it could prompt faintheartedness. It cites Saint Teresa of Calcutta, influenced by Marmion in this approach, as a contemporary witness to the grounded vulnerability, attentiveness to others, and fruitfulness it can produce.

There is a critical caveat to consider before moving forward: if some part of this work were to prompt excessive sadness or anger in your life, then you may have an open wound that first needs addressing. Yet I have surprisingly good news for you: Jesus desires to heal your emotions, anxieties, and traumas, here and now, just as he healed people in Galilee. When sought in a spiritual form, this emotional healing takes the form of healing and

---

96 Thérèse of Lisieux, "Letter 247, to Father Bellière, 21 June 1897," in *Archives du Carmel de Lisieux*, last accessed August 29, 2014. http://www.archives-carmel-lisieux.fr/english/carmel/index.php/lt-241-a-250/1155-lt-247-a-labbe-belliere; see also Jamart, *Complete Spiritual Doctrine of St. Thérèse of Lisieux*, 110.

97 According to Tierney, *Blessed Columba Marmion*, 132, the Roman Censor's estimation of Marmion can be summed up thus: he was "generous to the point of forgetting himself to an uncommon degree."

98 Marmion, "Letter to an unknown correspondent, 11 September 1897," in *Letters*, 80.

deliverance ministry, worked by the Holy Spirit through God's instruments. Indeed, the Church's renewed focus upon the healing charismatic gifts of the Holy Spirit in 1 Corinthians 12 has brought great progress in these areas in recent decades, to the point where parishes and dioceses are offering the special ministry of inner healing as part of their service to God's people.[99] With regard to the spiritual healing of emotions, the work done by Francis and Judith MacNutt and Christian Healing Ministries can be of great service.[100] The restorative work can go hand-in-hand with psychological work as well, as needed. Jesus wants you to feel free of whatever weight you have been carrying and also to enjoy the liberation of union with God.

Let us now return to whether Marmion's theological reflections may have expressed or concealed a depressive approach to life. While it is not within the sphere of spiritual theology to offer a diagnosis of depression, a spiritual theologian can analyze similar effects under the experience of faintheartedness. It must be emphasized that Marmion was not wallowing in fears about having been defeated by life, brooding about the evil of the world, or despairing about whether he would ever become the man God (or his parents) had wanted him to be. In fact, his biography presents a lively and courageous man who knew he was lovable and deeply loved by God, no matter what. When he wrote "our best actions are very miserable indeed," he was not offering a melancholic reflection on the state of fallen humanity; rather, he was expressing a theological fact — "it is of faith" — namely we are not able to merit anything on our own and that only our sins, which are inherently miserable, are uniquely our own.[101] Here Marmion was merely leaving behind confidence in his own unaided activity, so as to be transformed into a person on fire with the Spirit of God.

---

99   See 1 Cor 12:1, 4–11: "Now concerning spiritual gifts, brethren, I do not want you to be uninformed.... Now there are varieties of gifts, but the same Spirit; and there are varieties of service, but the same Lord; and there are varieties of working, but it is the same God who inspires them all in every one. To each is given the manifestation of the Spirit for the common good. To one is given through the Spirit the utterance of wisdom, and to another the utterance of knowledge according to the same Spirit, to another faith by the same Spirit, to another gifts of healing by the one Spirit, to another the working of miracles, to another prophecy, to another the ability to distinguish between spirits, to another various kinds of tongues, to another the interpretation of tongues. All these are inspired by one and the same Spirit, who apportions to each one individually as he wills."
100   Judith MacNutt and Christian Healing Ministries, last accessed June 19, 2020. www.christianhealingmin.org/; for example, see "Worship in Community: Healing Conference, Session 3: Inner Healing, Sept. 21, 2007," last accessed June 19, 2020. vimeo.com/341085381.
101   Marmion, "Letter to an unknown correspondent, 11 September 1897," in *Letters*, 80.

We must always balance humility with acknowledging the power of God at work in our lives. It would be literally worthless and really detrimental to ourselves to focus upon our nothingness apart from a context in which we want to increase some already-present divine graces, gifts, and merits. After all, to go to God with empty hands is to hope to have them filled! "But let thy hand, [O Lord], be upon the man of thy right hand, the son of man whom thou hadst made strong for thyself. Then we will never turn back from thee; give us life, and we will call on thy name" (Ps 80:17–18). We have previously given careful attention to the divine plan for our lives and to the divine means for grace, for those concepts reinforce the reality that we are each beloved of God, worthy of gifts. In the right context and with those who would not distort its meaning,[102] the grace of nothingness can transform us into a vessel of divine gifts. (You can even, *Deo volente*, become a healer or someone who prays for healing for others.)

Keep in mind that Marmion here counseled someone he was accompanying to reflect daily on her own nothingness. At the start of this letter, he explicitly stated that these three stations were meant to help her to grow in the humility that would open her to union with God:

> Your letter was a joy for me; for I see that despite your unworthiness, God is guiding you, and is full of mercy and love in your regard. Your great object ought to be, to become very humble. This is the sure road to God's love; for He is so powerful that he can change even our corruption into the pure gold of His love, if He finds no obstacle in pride. Believe me, my dear child, if you are sincerely humble, God will do the rest. To become humble, a practice I have may aid you: it is to make three stations every day.[103]

This introduction to his daily meditation on his nothingness was, therefore, one filled with the following aspects: the recognition of a unique and challenging goal, the hope necessary for the fulfillment of that goal, the recognition of a specific blockage with regard to the fulfillment of that goal, and a specific recommendation on the way to overcome the root-cause of the problem. Far from being fainthearted, Blessed Columba expressed a notable confidence both in this practice and in his friend's preparation for it.

102 Indeed there may be persons suffering from certain types of depression who may not benefit from this practice and who may need to consult professionals before considering it.
103 Marmion, "Letter to an unknown correspondent, 11 September 1897," in *Letters*, 79.

It is of great value to be properly prepared for this practice, in order to distinguish it from anything that would make you feel truly miserable. This truth applies to any practice that is oriented toward helping you "to die to self" spiritually, for any such counsels will necessarily lead you into instances of anxiety (cf. Gal 2:20, Lk 9:23, Jn 12:24). If a practice, whether this one or an ascetic one, does not lead you to a sense of liberation, then it should be abandoned. While this practice is sound in itself, to undertake it requires a deep faith, a sound theological preparation, a reasonably balanced psychology, and a deep supply of spiritual confidence. In order to undertake it, you should be able to distinguish between depression and theological reflections about your weakness/misery. This weakness/misery is the weakness that looks to a higher power for help, recognizing it cannot do it on its own. Real mysticism should cause neither confusion nor dejection; it should not mystify. Yet an individual unprepared for this practice could stray into faintheartedness or pusillanimity during its more perplexing and challenging moments. Such a risk is indeed greater for those unprepared to sacrifice for the reward.

The following quotation from Gionta encapsulates the risk of only accepting humility without finding in it the plenitude of the necessary confidence in God:

> Still Dom Columba [knew] well that the confidence is not the auto-matic outlet from the abasement provoked by the understanding of one's proper miseries, since the soul understanding its nothingness is able to close itself in mistrust and hopelessness. In such a case, humility would not have reached its final goal, but would have only completed the first pass, not having reached the goal. So, the Author, after having insisted much about the necessity of humility and compunction, impels with greater vehemence to cross past dejection and reach *confidence in God*; he does not propose in the least a gloomy or gray piety but spurs one to pour out one's heart before the Father that loves us.[104]

Note that Gionta supports the view that Marmion's advice is not itself depressive. But he is careful to observe the risk of putting this advice into practice only by halves, and he admonishes the reader against it.

To progress deeply in the spiritual life, though, is to find that you have nothing on which to take any security. If you were committed to going

---

104 Gionta, *Le Virtù Teologali*, 237. My translation.

deeply through the dark nights, then you would naturally risk such dejection and Marmion's advice would be highly pertinent to you. Marmion discussed this point with someone he accompanied in the following way:

> In your letter there is a phrase which pleases me very much, because I see in it the source of great glory for Our Lord. You say, "There is nothing, absolutely nothing in me upon which I can take a little security. Therefore I do not cease to cast myself with confidence into the heart of my Master." That, my daughter, is the true way, for all that God does for us is the result of His mercy which is touched by the avowal of this misery; and a soul that sees her misery and presents it continually to the gaze of Divine Mercy, gives great glory to God by leaving Him the opportunity of communicating His goodness to her. Continue to follow this attraction, and let yourself be led, in the midst of the darkness of trials, to the nuptials of the Lamb to which He destines you.[105]

In truth, in this passage are apparent the depths of anxiety you could encounter. Yet, before discussing distrust of God in greater detail, let us remain here a moment to recognize Marmion was here "please[d]" with the news that the person he was accompanying had moved beyond insecurity to true trust in God.[106] To acknowledge our nothingness *and* to have confidence in God *together* form the "true way"[107] toward the deepest spiritual rewards and interior liberation.

Our spiritual theologian concluded: "Let yourself be led, in the midst of the darkness of trials, to the nuptials of the Lamb to which He destines you."[108] The analogy of a bridal chamber is perhaps the least deficient image for union with God, and it served Saint John of the Cross well in his descriptions of the soul's adventurous search for union in the dark night.[109] In God's way of acting, to feel the darkness of being without support is in some way to begin to enter into the nuptial encounter. To employ further the analogy of the bridal chamber, to accept our nothingness is to accept to be disrobed by God, first of our self-reliance and then of our other obstacles to union. When the soul has surrendered herself entirely to God, God surrenders Himself entirely to her, to the extent that she can receive this gift in

---

105   Marmion, *Union*, 102.
106   Ibid.
107   Ibid.
108   Ibid.
109   Cf. John of the Cross, *Ascent of Mount Carmel*; John of the Cross, *Dark Night*; and John of the Cross, *The Spiritual Canticle*, passim.

this life. What is required is to allow God to guide and direct the necessary process of detachment with regard to our obsessive attachments.[110] God desires this union with us more than we desire it with Him, and so He will work to achieve it in us, if we allow Him to do so. We often refuse to give God the lead, because we do not trust in His objective love for us. We may also need to be stripped of our false conceptions about the process, such as any false notions about the way in which the bridal encounter will occur (to be discussed later). In this encounter, we permit ourselves to be hidden within ourselves with the Hidden One in infused contemplation, and such an encounter would not make for dramatic cinema. Since its rewards are difficult to grasp from the outside, those being initiated into them need reassurance about "[letting themselves] be led, in the midst of the darkness of trials, to the nuptials of the Lamb to which He destines [us]."[111] To consider the bridal analogy can help us to overcome our fears and hesitations.

This is the point: faintheartedness is merely to accept your incapacity without trusting in God to bring about the desired transformation. Perhaps it isn't so much to fear God's inability to transform you as it is to fear that your life is about as significant as a lottery card. Marmion knew this fear well:

> Why then is it that pusillanimous souls are to be found who say that holiness is not for them, that perfection is something beyond their power, who say, when one speaks to them of perfection: "It is not for me; I could never arrive at sanctity." Do you know what makes them speak thus? It is their lack of faith in the efficacy of Christ's merits. For it is the will of God that all should be holy: *Haec est voluntas Dei, sanctificatio vestra* ["For this is the will of God, your sanctification"] (1 Thess 4:3). It is the Lord's precept: "Be ye therefore perfect, as also your heavenly Father is perfect" (Matt 5:48). But we too often forget the Divine Plan; we forget that holiness for us is a supernatural holiness, of which the only source is in Jesus Christ, our Chief and our Head; we do a wrong to the infinite merits and inexhaustible satisfactions of Christ. Doubtless, by ourselves, we can do nothing in the way of grace or perfection; Our Lord expressly tells us so. *Sine Me NIHIL*

---

110 Cf. Marmion, *Soul*, 200; on attachments, see also Gionta, *Le Virtù Teologali*, 305.
111 Marmion, *Union*, 102; in a separate but complementary context, Gionta (*Le Virtù Teologali*, 234) comments on Marmion's general teaching about overcoming self-reliance with the following words: "The trials, the sufferings, the pains and even faults of which one repents enter into a divine pedagogy brought about by the Lord to strip one of every auto-sufficiency about the plan of salvation and to dispose one to receive grace fruitfully." My translation.

potestis facere (Jn 15:5) and St Augustine, commenting on this text, adds: *Sive parum, sive multum, sine illo fieri non potest sine quo nihil fieri potest.* [Whether little or much, without him you cannot do it; without him, nothing, you are able to do.] That is so true! Whether it concerns great things or small, we can do nothing without Christ. But by dying for us, Christ has given us free and confident access to the Father (Eph 2:18; 3:12) and through Him there is no grace, for which we cannot hope.

Souls of little faith! Why do we doubt of God, of our God?[112]

While the recognition of a person's incapacity brings about despair in the fainthearted, it is simultaneously the point at which those confident in God make great progress.

If you suffer from faintheartedness, you may have a distorted image of God, especially if you transpose the experience of bad parents onto your image of God. If, for example, your father was demanding, then you may suffer from scrupulosity, fearing a demanding God. A daughter of an inattentive father may well doubt whether God is invested in helping her to grow spiritually. Here is an exercise: if, questioned by someone completely ignorant of Christianity, you had, without the use of any technical language, to give testimony about God's personality, what would you say? Jesus's answer is the Parable of the Good Father / Prodigal Son (cf. Lk 15:11 – 32). If your answer is something other than a father wanting unconditionally to bless you, then that may be some of the reason for your faintheartedness.

With trust in a father who wants to bless you, turn your weaknesses into divine strengths by making them signs of divine mercy. Consider Marmion's words carefully: "That, my daughter, is the true way, for all that God does for us is the result of His mercy which is touched by the avowal of this misery; and a soul that sees her misery and presents it continually to the gaze of Divine Mercy, gives great glory to God by leaving Him the opportunity of communicating His goodness to her."[113] The trial is to remain patiently faithful as best as you can while perceiving the true and constant state of your misery and unworthiness.

To accept your misery is the point at which the grace of nothingness becomes a deep reality and a true disposition. It is also the point at which deep growth occurs, according to this letter of spiritual accompaniment by Marmion:

---

112   Marmion, *Soul*, 69.
113   Marmion, *Union*, 102.

You are on the right road to God; a road which ever leads to Him, despite our weakness. It is the road of duty accomplished through love despite obstacles. Jesus is our strength. Our weakness assumed by Him becomes divine weakness, and it is stronger than all the strength of man: *Quod infirmum est Dei, forties est hominibus* [The weakness of God is stronger than men] (1 Cor 1:25). This is a great, but profound truth. Our dear Lord's Passion is nothing else than this triumph of divine weakness over all the strength and wickedness of men. But for this we require great patience, and the loving acceptance of God's will at every moment. For *passionibus Christi per patientiam [participemur]* ["we shall through patience share in the sufferings of Christ"] [Benedict of Nursia, Prologue, no. 50]. Think well over this in prayer and you will make great progress. You must be very prudent, and take care of your health in order to perform your duty. [114]

Note that Marmion taught that the acceptance of your misery normally occurs within the loving accomplishment of the normal duties of your life. In no way can you force God's hand by meditating at length on your nothingness or by leaving behind your duties. You must trust in God and dare to be all God wants you to be within the normal rhythm of your state of life. Marmion's attentiveness to a person's duties is another sign that his counsel was itself neither depressive nor negative in nature.

SAINT TERESA OF CALCUTTA: AN APT WITNESS FOR BEING "NOTHING." Given how difficult it is to accept the disposition of nothingness, it is worth including here a contemporary witness to corroborate the value of this practice. Saint Teresa of Calcutta (1910 – 1997) is a most relevant witness for having been deeply influenced by the writings of Blessed Columba Marmion and for having extensively employed the evangelical sense of nothingness. David Toups, in his foreword to a recent edition of *Union with God: Letters of Spiritual Direction by Blessed Columba Marmion*, wrote, "Mother Teresa would quote from [Marmion] extensively, even citing him in her original handwritten copy of the Constitutions of the Missionaries of Charity." [115] In one of her letters, she reported having reflected upon her nothingness after having read one of Blessed Columba's works: "Today I read something in

---

114   Marmion, "Letter to the mother of a family, no. 6, 21 November 1922," in *Letters*, 217–18; Benedict of Nursia, prologue to *The Rule of Saint Benedict*, no. 50. This letter is also quoted in Marmion, *Union*, 79. On this topic, it is also well worth reading Marmion, *Mysteries*, 461 and Marmion, *Union*, 74–79.
115   David Toups, Foreword to *Union*, x.

Abbot Marmion, 'Suffering with Christ': 'when this fire (God's love) comes into contact with imperfection, it produces suffering.' There must be so much of nothingness in me and so this fire causes so much pain . . . Pray for me."[116] Indeed, Saint Teresa of Calcutta spoke and wrote so prolifically about her nothingness that the editor of *Come Be My Light* dedicated its twelfth chapter to the topic: "God Uses Nothingness to Show His Greatness."[117] Finally, she explicitly used nothingness in an evangelical sense. "Father [van der Peet], Jesus has given me a very great grace and that is: the deepest conviction of my total nothingness," reported Saint Teresa of Calcutta; "If He could find a poorer woman through whom to do His work, He would not choose me, but He would choose that woman."[118] This evangelical sense of nothingness is most powerfully seen in her comments about her own leadership:

> I have already written to our Sisters to pray and to vote for somebody else in my place. There are many Sisters who can do even better. I have done with God's grace — much — because I gave Jesus a free hand — knowing that I can't do anything by myself. — The conviction of my nothingness has made the work & the whole Society completely His. He will do still greater things if He finds somebody more nothing than I. (I don't think there is one.) I will be happy, very happy to be free — and to be just a simple Sister in the Com. [community] — after nearly 35 years. — I am longing for this. — I will always do what the Church — through the Holy Father & you [Cardinal Picachy] — want me to do but I am longing to be only all for Jesus — through Mary, a simple MC [Missionary of Charity].[119]

---

116 Teresa of Calcutta, "Letter to Father Neuner, 30 March 1966," in *Come Be My Light: The Private Writings of the "Saint of Calcutta,"* by Teresa of Calcutta, ed. Brian Kolodiejchuk (New York, NY: Image/Doubleday, 2007), 255.
117 Teresa of Calcutta, *Come Be My Light*, 267ff., see especially 271: "The mystery of God's greatness and her nothingness had become a recurrent theme in her speaking and writing. Her smallness, an essential element of the way she related to God and to others, had shaped her way of praying and acting, her very life. She even welcomed the growing publicity from His hand, since in her smallness she neither made any claims nor wished to place any obstacles in the way of His action."
118 Teresa of Calcutta, "Conversation with Father van der Peet," in *Come Be My Light*, 294; it is also notable that Saint Teresa of Calcutta praised Father van der Peet, one of her confidants, for his ability to write about nothingness; see "Letter to Father van der Peet, 6 March 1976," in *Come Be My Light*, 270: "You write so beautifully of nothingness, we — and fullness — God. — And to think that those two are so apart — and yet the humility of God has made it one — Jesus . . ."
119 Teresa of Calcutta, "Letter to Cardinal Picachy, 16 September 1985," in *Come Be My Light*, 305.

For many reasons, then, Saint Teresa of Calcutta is a most apt contemporary witness.

So, let us attend to Saint Teresa of Calcutta's comments about "being nothing" in the following account from Father Paul Murray:

> I remember her remarking on three or four occasions: "In this age, more than in any other, God wants to use nothing!" "Nothing," I discovered, as time passed was a word she liked to use a lot. On another occasion she declared: "Father Paul, when you discover you're nothing, rejoice!" Here, as much as the accent of joy, the note of liberation is telling. For what Mother Teresa means by "being nothing" is in no way connected to the cold imprisonment of self-mistrust, or to what is called nowadays "low self-esteem." It is true Mother Teresa always approached God in deep poverty of spirit. But, at the same time, with an equal profundity of spirit, she trusted absolutely in his love for her.[120]

Why should you rejoice at having become nothing in your own eyes? After all, did not Saint Teresa of Calcutta also write, "There must be so much of nothingness in me and so this fire causes so much pain"?[121] To have become nothing in the eyes of others could be a release from the anxiety to meet some imposed standard. That was not, however, the way in which Saint Teresa of Calcutta was probably speaking, although she must have suffered much from the standards set for her. Given the great affirmation she had received, she was probably discussing a sense of rejoicing at having fully accepted her own sense of her nothingness. Why, though, would she have rejoiced at her nothingness and have even counseled a well-established professor of spiritual theology to do so as well? Let us speculate that this spiritual joy of hers was the result of having found either some sign of progress in the spiritual life or some way toward opening herself to true transformation in it — perhaps even after years of frustrating mistakes in it. Since Saint Teresa of Calcutta was talking to a spiritually reflective person, himself already well instructed in the finer points of spirituality, her counsel on this topic likely must have spoken to some point of transformation that was normally to occur years into the process of spiritual development. Whether she had had years of frustrating mistakes cannot be fully known,

120   Paul Murray, I Loved Jesus in the Night: Teresa of Calcutta, A Secret Revealed (2008; rpt., London: Darton, Longman, and Todd, 2010), 21–22.
121   Teresa of Calcutta, "Letter to Father Neuner, 30 March 1966," in Come Be My Light, 255.

but the context for this conversation seems to indicate a long-felt need for the liberation brought by having accepted her nothingness. Brian Kolodiejchuk, editor and compiler of *Come Be My Light*, gives some indications of this need, saying:

> By the latter part of the 1970s the distressing thoughts that had been puzzling her in the early 1950s and tormenting her in the 1960s had given way to serenity and peace. In her relationship with Jesus she wanted Him to be at ease with her, not even to mind her feelings. While the painful darkness persisted, a deep joy permeated her words and deeds. She was able to communicate her understanding to others and to encourage them to surrender completely.[122]

Note well, it was in 1966 when she had written, "There must be so much of nothingness in me and so this fire causes so much pain."[123] Kolodiejchuk cites the following letter of counsel she penned in 1974 as evidence of her deep transformation:

> You had said "Yes" to Jesus — and He has taken you at your word. — The Word of God became Man (cf. Jn 1:14) — Poor. — Your word to God — became Jesus — poor and so this terrible emptiness you experience. God cannot fill what is full. — He can fill only emptiness — deep poverty — and your "Yes" is the beginning of being or becoming empty. It is not how much we really "have" to give — but how empty we are — so that we can receive fully in our life and let Him live His life in us.
>
> In you today — He wants to relive His complete submission to His Father — allow him to do so. Does not matter what you feel — as long as He feels alright in you. Take away your eyes from your self and rejoice that you have nothing — that you are nothing — that you can do nothing. Give Jesus a big smile — each time your nothingness frightens you.
>
> This is the poverty of Jesus. You and I must let Him live in us and through us in the world.[124]

That Saint Teresa of Calcutta had profoundly accepted a disposition of nothingness is the most probable explanation for her "accent of joy" and

122 Brian Kolodiejchuk, commentary in Teresa of Calcutta, *Come Be My Light*, 274–75.
123 Teresa of Calcutta, "Letter to Father Neuner, 30 March 1966," in *Come Be My Light*, 255.
124 Teresa of Calcutta, "Letter to Father Don Kribs, 7 February 1974," in *Come Be My Light*, 275–76.

"note of liberation" while telling Father Paul Murray to rejoice upon feeling his nothingness.[125]

It is doubtful, though, that she was rejoicing at a sign of progress, for we must eventually relinquish even affirmation from God about our spiritual progress. Many spiritual men and women try to measure their spiritual progress so as to feel affirmed by God in it, but to accept our nothingness is not a mere replacement for the spiritual person's favorite system of measurement, such as Saint Teresa of Avila's stages of prayer or redeeming those around them or some other accomplishment. Rather, to accept our nothingness is the real development of surrendering to God both our measurement of accomplishment and our fears about feeling our nothingness. In other words, Saint Teresa of Calcutta's joy at having accepted her nothingness, which could have occurred years before her conversation with Father Murray, must have been the result of a real development in her spousal relationship with Christ, albeit not one measured in anything but surrender to God.[126]

Her surrender was real, based upon these words: "I am at His disposal — He can do with me just as it pleaseth Him, without even a thought of consulting me. I just want to be His own little one — if He so wants, otherwise I will be happy to be just nothing & He everything."[127] Indeed, the joyful testimony she expressed to Father Murray demonstrated that the acceptance of her nothingness was for her an entryway into a transformed life with Christ. She gave testimony to this fact because she didn't want Father Murray to have missed that entryway. If nothingness had indeed been for her a "narrow gate" — one, however, that had eventually "[led] to life" — then she knew well the value of reassuring one of the "few" who would find it to enter into its confining entrance (Mt 7:13–14). From this point of view, we can now see Saint Teresa of Calcutta indeed offers us a most apt testimony to the disposition of nothingness. We shall return to the above passage, which is worthy of multiple readings, after having made more progress.

Saint Teresa of Calcutta's joyful witness to the disposition of nothingness should encourage any who remain in doubt about whether a proper interpretation of it might be harmful. She certainly thought love was good and she was lovable. She was neither depressive nor philosophically nihilistic.

---

125 Paul Murray, I Loved Jesus in the Night: Teresa of Calcutta, A Secret Revealed, 21–22.
126 In Teresa of Calcutta, Come Be My Light, 276, see also Kolodiejchuk's interpretation of "Letter to Father Don Kribs, 7 February 1974" (quoted above) as an expression of Saint Teresa of Calcutta's surrender.
127 Teresa of Calcutta, "Letter to Father van der Peet, 17 February 1978," in Come Be My Light, 282–84, esp. 284.

On the contrary, the acceptance of her nothingness was for her a liberating, life-giving truth. This disposition is meant to help you to turn your weaknesses into divine strengths and turn your thoughts to a more confident hope in the God who incessantly loves you with predilection. Since it is your obsessive attachments that sadden you and distract you from God — robbing you of poverty of spirit — to be liberated from them is life-giving.

We can also see from Saint Teresa's witness that this disposition can make us into a messenger of life-giving love and healing. The editor of a recent version of *Christ the Ideal of the Priest* speculates that statements in Marmion such as "Jesus is the herald of infinite mercy to human misery"[128] may have influenced her initial desires to help the poorest of the poor. Her desire to bring Christ's love to those most in need of it has long been common knowledge, but these private thoughts now connect her motive with her own thoughts on humility:

> More and more I begin to learn why Jesus wants us to learn from Him to be meek and humble of heart. For because without meekness we can never be able to accept others nor love the other as He loves us. — And so before we learn humility, without which we cannot love God — we have to learn to love each other. — We need meekness & humility to be able to eat the Bread of life. — We need meekness & humility if we want to feed Him in the hungry One. I would be happy if you wrote about the hunger of man and the Bread of life, the hunger of God and the Hungry One in the distressing disguise of the Poor.[129]

In an unrelated but strikingly similar phrase, Saint Teresa of Calcutta connects accepting our nothingness with giving to others from God's fullness: "It is only when we realize our nothingness, our emptiness, that God can fill us with Himself. When we become full of God then we can give to others, for from the fullness of the heart the mouth speaks."[130] Due to the difficulties inherent in her work, Saint Teresa of Calcutta would have needed both an abundance of grace and a theological framework in which she could have humbly served Jesus in her extraordinary way. To have accepted her own nothingness undoubtedly helped her to accept others

---

128 Marmion, *Priest*, 137.

129 Teresa of Calcutta, "Letter to Father van der Peet, 26 November 1976," in *Come Be My Light*, 278–79.

130 Teresa of Calcutta, "instruction to the M. C. Sisters, 17 May 1978," in *Come Be My Light*, 273–74.

whom no one else wanted to serve.

To consider "who we are," then, leads us to share the mercy we have received, especially to the poorest of the poor. Considered in this light, the disposition of nothingness is neither a depressive nor a nihilistic term that would close you in on yourself. It is quite the opposite. It is a life-giving term that liberates you of your false securities in order to open you toward a joyful, gracious interaction with everyone. To be one with God means to be one with everyone.

Third Station: Consider What You Could Become.

> 3rd station: what we may become. If God takes away His hand from us, we are perfectly capable of becoming what we were before, and worse. God sees this. He knows what depths of treachery we are capable of. How can we be proud?[131]

Marmion's final station considered presumption, which is the other extreme in the spiritual life. Just as faintheartedness is to go to defect in the spiritual life, so presumption is to go to excess in it. Marmion's private notes contained additional reflections on this tendency:

> I have received recently a light which seems to me very precious: God is contemplating me at this moment. He sees the depths of my wretchedness. He knows everything, even the contingent future. He knows clearly to what depths I would sink if He withdrew from me His grace. He knows exactly what I am capable of. For my part I can guess it from the experience of my own past, and indeed I would fall still lower, because the abuse of His grace would in itself be so great that I would be led to commit the greatest crimes. This is strictly true every moment of my life even when I feel myself on fire with the desire to please God. I am so changeable! This thought humbles me and makes me to realize how good God is to sustain me, and to understand that I must put all my confidence in the merits of Jesus Christ. Humility, as St Francis de Sales tells us, is simply the courage to face the full rigour of the truth in regard to oneself with all its consequences.[132]

Just as God has saved us out of a state of sin, he also continues to save us from becoming grievous sinners, as long as we continue to cooperate with

---

131   Marmion, "Letter to an unknown correspondent, 11 September 1897," in Letters, 80.
132   Marmion, "Notes, Retreat, May 1889," quoted in Philipon, Spiritual Doctrine, 151.

His grace. Sometimes we don't cooperate with his grace. Sometimes we say to ourselves, "[God] will never see it" (Ps 10:11) or, worse yet, "There is no God" (Ps 10:4). To sin, is it not at some level to say, "God is nothing"?

It is worth taking a moment to unpack the ways in which thinking of the future can prompt a fall of the type just described. Anxious to succeed, if only spiritually, we get ahead of ourselves. Marmion has keen insights on these tendencies:

> God is essentially the first cause. Our homage consists in acknowledging Him as the source of all good: *Omne datum optimum et omne donum perfectum desursum est descendens a Patre luminum* [Every good endowment and every perfect gift is from above, coming down from the Father of lights] (Jas 1:17). The man who tries to act on his own initiative is, in practice, denying this. Every creature is in a state of complete dependence in relation to God. *Tota a Deo et ad Deum* [Everything from God and to God]. Humility is the practical recognition of this relation. God has destined us to an elevation which is infinite and which He alone can accomplish in us. Humility is the habitual acceptance of this fact. The proud man is, more or less unconsciously, putting himself in the place of God. In his thoughts, in his words, in his actions, he is exalting himself, giving primacy of place to his own ego. Gradually he begins to seek admiration and makes of himself the final end and the centre of everything.[133]

To act on our own initiative makes us feel as if we are in control, as if we are marching toward our destiny, but it is a false construct of our own imagination. The key to acting upon God's initiative, and therefore the key to reaching "an elevation which is infinite and which [God] alone can accomplish in us,"[134] is to embrace the awkwardness and vulnerability of the grace of the moment.

Over time, the focus upon the grace of the moment will lead you step by step to finding your own unique path to union with God:

> I do not say to you: "Aspire straightaway to the highest sanctity." But I do recommend you strongly — for it is of the utmost importance — to try to walk in the way of sanctity which God has chosen for you. He alone knows your weakness: *ipse cognovit figmentum*

---

133 Marmion, "Retreat, Erdington, December 1907," quoted in Philipon, *Spiritual Doctrine*, 152.
134 Ibid.

nostrum [for he knows our frame] (Ps 103[102]:14), and in His
wisdom, He has measured exactly what you are capable of, and
what is the power of the graces destined to support your progress.
It is from this desire of sanctity that all true spiritual life proceeds:
by it the soul prepares itself to receive the gift from on high; in
its acknowledgement of its powerlessness and in its expectation of
the help of grace, it lays itself open to the influence of the Lord,
and increases its capacity for the divine.[135]

In other words, in remembering your weakness and dependence upon
God and in staying present to the grace of the moment, you allow God to
increase your work or asceticism or prayer life as He deems fit to do so. It
never works to push yourself beyond your own state by your own powers.

Even a spiritual person must constantly pray that God "lead us not into
temptation" (cf. Mt 6:13), otherwise "[he is] perfectly capable of becoming
what [he was] before."[136] But how is it that a spiritual person, striving to
please God, diverts from the right path? In many hidden ways — sometimes
even hidden to ourselves — our false motives corrupt our aim and spur
self-reliance. Ruth Burrows, a contemporary commentator on Carmelite
spirituality, sums up the various temptations of spiritual strivers in stating
that importance is what they are tempted to seek under a spiritual guise:

> It might seem that we Christians who are striving to live out what
> we believe, who see our meaning in God, who know, in faith, the
> grandeur and security of man in God, can let go this craving for
> importance. Oh, but we can't. We carry on the pursuit in a far
> more subtle and dangerous way. We want spiritual importance.
> We want our interior life, our way to God, to have elements which
> make us feel important. We want to rise above the mediocrity
> of the common lot. This might seem justifiable but in reality it
> could mean nothing but a desire to escape from the sheer drabness
> of the ordinary, seeking a short-cut from the drudgery... back
> again to that secret coveting of spiritual riches, beauty, glory, and
> achievement.[137]

If you are not focused upon God (and upon your own nothingness), then
you can be lured into living for yourself in some way. This is all a pursuit
of nothingness: "[Those not seeking God in all things] are either attached

---

135 Marmion, *Priest*, 44–45.
136 Marmion, "Letter to an unknown correspondent, 11 September 1897," in *Letters*, 80.
137 Burrows, *Guidelines for Mystical Prayer*, 128.

to created things or seek themselves, by egoism, self-love, levity; and it is themselves too that they find — themselves, that is to say nothingness."[138] Behold Marmion, the new *Qoheleth*. Since a quasi-state of self-reliance follows upon even weakly held false motives, over time a type of accommodation to mediocrity and lesser goals causes a person to shrug off contemplative union with God as unattainable. Then, you truly find only yourself. The opposite is to find yourself to be an amazingly graced person, guided by God's love and filled with glory. Now is the moment to take an inventory of yourself and admit whether God or the pursuit of importance reigns in your life — not that they are mutually exclusive.

RETURNING TO THE TOPIC OF ASCETICISM. Even within an ascetical framework in which we want our actions to serve growth in humility, we can still make the error of adopting an untrusting approach. On the side of faintheartedness, we stop trusting and discontinue the pursuit of union — sometimes only in interior ways — or become despairing. On the side of presumptuous action, we turn to self-reliance in order to try to answer our anxieties about the pace, progress, or means of our sanctification toward union (or our importance).[139] Both types of distrust complicate the process, and the latter can lead to the former.

Faintheartedness can indeed express frustration at not having become the "perfect" saint you may want to become. To the extent that such selfishness is at play, the breaking down of the false self may indeed approach or somehow overlap with depression. Yet to become a perfect self-glorifying "saint" is not Marmion's way. The appropriate response is to allow Christ to lead, and we do it by confidently surrendering to Christ our inability to bring the process to completion.

Similarly, we can find no security in presumptuous action. While we should do our part through typical asceticism to remove obstacles to union with God, in the end we cannot make ourselves worthy of God. If you discern a typical ascetic practice to be liberating, then you should follow it. The problem here discussed pertains to ascetic practices viewed as perfective or meant to build up status. There is a great difference between dieting and

---

138   Marmion, *Monk*, 12.
139   In Marmion, *Monk*, 226, Marmion wrote of a similar dynamic in our prayer life: "If forgetful of our nothingness, we come before God, full of confidence, but with little reverence; or if, on the contrary, we are penetrated with fear, but have only a slight confidence, our relations with God are not what they ought to be. The self-abasement of the creature should not be to the detriment of the confidence of the child; the quality of child ought not to cause forgetfulness of the condition of creature and sinner."

turning yourself into the emaciated figure of Saint Jerome depicted in many paintings after the Council of Trent. Contrary to some views, our asceticism does not need to be all-consuming in quite that way, even as we strive to turn our attention to "the things that are above," rather than "the things that are on earth" (Col 3:1–2).

Early in the prologue of the *Rule of Saint Benedict* is a quote from Psalm 34:14, which expressed to Marmion the characteristics of proper asceticism:[140] "If you desire true and eternal life . . . turn away from evil and do good; let peace be your quest and aim."[141] In emphasizing this text, Marmion highlighted that we should peacefully and discretely aim our asceticism at overcoming vices and building virtues. As the previous section attested, it is in accepting your misery and weakness that you allow the deepest progress in interior virtue to occur, for it is then that you allow God to divest you of your obsessive attachments. Under this scheme, it is easier to accept peacefully whatever circumstances or practices are truly liberating.

To shift the primary focus of your asceticism toward a passive asceticism that trusts in God to bring about the trials or calls necessary for growth is the way by which to avoid excess — at least until you clearly discern an unmistakable call to undertake atypical ascetic acts or penances. With regard to being led "to the nuptials of the Lamb," Marmion was confident that the "true way" was to have nothing "upon which [you] can take a little security;" and this advice applied above all to the security sought in excessive spiritual practices.[142] These lessons are not new. Saint Benedict himself counseled humility with regard to asceticism: "The eighth step of humility is that a monk does only what is endorsed by the common rule of the monastery and the example set by his superiors."[143] It was for these reasons that Marmion counseled the following approach on mortification: "For you it will consist above all in the perfect observance of the Rule and the regular discipline, and in the mortification of the common life generously accepted."[144] Anyone who were to find this advice to be a restricting imposition would need to review both his generosity to the community and his trust in God's ability to further his interior development. "It is not always on account of the lack of afflictive mortifications that inward progress is retarded in so many souls,"

---

140 Cf. Marmion, *Monk*, 125.
141 Benedict of Nursia, prologue to *The Rule of Saint Benedict*, no. 17.
142 Marmion, *Union*, 102.
143 Benedict of Nursia, *The Rule of Saint Benedict*, chap 7, no. 55.
144 Marmion, *Union*, 55.

wrote Marmion; "this cause must often be sought for in the selfishness that makes them indifferent to the needs of their brethren."[145]

In guarding against presumptuous self-reliance, you allow God to guide the subtler parts of the process of overcoming your egoism. Indeed, to reflect daily upon your nothingness is a great aid in that regard, for it helps you to navigate the many temptations to "seek admiration and make of [oneself] the final end and the centre of everything."[146] It is the practical way by which to accept yourself as already being loved — favored — by God. Until you accept your nothingness — deeply accept it with adult theological reflection — you will either relentlessly try to prove your worth to yourself and to others or give up. To accept this fact is not as simplistic as a Protestant's acceptance of "saving faith" through an altar call. It requires ongoing attention, lest the pursuit of a transitory importance lead you to pusillanimity and to becoming "what we were before, and worse."[147] If a graduate of a twelve-step program cannot recognize your definition of grace as that action of a High Power that saved him from addiction and realized real gains in his life, then it needs revision.

The path of spiritual childhood (i.e., of accepting your nothingness) reverses the fundamental arc of spiritual presumption, spiritual cowardice, and decline by humbly and confidently accepting yourself as already being loved by a God who wants to transform you. In wanting merely to return the love already received, you then measure your life by the love you give. Your life, then, becomes about receiving the graces that increase those loves (received and given).

To Have Confidence in God

The next step is to have confidence that the merciful God will bestow on us everything necessary for spiritual progress. "Acknowledge your utter nothingness then before this Word, unite yourself to Him in faith,"[148] taught Marmion. Note well, we give ourselves to Christ in this way. There is, then, an orientation to the disposition of nothingness:

> Each degree of humility itself only increases with faith and confidence in God. With every degree of inward humility, our Blessed

---

145 Marmion, *Monk*, 409; Gionta, *Le Virtù Teologali*, 313.
146 Marmion, "Retreat, Erdington, December 1907," quoted in Philipon, *Spiritual Doctrine*, 152.
147 Marmion, "Letter to an unknown correspondent, 11 September 1897," in *Letters*, 80.
148 Marmion, *Union*, 141.

Father gives hope of a special correspondence of Divine grace.
Have we not shown how with him humility finds its completion
in invincible confidence in the merits of Christ Jesus Who brings
grace to us? It is for God then to direct us by His will, by that of
His Church, by events; it is for us to do this will each time that
it is manifested to us, trusting ourselves to God, for the rest, and
holding ourselves assured that we shall infallibly come to perfect
charity: "Mox ad caritatem Dei perveniet . . . perfecta[m] [(the monk)
will quickly arrive at the perfect love of God]" (Rule of Saint Benedict,
Ch. 7, no. 67). This is the whole aim of the asceticism of humility.[149]

So, just as Saint Benedict oriented his ladder of humility to the goal of
coming to "the perfect love of God [that] casts out fear (1 Jn 4 : 18),"[150] in
a similar manner Blessed Columba oriented his advice about accepting our
nothingness to growing our confidence in God.

Not surprisingly, then, Marmion's explanation of Benedictine spirituality is an updated and detailed account of the core spiritual message of his
patriarch. As Gionta observes, the updated aspect of this approach makes
his teaching original: "We touch in this convergence [between trust in
God and humility] one of the aspects not only strongly and at length valued by Dom Columba, but also [one of the aspects] most original in his
thought."[151] Gionta also notes that "in [faith and charity], united to filial
confidence, Dom Columba . . . assigns the secret to spiritual progress."[152]
Part of the brilliance of Marmion's new combination of these themes lies
in his understanding of putting on Christ's filial confidence:

> Our souls ought to be full of great confidence. In our relations with
> our Heavenly Father, we ought to remember we are His children
> through being partakers of the filiation of Christ Jesus, our Elder
> Brother. To doubt of our adoption of the rights it gives us is to
> doubt Christ Himself. Let us never forget we put on Christ on the
> day of our baptism: Christum induistis [you have put on Christ], or

149 Marmion, Monk, 379; Benedict of Nursia, The Rule of Saint Benedict, chap. 7, no.
67; see also Marmion, Union, 141: "In prayer, my dear child, give yourself often to Jesus
Christ. You must cast yourself down in your utter nothingness before Him, that will
do great good to your soul."
150 Benedict of Nursia, ch. 7, no. 67.
151 Gionta, Le Virtù Teologali, 231. My translation. See also ibid., 250: "From the
beginning until the end of his monastic career [Marmion] kept on about the same
points . . . [including] the necessity of humility together with the expansion of the soul
into total confidence." My translation. On this topic, see ibid., 231–54.
152 Ibid., 337.

rather we have been incorporated with Him. We have therefore the right to come before the Eternal Father, and say to Him: *Ego sum primogenitus tuus* [I am your Firstborn Son]: to speak in the name of His Son, to ask Him with absolute confidence for all we need.[153]

In Blessed Columba's mind (as later in that of Saint Pio of Pietrelcina), we can take on the confidence of a son or daughter who is preferred by the Father.[154] We, in Christ, are favorites.

To explore Marmion's approach to trust in God, let us be guided by the passage from which we extrapolated our guiding tripartite scheme; it reads: "A tending toward God in Himself with a sense of confusion at our unworthiness and confidence in His goodness and in the Precious Blood of Jesus Christ are the three notes of real union with God. Do not fear. This way is sure."[155] We have already covered the reasons to have confidence in God's objective goodness. Let us now consider in greater depth the ways by which we place our "confidence . . . in the Precious Blood of Jesus Christ."[156] The source of our confidence is the unfailing desire and ability of Jesus Christ to sanctify us, the Father's adopted children. Accordingly, our confidence is

---

153   Marmion, *Life*, 164.

154   Cf. Pio of Pietralcina, *Correspondence with His Spiritual Daughters*, trans. Geraldine Nolan, ed. Gerardo Di Flumeri, vol. 3, 2nd ed. (San Giovani Rotondo: Edizioni, 2001), lxxv. E.g., see Saint Pio's words about divine predilection in letters of spiritual accompaniment to various individuals [my translations]. "Letter 17 to Annita Rodote, 28 July 1918": "Jesus continues to regard you as his favorite (predilected) daughter and makes you entirely his own." "Letter 8 to Margherita Tresca, 9 July 1918": "Jesus continues to regard you as his predilected one and transforms you entirely in him." "Letter 37 to Maria Gargani, 13 December 1918": "How are you able to fear the repulsion of him who has sealed his heart with the sign of his predilection?" "Letter 43 to Maria Gargani, 20 March 1919": "Oh how I am grateful to this lovable Savior in seeing the love with which he favors (predilects) your soul!" "Letter 18 to Assunta di Tomaso, 26 November 1919": "I receive your blessing and while on the one hand I am afflicted that you feel so intensely afflicted by suffering, on the other hand, I rejoice in the spirit, knowing that it is all desired directly by the divine spouse in the predilection he has for your soul." "Letter 17 to the Sisters Ventrella, 24 January 1919": "Your present state has brought my bitterness and martyrdom to an apex, but pronouncing the fiat!, I am resigned, comforting myself with the thought that Jesus permits this storm in my most dear daughter out of pure predilection and not out of chastisement." From the point of view of merits, Jesus is the Father's favorite and the most beloved Son (cf. Mt 3:17; 17:5; Aquinas, *Summa Theologica*, i., q. 20, a. 3; vol. 1, 115). Clothed in Christ, we, adopted children and chosen ones, can participate in his privileges and rewards, to differing degrees. Yet, the Father's gaze falls, like the rays of the sun, on each of us in full intensity. In heaven, each soul receives a unique and special love of undivided attention (cf. Rev 2:17). Is that attentiveness not favoritism from that individual's point of view — not relative to other people but merely within that relationship?

155   Marmion, *Union*, 197.

156   Ibid.

Christocentric, for He is the pledge of our sanctification and the principle of our hope for it. Since Christ is our mediator, in Him we have the confidence to "dare to [ask]"[157] for what we need. Were he not our Mediator, to ask for union with God would be brazen. Due to our divine adoption, however, we can say: "If without Him we can do nothing, in Him we are 'made rich,' and nothing is wanting to us: *ita ut nihil vobis desit in ulla gratia* [so that you are not lacking in any spiritual gift] (1 Cor 1:5, 7)."[158] Christ, then, is our hope for attaining union with God.

Yet this confidence must also be humble, for to fail to request our needs in Christ's name can presume God exists merely to serve us. This reality prompts a question: does a request for union with God require some special confidence on our part? It probably requires a higher degree of confidence than normally given, and Marmion's writings indicate that fact as well.[159] Since to open ourselves to union with God requires a high level of confidence in and commitment to God, we must consider confident prayer from two points of view, namely of putting our confidence in God in a high degree and of maintaining that confidence. So, what are the generic attributes (or form) of these interrelated acts of confidence, and what were the ways in which Marmion realized them (or the specific matter of this confidence in Marmion's life)? With regard to its form, let us consider four qualities, namely that it should be committed, pure, persevering, and simple. The former two qualities, that our prayer for union be committed and pure, pertain primarily to the act of putting our confidence in God; the latter two, that the prayer be persevering and simple, pertain to maintaining that confidence. With regard to the concrete ways in which Marmion manifested such confidence, we shall consider three of his practices: his consecrations, his practice of the presence of God (i.e., his prayer of participating in Christ's state of being *in sinu Patris* [in the heart/bosom of the Father, Jn 1:18]), and his refusal to overcomplicate the process.

A COMMITTED CONFIDENCE. At some point we must assuredly make this request for union with God in a way that definitively opens ourselves to its fulfillment, and that way must include some notion of respect for both the blessed Trinity and the content of this audacious prayer. In short, we must commit to God, in order for Him to bestow the gift of union upon us.

---

157 "Communion Rite" in *The Daily Roman Missal: Complete with Readings in One Volume*, 7th ed. (Woodridge, IL: Midwest Theological Forum, 2012), 811.
158 Marmion, *Soul*, 368.
159 Cf. Marmion, *Monk*, 358, 395; Marmion, *Union*, 69–70.

How, then, do we commit to God in a more profound way than our standard conversion? There is no easy answer to this question, but presumably you do not request union with God in a definitive way while reading a spiritual book in bed in your pajamas. While you should act on any such impulse to commit to God, you should probably formalize it in some way, at least by getting out of bed and onto your knees. In speaking of reverence in prayer, Saint Benedict taught the following: "Whenever we want to ask some favor of a powerful man, we do it humbly and respectfully, for fear of presumption. How much more important, then, to lay our petitions before the Lord God of all things with the utmost humility and sincere devotion. We must know that God regards our purity of heart and tears of compunction, not our many words."[160] This advice applies more forcefully still when the content of your request is not a mere favor but the most divine gift.

Were it not itself desired by God, such a request would be preposterous. How, then, do we properly make it? To answer that question, let us turn to an insight from Saint Thomas Aquinas on the significance of our gestures while at prayer: "When we genuflect we signify our weakness in comparison with God and when we prostrate ourselves we profess that we are nothing of ourselves."[161] In a prayerful reflection on Psalm 38, Aquinas wrote a similar but unrelated statement that perhaps clarifies the type of dedication he there expressed: "Although I am nothing of myself, nevertheless all that I hope to be, and all that I am, is in you [my God]."[162] Such an interior prostration that disavows itself of its own power and places all of its hope in God's power is the type of commitment that opens the process of placing all of our confidence in God. This notion of a committed confidence corresponds closely with Marmion's teaching, for he taught that the "general disposition" necessary for a "habitual preparation for our union with Jesus Christ, and, above all, for the perfection of this union is the total gift, frequently renewed, of ourselves to Jesus Christ."[163]

It is now possible to examine the concrete ways in which Marmion embodied a committed confidence. The (interior) prostration mentioned above recalls the prostration Marmion made during his mystical death at his profession as well as the one he made during his ordination to the

---

160 Benedict of Nursia, *The Rule of Saint Benedict*, chap. 20, nos. 1–3.
161 Aquinas, *Summa Theologica*, ii–ii, q. 84, a. 2, ad 2; vol. 3, 1547.
162 Aquinas, "Psalm XXXVIII," in *In Psalmos*, Parma ed., 298, quoted in Paul Murray, *Aquinas at Prayer: The Bible, Mysticism, and Poetry* (London: Bloomsbury, 2013), 146.
163 Marmion, *Soul*, 270–71.

priesthood. It also brings to mind personal consecrations, such as the one Marmion made to the Blessed Trinity.[164] While lay men and women are free to find their own ways to express this type of commitment, these were nonetheless the ways by which Marmion probably initiated a complete confidence in God. These ways, after all, may have only been the ways in which Marmion re-expressed or reinforced the promises made at baptism and confirmation. Admittedly, it is impossible to pinpoint the deliberate, complete dedication of self that begins this type of confidence.

A PURE CONFIDENCE. Both Marmion and Saint Benedict mentioned the criterion of purity of heart. This criterion is difficult to assess, for often we are prompted to greater confidence in God's mercy after having suffered a deeper sense of self-knowledge.[165] While we must do our part to remove our obstacles to union, or purify our hearts, to presume upon our purity in our prayer for union would be a tragic mistake. We are not entitled to union with God.

For the moment, then, let us consider purity under the lens of purity of intention.[166] If God does not will something, then no amount of confidence or commitment will bring about the graces necessary for obtaining it. In searching for God's will, you acquire peace. In contrast, to persist toward an unattainable false goal only brings you dismay. Marmion examined this relationship in the following passage of spiritual accompaniment:

> I very much wish that you could acquire calm and peace, and it is certainly an inspiration of the Holy Spirit that is urging you in this direction. Only do it very gently and quietly and don't be too much distressed if you don't succeed straight away. The best means of acquiring this calm is an absolute resignation to God's holy will, there you will find the region of peace and . . . Try to wish for nothing, to attach your heart to nothing without having first presented it to God and placed it in the Sacred Heart, in order to wish it in Him and with Him.
>
> One of the chief reasons why we lose peace of soul is that we desire something, our hearts cling to some object, without

---

164 Cf. Marmion, "Notes, Christmas 1908," quoted in Thibaut, Dom Columba Marmion, 155–56.

165 See Marmion, Union, 55: "To arrive at this union, we must pass through many sorrows and trials and above all that of feeling how weak we are in ourselves."

166 Gionta also has a short section on Marmion's point of view on intention; see Gionta, Le Virtù Teologali, 281–83.

knowing if God wills it or not, and then, when an obstacle is opposed to our desires, we are troubled, we are no longer in conformity with His holy will, and we lose peace.[167]

So, to have confidence in God's plan for your holiness is not to trust that God will repay your gift of self with some specific gift, such as a hundredfold of exteriorly recognized greatness in this life. Even God could not provide such a narrative for everyone. Rather, to have confidence in God is to have the confidence to allow yourself to be conquered by God. When you surrender to God, you allow the deepest lies within yourself to be healed and you allow yourself to be transformed into someone on fire with the Spirit of God.[168] Our joy and our "hundredfold" in this life (cf. Mt 19:29) are to be found in union with God: "[God] says to us," according to Blessed Columba, "It is I Myself Who will be Thy reward, a reward 'exceeding great': *Ego merces tua magna nimis* (Gen 15:1)."[169] That is a narrative God can provide for everyone and to which anyone can aspire, since God has opened the way to it.

A PERSEVERING CONFIDENCE. Like the persistent widow in Jesus's parable of the widow and the unjust judge (cf. Lk 18:1–8), we intensify our prayer by persevering in it. To persevere in serving God is the key to surrendering to Him. To maintain our confidence during difficulties is, therefore, of equal significance to accepting our nothingness, otherwise we would eventually fall to discouragement. This temptation to discouragement is greatest in the aridity felt during the dark nights, yet those trials are designed, according to Marmion, to bring us to "ABSOLUTE resignation and submission."[170] Think of it this way: if you have properly aimed at union with God, if you have really accepted your nothingness, and if you have placed your confidence in God, then what difficulties — indeed, what fears — can truly dissuade you? None should. Every trial can be turned to spiritual profit; each of them can be offered as a redemptive sacrifice in cooperation with Christ's cross.[171] In practice, though, we do often allow difficulties to dissuade us from persevering.

---

167 Marmion, *Union*, 11–12.
168 On Marmion's explanation of the value of surrender to God, see Marmion, *Monk*, 436.
169 Marmion, *Monk*, 116; see also ibid., 104 (quoted below on 143).
170 Marmion, *Union*, 62–63.
171 On the role of sharing in Christ's sufferings, see Marmion, *Monk*, 384–85.

THE GRACE OF "NOTHINGNESS"

In the pursuit of union with God, the greatest difficulties generally come from within a person, especially with regard to wanting to measure our progress. When we follow these three simple counsels of Marmion, we need not further complicate the process by worrying about indicators of progress. Anxiety is, after all, opposed to the confidence necessary for bringing this process to completion. We need merely to remember that God will infallibly complete the process for anyone truly tending toward union with Him in this way. Although the spiritual masters have astutely written of a progression in the spiritual life, such an ordering is meant not so much as a system of measurement than as a means for cataloging information on a complicated transformation that God controls. Those schemes are very helpful in allowing us to efficiently find solutions to specific problems along the way. But you cannot force God to bring you through them at any specific pace. In giving too much attention to the scheme and to your preconceptions about where you should be in it, you risk producing doubts, complacency, and discouragement.

In one of the final sections of *Christ in His Mysteries*, Marmion argued that humility and confidence are the two dispositions necessary for holiness: "Feelings that ought to animate our seeking to be holy: a deep humility and an absolute confidence."[172] As a necessary interior disposition, trust is of equal value to humility, for it overcomes our doubts and the complacency that results from them. Marmion was adamant about the need to desire and strive constantly for holiness with ever-greater trust in God. Here is my favorite passage from him:

> When we celebrate the Feast of All Saints, we ought to repeat to ourselves the words St Augustine heard: "Why cannot you do what those did?" What motives have you for not aiming at holiness? Oh, I know very well what each of you is tempted to say: "I have such and such a difficulty, there is such and such an obstacle standing in my way; I would never be able to become a saint." But be assured that all the saints have met with "such a difficulty" or found "such an obstacle standing in their way"—and much bigger ones still than yours!
>
> So, therefore, no one can say, "Holiness is not for me." What is it that can make it impossible? God desires it for us; He wants us to be holy for His glory and for our joy: "This is the will of God, your sanctification" (1 Thess. 4:3). God isn't making fun of

---

172 Marmion, *Mysteries*, 455 (see Appendix 1).

us. When Our Lord says to us, "Be perfect" (Mt 5:48), He knows
what He is asking of us, and He does not demand anything that
is beyond our power when we lean upon His grace.

One who claimed to arrive at perfection through His own
strength would be committing the sin of Lucifer, who said: "I
will raise myself up, I will place my throne in heaven... I will
be like the Most High" (Cf. Isaiah 14:13–14). Satan was struck
down and hurled into the abyss.

As for us, what shall we say? What shall we do? We nourish
the same ambition as this prideful angel; we wish to reach the
objective aimed at by this proud one. But whereas he claimed to
attain it for himself, we shall declare that without Christ Jesus we
can do nothing. We shall say that it is with Him and through Him
that we can enter into heaven. O Christ Jesus, I have such faith in
you that I believe you are powerful enough to effect this marvel
of raising a lowly creature like me, not simply to the hierarchies
of angels but up to God Himself; it is only through you that we
can arrive at this divine summit.[173]

This confidence in God is opposed to the false humility of wallowing in your
nothingness. If you believe you are no more suitable for holiness than gym
shorts are for one's Sunday best, then listen up. Some fall into a false humility by saying to themselves, "I would never be able to become a saint,"[174]
others by "[declining] every function, even those that they naturally feel
themselves capable of exercising well."[175] These points of view falsely reject
that God has selected you for a special mission in this life! If you are chosen
to be Agent 008, then accept the suit and the car that you need; if chosen
to be God's instrument in some other way, accept the gifts that will fit you
and your mission better than any bespoke suit. You'll look dazzling, both
in the suit and in your proper holiness, especially on Sunday. Furthermore,
in persevering in confidence you can deepen your humility: "Each degree
of humility itself only increases with faith and confidence in God."[176] The
two steps described here are mutually reinforcing, and together they form
a virtuous cycle — when we finally accept our nothingness fully, we then

---

173 Marmion, *Mysteries*, 457–58.
174 Ibid.
175 Marmion, *Monk*, 241; Gionta first extrapolated this connection, *Le Virtù Teologali*,
240: "In fact, Dom Columba speaks of 'false humility' when it refers to the feeling
of not being able to do anything of good even with the help of God, because in this
case one offends His grace that truly assists us and gives us strength." My translation.
176 Marmion, *Monk*, 379.

pray with absolute confidence.[177] So, move from contemplating your spiritual nothingness to imagining your spiritual richness, from appreciating Christ's richness within you to giving Him all of the glory.

In Sinu Patris. Blessed Columba's principal aid for persevering in confidence in God was to participate mentally in Christ's state of being *in sinu Patris* ("in the bosom of the Father" of Jn 1:18). To understand this idea, we must realize Marmion held that each believer re-experiences particular aspects of Jesus's life (e.g., each Lent each believer dies to himself or herself a little). Here is his explanation of participating in Christ's mysteries:

> The life of Christ, the divine but at the same time accessible Exemplar of the Christian life, was manifested to our sight by the states and the mysteries, the virtues and actions, of the sacred humanity. Human in its outward expression, the life of the Incarnate Word is wholly divine in its origin.
>
> And so the mysteries of the God-man are not only models that we ought to ponder; they also contain within themselves treasures of merit and of grace. By His almighty power Christ Jesus, ever living, produces the interior and supernatural perfection of His states in those who are moved by a sincere desire to imitate Him, and who put themselves in contact with Him through faith and love.[178]

So, as a believer can unite himself to Christ's cross (cf. Col 1:24), so too a believer can, in a certain sense, participate in Christ's other mysteries (think of those of the rosary and those celebrated in special liturgical solemnities).

Thibaut found the following private note on the matter of participating in Christ's mysteries to express the "fundamental orientation of [Marmion's] interior life":[179]

> Each state of Our Lord works in us as a sacrament according to our faith and produces the effects that respond to that state. But Jesus's fundamental state, which is found at the base of the others, is: "the only Son, who is in the bosom of the Father" (Jn 1:18). There is his sanctuary that he never leaves: in the crèche at Nazareth, on the Cross — even at the moment when he cried "My God, my God, why have you abandoned me?" (Mk 15:34). He was always in the bosom of the Father.

---

177 Cf. Marmion, *Monk*, 380.
178 Marmion, *Mysteries*, xiii.
179 R. Thibaut. *L'Idée Maîtresse de la Doctrine de Dom Marmion*, 174. My translation.

United to Jesus, we are *in sinu Patris*, "in the bosom of the Father," the bosom of love and of infinite mercy. It is the way of pure love that supposes the effort always to do that which is the most agreeable to the Father: "He has never left me alone, because I always do that which pleases him" (Jn 8:29). Our weaknesses, our miseries do not stop us from being *in sinu Patris*, because it is the bosom of love and of infinite mercy, but this repose supposes a profound annihilation and contempt of ourselves, so much greater when we are so close to this infinite sanctity; it also supposes that we lean on Jesus, "whom God made our wisdom, our righteousness and sanctification and redemption" (1 Cor 1:30). Everything that one does in the bosom of the Father, with the spirit of adoption, is of an immense price. But this state supposes the absence of every deliberate fault, and of every refusal to follow the inspirations of the Holy Spirit. Because if Jesus were to take on himself "our infirmities and our miseries," he would not accept the least deliberate sin: "Who among you convicts me of sin?" (Jn 8:46). In this sanctuary, one receives graces, and often the repose of contemplation.

Sometimes the thought of our weakness, of our stains, of our unworthiness will come to terrify us. That thought must humble us, profoundly bring us to nothing before God, but not put us off, because if we are *in sinu Patris*, it is with Jesus and it is in him that we are there, and the greater are our miseries, the more our faith and our confidence honor Him. Because Jesus identified himself so much with us, it is his illness and weakness — [he is] even coated in our miseries. When, in the force of our faith, we present ourselves before God in the name of Jesus, it is his well-beloved Son that he sees poor, weak, and miserable (such as he was in his Passion) in us.[180]

What exactly did Marmion mean by participating in Christ's state of being *in sinu Patris*? He intended it to be some sort of similitude to Christ's beatific vision, but what form did it take? Based upon his correspondence, he intended it as a practice, a feeling, a dwelling, for nine years later he wrote: "I have the sentiment that Our Lord wants to introduce to you a new dwelling where you will be able [to do] much for the glory of God and for the Church.... When you will be there, *in sinu Patris*, you will smuggle [with

180 Marmion, "Notes, 22 Avril 1906," quoted in Thibaut, *Dom Columba Marmion*, 152–53; quoted in part in R. Thibaut, *L'Idée Maîtresse de la Doctrine de Dom Marmion*, 173–74. My translation.

you] the one who would not be able anymore to be separated from His sister in Christo."[181] This counsel presents Marmion's practice as a form of the practice of the presence of God.

Certainly, Marmion only practiced the presence of God by way of the "simple attentiveness," recommended by Blessed Lawrence of the Resurrection, not by the beatific vision.[182] Still, to approach this prayer from the point of view of finding therein Christ's constant confidence in the Father enriches it. Indeed, to make Christ the mediator of this prayer builds our confidence in it.[183] In attending to the Father's presence in Christ, anyone, regardless of the state of his soul, could confidently turn again to God for help and find confidence in this practice. Let us not be afraid of praying! Indeed, Brother Lawrence had already explained this practice as a way by which to build our confidence in God,[184] but hopefully this reframing of the practice further assuages any hesitations you may have about searching for God in this way. Furthermore, Marmion's practice of the presence of God places himself in the bosom of the Father, i.e., in a place of glory where we can already recognize ourselves as beloved children of God and amazing persons, independent of external standards. This practice is similar, then, to those in which persons mentally and spiritually take refuge in the Sacred Heart of Jesus, confident no evil thought can overwhelm them there.

Let us note briefly that Marmion's description of the setting for this prayer validates our chosen organizing scheme for Marmion's subjective response. In order to enter into this prayer — and whatever "repose of contemplation"[185] may follow from it — Marmion presupposed four things:

---

181 Marmion, "Letter to Mother Marie-Joseph van Aerden, 9 May 1917," in *Correspondance*, 855. My translation.

182 Brother Lawrence of the Resurrection, *The Practice of the Presence of God*, trans. Donald Attwater (Springfield, IL: Templegate, 1974), 76. Also of note is the following report of Brother Lawrence's descriptions of this prayer in ibid., 118–19: "Sometimes he calls it a simple act, or a clear and distinct knowledge of God: sometimes an impression or a loving gaze or a sense of God; yet other times he calls it a waiting on God, a silent conversation with Him, a divine repose, the life and peace of the soul. He says, however, that all these expressions are synonyms."

183 Cf. Marmion, "Letter to Mother Marie-Joseph van Aerden, 9 May 1917," in *Correspondance*, 855.

184 Cf. Brother Lawrence, *The Practice of the Presence of God*, 82: "A little lifting-up of the heart is enough; a short remembrance of God, an interior act of worship, made in haste and sword in hand, are prayers which, short as they may be, are nevertheless most pleasing to God; and far from lessening a soldier's courage in moments of danger, they increase it."

185 Thibaut, *Dom Columba Marmion*, 152–53.

1) the attitude of tending to God in Himself: "It is the way of pure love that supposes the effort always to do that which is the most agreeable to the Father"; [186] 2) the self-abasement of seeing ourselves as nothing: "This repose supposes a profound annihilation and contempt of ourselves"; [187] 3) confidence in Christ Jesus: "It also supposes that we lean on Jesus, 'whom God made our wisdom, our righteousness and sanctification and redemption' (1 Cor 1:30)"; [188] and 4) purity of heart: "[It] supposes the absence of every deliberate fault, and of every refusal to follow the inspirations of the Holy Spirit." [189]

The last paragraph in the above passage reflects upon the way by which the third attribute, that of leaning on Jesus, supplies for the fourth, that of purity of heart. As such it reflects on the way by which to acquire a persevering confidence: "Sometimes the thought of our weakness, of our stains, of our unworthiness will come to terrify us. That thought must humble us, profoundly bring us to nothing before God, but not put us off." [190] Specifically, the more bitter our self-knowledge were to become — "so much greater when we are so close to this infinite sanctity" [191] — the more we could thereby grow in confidence in Jesus: "The greater are our miseries, the more our faith and our confidence honor Him." [192] Since to present yourself to the Father through Jesus is the way by which to rely no longer on your own merits, it serves as the key for overcoming discouragement. This is evident in Marmion's phrase, "[W]hen, in the force of our faith, we present ourselves before God in the name of Jesus, it is his well-beloved Son that he sees poor, weak, and miserable (such as he was in his Passion) in us." [193] It is from this mental practice, then, of presenting himself in a sense clothed in Christ (cf. Gal 3:27) in the bosom of the Father that Marmion maintained a prayerful confidence in the Father's mercy.

---

186 Ibid.; for similar thoughts, see Brother Lawrence, *The Practice of the Presence of God*, 47; see also Gionta, *Le Virtù Teologali*, 307: "These are the notes of perfect charity that permit you to repose *in sinu Patris*." My translation.
187 Thibaut, *Dom Columba Marmion*, 152–53; for similar thoughts, see Brother Lawrence, *The Practice of the Presence of God*, 35, 50–51.
188 Thibaut, *Dom Columba Marmion*, 152–53; for similar thoughts, see Brother Lawrence, *The Practice of the Presence of God*, 48.
189 Thibaut, *Dom Columba Marmion*, 152–53; for similar thoughts, see Brother Lawrence, *The Practice of the Presence of God*, 73, 111.
190 Thibaut, *Dom Columba Marmion*, 152–53.
191 Ibid.
192 Ibid.
193 Ibid.

In this reframing of the practice of the presence of God, Blessed Columba not merely adverts to God's Presence but identifies with Christ's being and makes the gaze of Christ his own. Above all, this practice strives to replicate Christ's loving obedience to the Father at times in which our humanity has the temptation to recoil from suffering.[194] By way of it, we associate ourselves with Christ's own loving response, which was at times imbued with human fear. This is notable in two ways. First, to "put on Christ" (Gal 3:27) in this meditation allows you to have confidence in presenting yourself before God. Second, to associate with Christ's loving response avoids misinterpreting this prayer as a merely one-way, top-down experience. This practice is not like that of a child playing in a park who is comforted by averting occasionally to his mother's safeguarding presence, nor is it like the experience of a sunbather blithely taking in the rays; it is something more; it is an exchange of loving glances.[195]

To cooperate in Christ's state of being *in sinu Patris* is but the foundation of a series of profound meditations in *Christ in His Mysteries*. Since "[t]he love of Jesus for His Father is the basis of all His states and explains all His mysteries,"[196] our participation in that fundamental state is the basis for participating in Christ's other states.[197] Coming after the first two preliminary chapters in *Christ in His Mysteries*, the following paragraph states Marmion's reason for reflecting on the liturgical year's representation of Christ's mysteries:

> The mysteries of Christ are ours; the union that Jesus Christ wishes to contract with us is one in which everything He has becomes ours. With a divine liberality, he wants us to share in inexhaustible graces of salvation and sanctification that He has merited for us by each of His mysteries, so as to communicate to us the spirit of His states and thus to bring about in each of us a resemblance to Him — the infallible pledge of our destiny planned from eternity.[198]

---

194   Cf. Marmion, *Mysteries*, 51: "In the first gaze of His life on earth, the soul of Jesus saw the whole succession of His mysteries — the abasements, the wearinesses and the sufferings of which they were formed, and, by one act of love, His soul agreed to carry out that program."

195   See Brother Lawrence, *The Practice of the Presence of God*, 118–19; there he also mentioned similar ideas of a mutual gaze or communion.

196   Marmion, *Mysteries*, 52.

197   Cf. ibid., 63.

198   Marmion, *Mysteries*, 41. See also ibid., 52: "We should imitate the Divine Word in His 'states.'"

While these meditations about Christ's mysteries expanded beyond merely participating in Christ's state of being *in sinu Patris*, they nonetheless also reinforced his confidence when facing the practical concerns of each day. Specifically, he was able to adapt these meditations to the varied experiences of his life: "Each state of Our Lord [can work] in us as a sacrament according to our faith and [produce] the effects that respond to that state."[199] For example, he could be in the bosom of the Father according to the Passion during a difficult day. These meditations, therefore, were an aid in his daily perseverance in diverse ways.

Saint Francis's Sermon on Perfect Joy. As promised, let us now return to the passage that demonstrated Saint Teresa of Calcutta's transformation, the one in which she said, "You and I must let [Jesus] live [his poverty of spirit] in us & through us in the world."[200] Saint Teresa used her nothingness to flip her perspective from one of spiritual acquisitiveness to one of spiritual emptying and submission to Divine Providence: "It is not how much we really 'have' to give — but how empty we are — so that we can receive fully in our life and let Him live His life in us," wrote Saint Teresa.[201]

Let us analyze this point of view with Saint Francis's celebrated "Sermon on Perfect Joy" in the collection of his Little Flowers.[202] Saint Francis tells Brother Leo that perfect joy is to be found neither in having all of the brothers give the perfect example of holiness, nor in knowing every science, nor in learning the Bible perfectly, nor in casting out demons, nor in revealing consciences, nor in prophesying, nor in raising the dead (after four days), nor in converting all unbelievers. As you can see, Saint Francis expressed and denied spiritual acquisitiveness in its fullest extent. When Brother Leo eventually asked in what perfect joy consisted, Saint Francis summarized it as accepting joyfully the rejection of the brethren; he gave the hypothetical case of having the brothers throw them back out into the snow after their long journey, beat them, and revile them as imposters. Saint Francis did not explain the story much, besides saying,

---

199 R. Thibaut. Dom *Columba Marmion*, 152–53; cf. R. Thibaut, *L'Idée Maîtresse de la Doctrine de Dom Marmion*, 173–74.
200 Teresa of Calcutta, "Letter to Father Don Kribs, 7 February 1974," in *Come Be My Light*, 275–76.
201 Ibid.
202 Francis of Assisi, "How St. Francis Taught Brother Leo That Perfect Joy Is Only in the Cross," in *The Little Flowers of St. Francis*, trans. Raphael Brown (Garden City, NY: Hanover House, 1958), 58–60.

> Above all the graces and gifts of the Holy Spirit which Christ gives
> to His friends is that of conquering oneself and willingly enduring
> sufferings, insults, humiliations, and hardships for the love of
> Christ. For we cannot glory in all those other marvelous gifts of
> God, as they are not ours but God's, as the Apostle says, "What
> have you that you have not received?"[203]

To that explanation, he added that he gloried only in the cross of Christ
(cf. Gal 6:14).[204]

Saint Teresa of Calcutta's self-emptying aligns well with the thrust of Saint
Francis's sermon, though there is probably no connection between these
passages. Her hope of still being filled with God's gifts also aligns with Saint
Francis's explanation that conquering yourself is the greatest gift of God.

You may, though, still be puzzled about the way in which this point of
view provides perfect joy. Saint Teresa of Calcutta continued:

> In you today — He wants to relive His complete submission to His
> Father — allow him to do so. Does not matter what you feel — as
> long as He feels alright in you. Take away your eyes from yourself
> and rejoice that you have nothing — that you are nothing — that
> you can do nothing. Give Jesus a big smile — each time your noth-
> ingness frightens you.[205]

She is a little more forthright that you may not feel perfect joy in difficult
circumstances, at least not at first. In a circumstance in which you are greatly
lacking in perfect joy, you could say to yourself, "Well, life is making me
feel like nothing today, but that's just fine, for I wanted to get close to God
anyway," but that partial response is neither going to overcome that initial
feeling nor result in perfect joy. Indeed, it is easier to see the joys associated
with the great victories Saint Francis theoretically rejected, and so we have
not yet found the answer.

Why, then, did the saints offer this counsel about perfect joy? This
question returns us to the topic of submission, which we are now prepared
to ponder in greater depth. To start, let us recognize that the saints know
they are beloved children of God, full of belonging and worthiness. That
is the case even when their nothingness is ridiculed by others. Also, they

203 Ibid., 60.
204 Ibid.
205 Teresa of Calcutta, "Letter to Father Don Kribs, 7 February 1974," in *Come Be My Light*, 275–76.

don't measure themselves by false measures, such as perfect mission work. They only want Jesus to live in them and to love through them. Furthermore, they are, by God's grace, willing to replicate any aspect of Jesus's life, if Jesus brings that aspect of their oblation to life. They can even rejoice at being chosen — at being found worthy — to replicate those aspects of Jesus's life in which a person truly excels at loving, if it were the Father's will. With the help of the Holy Spirit, they trust that the Father's plan has a special blessing for themselves and others.

So, if we participate in Christ's mysteries, it is not that we can merely rely on Christ to buoy us during our bad days — great though that is. It is rather that we can eventually appreciate, even rejoice over, the ways in which Jesus wants to relive all of his mysteries in us. "Now I rejoice in my sufferings for your sake," taught Saint Paul, "and in my flesh I complete what is lacking in Christ's afflictions for the sake of his body, that is, the church" (Col 1:24). Put another way, even though you may have already aligned yourself with the goal of glorifying God, you may nonetheless still need to refine the way in which to do so. If you, with all due discernment, are nonetheless overly zealous about using your talents in a specific way, then you could be falsely and harshly measuring yourself by that aspect of giving glory to God, to your own detriment. Trust that God values your unique role and wills your unique offering, whatever that may be. If you, having seemingly surrendered to God, still have a harsh judge within you, then you may need to reject that judge, seek healing for any wound associated with it, and reconsider the ways in which you can relive Christ's life. Please know this: God rejoices in your *existence* — then also in the ways you glorify Him.

Many Catholics have found meaning in the doctrine of the redemptive value of suffering, uniting their sufferings to Christ's cross as a result of it. [206] If our suffering, when properly offered, has spiritual value for others,

---

206 The redemptive value of suffering is a dogma that teaches that the faithful can cooperate in bringing the value of the Paschal mystery to the present situation by making a prayer/offering of their sufferings. Within this framework, God helps the faithful to profit from and find meaning in their difficulties. There is also a sense that God can endow generous souls with greater favors in this regard — that is, he does not send them suffering as a cruel or vengeful God. For example, Saint Thérèse made an oblation to God's merciful love to extend God the invitation to make use of her, according to her weakness and his grace, in this regard, and it seems as if God accepted her offering, gave her the grace to sustain a steady increase in that offering, and gained many souls through her in the process. To examine this topic, see John Paul II, *Salvifici Doloris: On the Christian Meaning of Human Suffering*, last accessed July 21, 2020. Vatican.va.

then we could desire the proper acquisition of that value. If Jesus in a sense wants to relive his cross in us, then we could celebrate that we have become his privileged coworkers, chosen to stand with Mary at the foot of the cross as monuments of God's mercy.[207] Mindful of Mary's powerful support, we could, perhaps even with joy, "run with perseverance the race that is set before us, looking to Jesus the pioneer and perfecter of our faith, who for the joy that was set before him endured the cross" (Heb 12:1–2).

It is one thing, though, to know of reasons for this transformation and another grace entirely to appropriate them at the level of perfect joy in one's heart. If that were not true, then Saint Teresa of Calcutta would not have written, "Does not matter what you feel — as long as He feels alright in you. Take away your eyes from yourself and rejoice that you have nothing."[208] The final step to persevering in perfect joy is to allow God to fill your heart.

Let us consider the test case of a victim soul. With great discernment, some souls carry the redemptive value of suffering to its fullness by making reparation for others through following Saint Thérèse's offering to Merciful Love. (Her offering is a beautiful one that should not be lightly discerned and undertaken.) Is such a soul filled with perfect joy? Given the weight she bears, the victim soul must desire at a deep level to make such an offering to God on behalf of others, but she too, despite her deep consecration to God, requires further transformation to acquire a pure heart that can live in this way peacefully and joyfully.

We here encounter a limit to our ability to trace the saints' path forward to perfect joy. On the other side of this limit is a grace that comes not from the result of any action or meditation but from God alone. It is as if our path in the woods is no longer marked by our pathfinders. We know that our much-desired refuge lies still deeper in the woods, that the principles we have learned will help us to reach it, that love is the path to it, but that Jesus is the only Pathfinder who can guide each person to its perfection as a mysterious act of mercy.

Yet before I sit back and put my fingers to my mouth with regard to this mystery, I call your attention to some of Saint Teresa of Calcutta's and Saint Paul's advice: "Take away your eyes from yourself"[209] and "[Look] to Jesus" (Heb 12:2). Some may include looking to heaven or living for

---

207   Cf. Marmion, *Priest*, 363.
208   Teresa of Calcutta, "Letter to Father Don Kribs, 7 February 1974," in *Come Be My Light*, 275–76.
209   Ibid.

heaven as part of this disposition. Marmion looked to Jesus for his path forward, and he imitated Jesus's own disposition of living *in sinu Patris* / in the bosom of the Father:

> The whole of [the Word's] personal Life consists of being *ad Patrem*, directed towards the Father. In giving Himself to us, he gives Himself as He is — entirely "oriented" towards His Father and His Father's glory. And that is why when we receive Him with faith, trust, and love, He makes real in us our own orientation towards the Father. It is this that we ought constantly to be asking and seeking: that all our thoughts, all our aspirations, all our desires, all our activity may go, by the grace of childship and love, to our Heavenly Father in His Son Jesus: "alive for God in Christ Jesus" (Rom 6:11).[210]

As we, with Jesus's and the Holy Spirit's help, orient ourselves entirely to the Father, the three Persons of the Blessed Trinity mysteriously transform all of our desires toward the Father, to the point that we come to perfect joy.

On Foretastes of Perfect Joy. There can be foretastes of perfect joy even for those who are acclimating to a life with the Holy Spirit and are still intimidated by pinpricks. So let us focus for the moment, by way of some tangible applications, on what gains may be made and felt today.

Let us reflect for a moment on the joy of requesting that your needs be met, of standing up for what is right, or of taking some other risk. In that context, you can also read these lessons as instructions on becoming more fully yourself, even when it feels weird. Saint Francis depicted perfect joy as staying true to oneself despite the rejection of others in an adverse circumstance. In the story, the saint doesn't choose suffering. He simply doesn't add to it by reacting badly to others; he simply doesn't lose his peace by losing himself. Furthermore, Saint Francis clearly, respectfully, and repeatedly advocates for his needs and those of his companion; in his hypothetical situation of being thrown out in the cold, he includes two long, detailed passages that follow the lines: "And if we continue to knock, and the porter comes out in anger, and drives us away with curses and blows" and "if later suffering intensely from hunger and the painful cold, with night falling, we still knock and call."[211] You too can encounter circumstances in which you can fear being locked out in the cold by loved ones. It is with

210 Marmion, *Mysteries*, 63; see also Marmion, *Monk*, 288–89.
211 Francis of Assisi, "How St. Francis Taught Brother Leo That Perfect Joy Is Only in the Cross," in *The Little Flowers of St. Francis*, 59–60.

some reason that many people struggle to open themselves to others, take principled stands, or take risks in this scary world. Yet advocating for your needs, being vulnerable, and saying what you need to say are all part of the process of coming to foretastes of freedom and perfect joy.[212]

Dr Gerald May, M.D., assessed the growth associated with just such risk taking:

> Grace empowers us to choose rightly in what seem to be the most choiceless of situations, but it does not, and will not, determine that choice. For this reason, the purest acts of faith always feel like risks. Instead of leading to absolute quietude and serenity, true spiritual growth is characterized by increasingly deep risk taking. Growth in faith means willingness to trust God more and more, not only in those areas of our lives where we are most successful, but also, and most significantly, at those levels where we are most vulnerable, wounded, and weak. It is where our personal power seems most defeated that we are given the most profound opportunities to act in true faith. The purest faith is enacted when all we can choose is to relax our hands or clench them, to turn wordlessly toward or away from God. This tiny option, the faith Jesus measured as the size of a mustard seed, is where grace and the human spirit embrace in absolute perfection and explode in world-changing power.[213]

Oh, how true this statement is! It is only when we can offer the open hand, versus the clenched fist, or it is only when we can accept to be thrown out in the snow by loved ones, that we can eventually realize, with perfect joy, that we are saying and doing the things we say and do responsibly for the right reasons, not out of fear, not out of addiction to power or security, not out of something someone can fault within ourselves, but only out of love and concern — it is their issues on display, not those of whoever is willing to make such a sacrifice. When you can see the purity of your own good desires, you are ready, with confidence in God's help, to bring healing to the dysfunction from a deep grounding in humble dignity. When you only

212 For an excellent introduction to the research on the topic of vulnerability, see Brené Brown, "The Power of Vulnerability" (lecture, Vancouver Convention Center, Vancouver, 2010), last accessed June 9, 2021. https://www.ted.com/talks/brene_brown_the_power_of_vulnerability?language=en; and Brené Brown, "Listening to Shame" (lecture, Vancouver Convention Center, Vancouver, 2012), last accessed June 9, 2021. https://www.ted.com/talks/brene_brown_listening_to_shame?language=en.
213 May, Addiction and Grace, 128.

want to charitably answer the call that burns within you, it will no longer be of as much consequence whether other people understand you. When you realize that readiness within yourself, then you embrace God's transformative graces for yourself and others in peaceful, responsible, yet radical ways.

If other people make you feel your nothingness after you have charitably made a necessary request, taken a stand, or taken a risk, then you have probably been a source of grace for them. Appreciate the immense spiritual benefit it can have for their redemption or deliverance. Of course, that great love always carries a benefit for you as well, making you that much more excellent on your true purpose/measure — "Greater love no man has than this, that a man lay down his life for his friends" (Jn 15:13). The experience can also prompt you to become more vulnerable with God, your true source of solace, allowing God's grace to unclog some hard-to-reach block in your relationship with Him. Look to God, befriend God in that spaciousness, let Jesus live in that vulnerable space inside of you.

One benefit for such emotional courage, at least when it is finally done well, can be a temporary sense of being at peace with God, yourself, and others. Even when the feeling of that peace fades, the memory of being emotionally courageous remains in your soul. As for any piercing vulnerability that may arise later, it is an exquisite jewel that can be offered to God: "Give Jesus a big smile — each time your nothingness frightens you."[214] To offer it to God does not make the pain or the feeling of spaciousness go away, but you can embrace it as a most treasured participation in Christ's deepest mysteries, looking to the Father the way Jesus did on the cross. Would not Jesus's Father value such a glance or smile from His beloved and hurting child and return it with yet a greater sign of appreciation? You can only see one side of a splendid exchange between you and a Father who will not be outdone by you. If you keep turning to God with deep vulnerability, giving him your desires and agonies, you will soon enough find a deeper freedom in yourself.

We need — and I'd like to say God desires — valiant men and women of communion who can steadfastly commit to bringing light and healing to their families and communities: "The wicked flee when no one pursues, but the righteous are bold as a lion" (Prv 28:1). You can find a peaceful boldness after having come to terms with the spaciousness or vulnerability of your situation. You do not need to be the savior of the situation, in the

---

214 Teresa of Calcutta, "Letter to Father Don Kribs, 7 February 1974," in *Come Be My Light*, 275–76.

sense of winning over everyone by some brash efforts (self-reliance); you just need to seek greater interior freedom for yourself and healing for the situation. There will come senseless times when you will simply encounter an evil that shoves you aside, perhaps even leaving its "reasons" unspoken and denied. When you find yourself telling God that it doesn't make sense, remember there is no rationale in evil — it doesn't make sense. At times evil must simply be tolerated, until grace abounds (cf. Rm 5:20) and God reveals his greater good (cf. Rm 8:28). When it feels as if you are the only one bringing the Paschal light into a dark domestic or local church, trust that divine mercy will overtake your misery, that a more deeply desired blessing remains in process, and that your flame will ignite a cascade of others, just as at the Easter Vigil. Jesus is coming (cf. Rev 22:20)!

Do these reflections already give you a slight foretaste of the freedom and joy of which the saints speak? Do you want a greater share of those blessings to occupy your heart and the hearts of others? If you say "I do," then trust the process and look to the Father in all you do. Persevere in this process, refining your spirituality of communion along the way, until you find yourself smiling both interiorly and exteriorly. You too will give a testimonial that Jesus does not forsake those who keep seeking healing, transformation, and union with Him. "Maranatha!"/"Our Lord, come!" (1 Cor 16:22; cf. Rev 22:20).

A SIMPLE CONFIDENCE. Allow me to tidy up a few important loose ends as we move toward a conclusion. Marmion's confidence was a simple confidence in God, based upon a simplified explanation of the interior aspects of the ascent to God. "According to the teaching of Saint Benedict, the spiritual life is very simple," wrote Marmion; "[w]e have only to prepare the ground, destroy sin, root up our vices, humble ourselves, and God will do the rest."[215] While Marmion's spiritual direction worked within the traditional models and did not negate them,[216] he did not emphasize detailed analyses of the three ways or of different grades of prayer.[217] He also did not offer complicated forms of asceticism. Furthermore, he separated extraordinary phenomena or visions from union with God: "Now it is not in

---

215 Marmion, "Conference, Louvain, before 1909," quoted in Philipon, *Spiritual Doctrine*, 150.
216 Cf. Marmion, *Soul*, 310–11; Marmion, *Monk*, 156, 346ff.
217 Although he did recognize different stages of prayer and briefly discussed them, such as at *Priest*, 284ff.

extraordinary means, in raptures, and ecstasies, that Our Lord has normally placed the life He wills to communicate to us in order to render us perfect, to make us saints, pleasing to His Father."[218] He did, nevertheless, value mysticism. Given how often he cited the mystics, he must have valued them very much and allowed them to teach and inspire him. His counsel, though, avoided anything that might distract from following a simple, persevering confidence in God. Just as humility provides the necessary foundation for undertaking active asceticism without incurring setbacks from it, so too a confident humility provides the necessary foundation for seeking mystical advice without thereby incurring drawbacks.

A simple approach, however, should not be confused with an exclusive or simplistic one. While Marmion's simple focus upon humility and confidence was similar to that of Saint Benedict, it was neither narrowly simplistic nor of an exclusively Benedictine character.

That it has an overall Benedictine character can be demonstrated in just a few lines:

> To every degree of ascension towards God, corresponds a degree of "the opening of self to God." How do we open ourselves to God? By more and more deepening humility. And this is how, definitively, the ladder, in the negative sense, of humility can serve as the ladder, in the positive sense, of perfection and charity. Upon the ladder of humility can be marked a gradation which doubtless admits of some convention and ingenuity, but which however well indicates all positive degrees in the supernatural life.[219]

Marmion later expanded on Saint Benedict's treatment of humility thus:

> It is that humility of which St Benedict treats with so much predilection that gives to Monastic spirituality its particular character of greatness, and invests it with a special splendour. The Holy Spirit harmonizes the two sentiments, the one of fear, the other of piety; and their accord causes the soul, selfless as it is before God and the neighbor, to be yet assured of the divine grace that comes to it through Christ, in Whom it finds everything which of itself it lacks. This invincible assurance fills it with the very power of God, and thus renders its life altogether fruitful. Knowing that without Christ it can do nothing, *Sine me nihil potestis facere* [Without me you can do nothing] (Jn 15:5), it knows with the same certainty that it

---

218 Marmion, *Soul*, 84.
219 Marmion, *Monk*, 219.

can do all things, as soon as it leans upon Him: *Omnia possum in eo qui me confortat* [I can do all things in him who strengthens me] (Phil. 4:13). Humility is the secret of its strength and vitality. [220]

A simple focus upon a confident humility is indeed the "secret" of the "strength and vitality" of Marmion's spirituality, and it is Benedictine in character. [221]

Yet Marmion did not follow Benedictine or monastic spirituality to the exclusion of insights offered by other teachers and ways — that would be a misreading of both Saint Benedict's and Marmion's simple approaches. At the conclusion of his rule, Saint Benedict encouraged his monks to read other spiritual works: "What book of the holy Catholic Fathers does not resoundingly summon us along the true way to reach the Creator?" asked Saint Benedict in rhetorical fashion. [222] The patriarch of western religious life continued by specifying a few recommendations: "Then, besides the Conferences of the Fathers, their Institutes, and their Lives, there is also the book of our holy father Basil." [223] So, just as Saint Benedict had been open to the insights offered by others, so too Marmion was undeniably open to the insights offered by the Doctors of the Church, saints, and commentators.

We should not confuse discretion with exclusion. Marmion, like Saint Benedict, merely wanted to focus his readers' attention on the most essential points, without distracting them unnecessarily. In this regard, Abbot Columba spoke as much of himself as of Saint Benedict in the following passage:

> It is because our Holy Legislator shines in discretion; he knows that nothing is more narrowing for souls than to regulate their intimate relations with God in too rigid and imperious a manner. He contents himself with indicating the fundamental attitude of the soul in the presence of God [and] the dispositions that are the condition of that fecundity of the divine action in the soul: purity of heart, humility, and compunction. [224]

So Blessed Columba neither imposed his own spirituality on others nor excluded other spiritualities as unhelpful. Within his simplified program, more advanced souls can always find further clarification elsewhere, as necessary and helpful.

---

220 Marmion, *Monk*, 227–28.
221 Ibid.
222 Benedict of Nursia, *The Rule of Saint Benedict*, chap. 73, no. 4.
223 Ibid., chap. 73, no. 5.
224 Marmion, *Monk*, 348.

ON UNION WITH GOD

We can now move toward the resolution of the great tension that began this work. In *Sponsa Verbi*, Marmion described the state of union with God as "surpassing that of all human desire":

> It is true that when the soul thinks of the infinite greatness of God, of His incomprehensible sanctity, and then considers her own misery and nothingness, she is seized with a sort of stupor at being the object of such a wonderful privilege. She cries out: "Is it not presumption, is it not temerity and foolishness to dream of aspiring to a condition which surpasses that of all human desire? How can these things be? *Quomodo fiet istud?*" (Lk 1:34)
>
> Certainly had it not been for Revelation, such an elevated thought would not have been born in the human soul. But God Himself desires this union; He makes the advances; He invites the soul both by words and works.[225]

While this union will reach its ultimate fulfillment in heaven, Marmion here described the union that can begin in part here below. "In Heaven the source of our joy will be the certain, perfect and inamissible possession of sovereign and immutable good, in the full light of glory," taught Marmion. "Here below, the source of our joys is the possession, already begun, of God, the anticipated union with God: this possession, this union is so much the more intimate the more we are bathed in the light of faith."[226] This foretaste of union is a "privilege" so "wonderful" that it "[seizes the soul] with a sort of stupor."[227]

Before we end with more of Marmion's thoughts on the subject of union with God, we must first clarify that union with God is on the ordinary path of grace, is the fullness of the Father's blessing, and is not an emptiness.

Union with God is in the Ordinary, Not Extraordinary, Path of Grace

Many may assume such a privilege would take the form of visions or other extraordinary phenomena. While Marmion did not include extraordinary phenomena in his definition of holiness, we need to consider whether extraordinary phenomena are, in his estimation, the reward for holiness. Considering Marmion did not, to our knowledge, experience any

---

225   Marmion, *Sponsa Verbi*, 17–18.
226   Marmion, *Monk*, 104.
227   Marmion, *Sponsa Verbi*, 17–18.

visions,[228] it would have been very strange from him to define a reward for holiness in that way. Four and a half years before his death he wrote: "During my sojourn here Our Lord has united me to Himself much, but in simple faith."[229] This sentence is very revealing for two reasons. First, Marmion acknowledged having come to a certain degree of union with God. Second, Marmion also specified its character and its rewards as within the bounds of a simple faith. Even more tellingly, Philipon's investigation of Marmion's unpublished retreats uncovered that Marmion even held the Blessed Virgin's life to have been without phenomena (excluding, presumably, the Annunciation from that statement).[230] From this point of view we can deduce two insights about the role of visions in his scheme: first, Marmion did not hold that extraordinary phenomena serve as rewards for holiness; second, Marmion accepted that God can offer visions and extraordinary gifts as He pleases. Were these facts to surprise some people, the following quotation from Saint John of the Cross's treatment of the ladder of ascent to God may help to clarify: "The secrecy of this ascent is evident, since ordinarily the losing and annihilation of self, which bring the most profit to individuals, are considered the worst for them, whereas consolation and satisfaction (which are of less value and in which one ordinarily loses rather than gains if attachment is present) are considered the best."[231] While both Marmion and Saint John of the Cross admitted the possibility of extraordinary phenomena, neither of them presented such phenomena as the best experiences. Therefore, while Marmion held visions to be possible, they were not the "wonderful privilege" of which he wrote in his description of that which "surpasses all human desire."[232]

Marmion, then, held that souls in union with God both do not ordinarily receive extraordinary phenomena as rewards yet receive divine touches of immense delight. How do we reconcile these ideas? To do so, let us review Marmion's private and public statements on contemplation. In a letter in which Marmion encouraged someone he was accompanying to practice putting herself *in sinu Patris*, he wrote:

---

228 See Philipon, *Spiritual Doctrine*, 84–85.
229 Marmion, "Letter to Mother Marie-Joseph van Aerden, 25 September 1918," in *Correspondance*, 938.
230 Cf. Marmion, "Retreat, Maredret, February 1914," noted in Philipon, *Spiritual Doctrine*, 207.
231 John of the Cross, *Dark Night*, bk. 2, chap. 18, no. 4.
232 Marmion, *Sponsa Verbi*, 17–18.

> I experience powerful graces and great lights in the depth of my
> soul; it seems to me, not only that Christ dwells in me, but that I
> am, as it were, buried in Him, spiritually surrounded by His sacred
> presence. I adore Him in response to the Father Who reveals His
> divinity to me, and I do so tranquilly, without effort, and more
> and more as a matter of habit. From this springs a great faith and
> unlimited confidence in the goodness of the heavenly Father in
> spite of the constant realization which He gives me of my wretch-
> edness, of my faults, and of my unworthiness. [233]

The "powerful graces" and "great lights" of which he wrote occurred "in the
depth of [his] soul," [234] which is another way of saying that they did not
occur in an extraordinary manner (or perhaps even in a manner directly
perceived). [235]

While Marmion here attested to having been "spiritually surrounded," his
spiritual awareness occurred in connection with being "buried in [Christ]." [236]
Let us define the latter in order to understand the former more fully. Since
in death we lose all of our faculties (as this bodily existence goes), this
expression of being "buried in [Christ]" [237] hinted at the classic descriptions of infused contemplation as the quieting of the faculties (i.e., of the
memory, intellect, and will). [238] In his section on prayer in the unitive way

---

233 Marmion, "Letter to Mother Marie-Joseph van Aerden, 9 May 1917," in *Correspondance*, 855, also printed in translation in Marmion, *Priest*, 383.
234 Ibid.
235 See John of the Cross, *Dark Night*, bk. 2, chap. 17.
236 Marmion, "Letter to Mother Marie-Joseph van Aerden, 9 May 1917," in *Correspondance*, 855; cf. Marmion, *Priest*, 383.
237 Ibid.
238 For example, see the second quotation of Blosius on 57–58 above; see Teresa of
Avila, "Fourth dwelling place" in *The Interior Castle*, 319–21: [no. 8:] "A little more than
four years ago I came to understand through experience that the mind (or imagination,
to put it more clearly) is not the intellect. I asked a learned man and he told me that
this was so; which brought me no small consolation. For since the intellect is one of
the soul's faculties, it was an arduous thing for me that it should be so restless at times.
Ordinarily the mind flies about quickly, for only God can hold it fast in such a way as
to make it seem that we are somehow loosed from this body. I have seen, I think, that
the faculties of my soul were so occupied and recollected in God while my mind on the
other hand was distracted. This distraction puzzled me . . . [No. 12:] Let us recognize
our misery [of distractions from the mind] and desire to go where no one will taunt
us . . . . So, Lord, bring us to the place where these miseries will not taunt us, for they
seem sometimes to be making fun of the soul. Even in this life, the Lord frees the soul
from these miseries when it reaches the last dwelling place." Also see John of the Cross,
Ascent of Mount Carmel, bk. 2, chap. 9., no. 1; for Marmion's acceptance of these points,
see Gionta, *Le Virtù Teologali*, 202–3, 329–30.

in *Christ the Ideal of the Monk*, Marmion offered a restatement of the classical definition of infused contemplation:

> Indeed in the measure wherein a soul is stripped of self, God acts more and more within it: He draws to Himself all the faculties of the soul that He may simplify their exercise. Prayer becomes more simple . . . the direct action of God is made deeper; the soul is motionless before God . . . ; it is intimately united to Him by an act of loving adherence, while yet this act is enveloped with the shadows of faith . . . . The soul puts aside all that the senses, the natural intelligence, even revealed truths, say of God: it rests in pure faith. [239]

He later added the following remarks about contemplation:

> What ought a soul to do? To give itself up, to let itself be taken; God touches the soul, He seizes its every fibre to make them all converge to Himself as to their centre; it is a Divine embrace, in which the soul, despite aridity, or darkness, or its own powerlessness, has nothing to do but yield itself up into the Divine Artist's transforming hand. [240]

Note that this "embrace," in which a soul "yields itself up," expresses the temporary loss of the faculties: "He seizes its every fibre to make them all converge to Himself." [241] Given that Marmion preferred to express his spiritual life as forms of participation in Christ's mysteries, it is hardly surprising that he described his "converging [to the indwelling Christ] as to [his] center" [242] as having been "buried in [Christ]"; this interpretation is even clearer from the context for his expression: "It seems to me, not only that Christ dwells in me, but that I am, as it were, buried in Him." [243] While the mystics have always regarded these mysterious encounters with Christ as profoundly positive, this description may nonetheless prove helpful to the many souls who remain timid about allowing themselves to enter into these mysterious encounters. So Marmion's public statements on contemplation coincide with his private statements about the manner in which he received his greatest graces in this marvelous but not extraordinary way.

---

239   Marmion, *Monk*, 358–59.
240   Ibid., 359.
241   Ibid.
242   Ibid.
243   Marmion, "Letter to Mother Marie-Joseph van Aerden, 9 May 1917," in *Correspondance*, 855; cf. Marmion, *Priest*, 383.

To hope for more mysticism is to misunderstand union with God. The manualists would here explain how extraordinary phenomena are not part of the normal growth of grace, whereas infused contemplation is.[244] The simple answer about visions is that we are unworthy of extraordinary gifts:

> Look at this portrait of a perfect monk that [Saint Benedict] draws for us when he comes to the 12th degree of humility: this monk, he says, has reached the point where the perfection of charity and divine union are about to be realised: *Mox ad caritatem Dei perveniet illam, quae perfecta foras mittet timorem* [(the monk) will quickly arrive at that perfect love of God which casts out all fear (1 Jn 4:18)] (Benedict of Nursia, Ch. 7, no 67). And what is this monk's attitude? He considers himself unworthy, on account of his sins, to appear before God.[245]

Some people may nonetheless hope such a spiritual posture might open them to a state in which God may grant them visions gratuitously. It is impossible to speculate in this matter, and it is unfitting to harbor that hope. Extraordinary phenomena may even occur more frequently than infused contemplation, but our true hope is to be filled with the gifts of the Holy Spirit while remaining "in simple faith."[246] If God wishes to give us consolation in extraordinary ways or to build up the Church through miracles and extraordinary gifts, then let us receive them with gratitude, but let us not seek them in such a way as to block our gratitude for our personal growth in holiness. Saint Teresa of Avila taught that we can receive both natural consolations and spiritual delights,[247] the latter of which, when distinguished from extraordinary phenomena, are received in infused contemplation.

Is a spiritual man or woman worthy of even those natural consolations and spiritual delights? Again, we are faced with the central paradox of "being nothing" while having merits. Let us put it this way: we are worthy of few of the best consolations, even though our virtues and supernatural merits allow us to receive many natural consolations and spiritual delights. If we truly accept ourselves as nothing, though, then we become quite abandoned about the ways in which God rewards us. As we move away from the notion of reward, our own mentality shifts from trying to win God's gifts

---

244   For example, see Garrigou-Lagrange, *The Three Ages of the Interior Life*, vol. 2, 580ff. (on extraordinary phenomena); ibid., 307ff., esp. 321 (on infused contemplation).
245   Marmion, *Monk*, 154–55.
246   Marmion, "Letter to Mother Marie-Joseph van Aerden, 25 September 1918," in *Correspondance*, 938.
247   Cf. Teresa of Avila, "Fourth dwelling place" in *The Interior Castle*, 316ff.

to receiving them as gifts. God rewards us, a hundredfold in this life and in the next (cf. Mt 19:29), but it is better for us to simply trust in his mercy and in the goodness of the Giver. If we were truly abandoned about the ways in which God takes care of us, then we could receive each and every aspect of every day as a grace. To approach God with empty hands is indeed to ask respectfully for them to be filled, but we must also respect the way in which God fills them and have gratitude for all God gives. So those who are "buried in [Christ]" in contemplation are also somehow revivified and filled in a new union with Christ, although not necessarily in some extraordinary way.[248]

Union with God is the Fullness of the Father's Blessing, Not an Emptiness

In his address to the World Congress of Benedictine Abbots in Rome in September 2000, Timothy Radcliffe, OP, beautifully re-expressed the topic of nothingness as the empty mercy seat / "Throne of Glory" on the top of the Ark of the Covenant (cf. Ex 25:17):

> I wish to claim that your monasteries disclose God not because of what you do or say, but perhaps because the monastic life has, at its center, a space, a void in which God may show Himself. I wish to suggest that the rule of Saint Benedict offers a sort of hollow center to your lives, in which God may live and be glimpsed.
>
> The glory of God always shows itself in an empty space. When the Israelites came out of the desert, God came with them seated in the space between the wings of the cherubim, above the seat of mercy. The throne of glory was this void. It was only a small space, a hand's breadth.... [On the cross] we see a throne of glory which is also a void, an absence, as a man dies crying out for the God who seems to have deserted him. The ultimate throne of glory is an empty tomb, where there is no body.[249]

Radcliffe's throne of glory is an even more powerful expression than that of Saint Thérèse's empty hands, for it references two of the Bible's most hallowed images.

The former master of the Dominican Order elaborates on this glory, describing the ways in which it outshines those who collect great public charisms:

---

248 Marmion, "Letter to Mother Marie-Joseph van Aerden, 9 May 1917," in *Correspondance*, 855; cf. Marmion, *Priest*, 383.
249 Timothy Radcliffe, "The Throne of God," in *I Call You Friends* (London: Continuum, 2001), 100.

We need Christians out there, shouting along with the rest, joining in the bustle of the market-place, trying to catch people's eyes. That is where Dominicans and Franciscans, for example, should be. But the monasteries embody a deep truth. Ultimately, we worship God, not because he is relevant for us but simply because he is. The voice from the burning bush proclaimed "I am who I am" [Ex 3:14]. What matters is not that God is relevant to us, but that in God we find the disclosure of all relevance, the lodestar of our lives. I think this was the secret of Cardinal Hume's unique authority. He did not try to market religion, and show that Catholicism was the secret ingredient for the successful life. He was just a monk who said his prayers. Deep down, people know that a God who must show that he is useful for me is not worth worshipping. A God who has to be relevant is not God at all. The life of the monk witnesses to the irrelevance of God, for everything is only relevant in relation to God. The lives of monks bear witness to that, by not doing anything in particular, except to abide with God. Your lives have a void at their centres, like the space between the wings of the cherubim. Here we may glimpse God's glory.

Perhaps the role of the Abbot is to be the person who obviously does nothing in particular. Other monks may get caught up in being bursar, or infirmarian, or running the farm or the printing house, or the school. But perhaps I can be so bold as to suggest that the Abbot might be the person who is guardian of the monks' deepest identity as those who have nothing in particular to do.[250]

The argument here is that God's glory is most evident in those pure hearts who single-mindedly turn toward God solely because He is the most captivating Beauty. Radcliffe's description of the mercy seat of the monk is reminiscent of what we could recognize as another type of mercy seat in Saint Paul's writings: "I know how to be abased, and I know how to abound; in any and all circumstances I have learned the secret of facing plenty and hunger, abundance and want" (Phil 4:12). If we further push Radcliffe's logic into Saint Paul's words, then his next line represents his throne of glory: "I can do all things in him who strengthens me" (Phil 4:13).

When we catch a glimpse of such God-centered poise in the saints, we intuit that which is possible by God's transforming power: "But the fruit of the Spirit is love, joy, peace, patience, kindness, goodness, faithfulness, gentleness, self-control; against such there is no law. And those who belong

---

250 Radcliffe, *I Call You Friends*, 102–3.

to Christ Jesus have crucified the flesh with its passions and desires. If we live by the Spirit, let us also walk by the Spirit" (Gal 5:22–25). If we truly seek God's blessing, then we seek the gifts and fruits of the Spirit. We can also welcome them, even, as the saints have not infrequently done, amid exterior difficulties and deprivations.

Radcliffe reminds us that our identity is that of a beloved son or daughter of God, not that of a workman. A workman may distort his or her status into something of a slave, whereas a beloved son or daughter knows his status of family member/friend. Jesus said, "No longer do I call you servants, for the servant does not know what his master is doing; but I have called you friends, for all that I have heard from my Father I have made known to you" (Jn 15:15). Above all, Jesus made known to us that our truest identity runs deeper than our occupations or ministries on His behalf. Let us rejoice at being God's friends.

So if God's glory most shines forth in a situation of a deeply abandoned confidence in Him, and if our lives are ultimately measured in heaven by our love, then you could find it to be a privilege to live a deep conformity to Christ as such a mercy seat. If this approach carries with it the blessings of abandonment, poise, and openhanded confidence in God, then everyone, in every call, can benefit from this approach. This is certainly not a prosperity Gospel, for our ultimate vocation is to relive Jesus's desire to fulfill his Father's will.

But does God leave a person in a void? In considering God's side of each of his covenantal relationships, it must be stressed again that the Good Father (cf. Lk 15:11–32) wills a fullness for you, his beloved child![251] As the Roman Office puts it on our lips, "If you hunger for holiness, God will satisfy your longing, good measure, and flowing over" (cf. Lk 6:38).[252] So let us never confuse our open-handed expectation as hoping for a void! On the objective side of the process, God is always working to bless and glorify each person in each context, amid little or plenty, according to his or her vocation and mission.

We do, though, occasionally lose our confidence in God's mercy and misconstrue holiness as a void. We can feel as if we are in a void when we

---

251   For a helpful reflection on this topic, see Neal Lozano, *Unbound* (Grand Rapids, MI: Chosen, 2010), Ch. 7, 110ff.
252   "Magnificat Antiphon of Evening Prayer of Thursday of Ordinary Time, Week II" in *Christian Prayer: The Liturgy of the Hours* (New York: Catholic Book Publishing Co, 1976), 833.

limit our perception of that blessing to a prosperity Gospel or to one particular grace or charism. We can also despair of receiving anything more than a passionless equanimity in a void.

Marmion counters these thoughts by teaching, "The more this soul gives itself, the more God acts and blesses its works, doubtless not always according to human foresight, but according to the good of this soul and the interests of His glory."[253] In other words, we do not believe in a God who leaves us empty-handed.

But what about those on the threshold of death? The "white-robed army of martyrs [praise God]" because they are united in charity to Christ, filled with interior blessings.[254] Those who live a non-bloody martyrdom can also recognize the power of God at work in them and praise God for the transformative gifts and charisms of that offering. If the mercy seat feels empty, then we hope all the more for God to abide there and for His graces to shine forth in radiant glory. Again, we hope to be monuments to God's mercy in every circumstance.[255]

As an aid to those whose confidence grows weak in the face of potential nothingness, let us recall Jesus's words to his disciples before He left the Upper Room:

> When Jesus had spoken these words, he lifted up his eyes to heaven and said, "Father, the hour has come; glorify thy Son that the Son may glorify thee, since thou hast given him power over all flesh, to give eternal life to all whom thou hast given him. And this is eternal life, that they know thee the only true God, and Jesus Christ whom thou hast sent. I glorified thee on earth, having accomplished the work which thou gavest me to do, and now Father, glorify thou me in thy own presence with the glory which I had with thee before the world was made" (Jn 17:1-5).

As some of Jesus's last words of instruction to his disciples, these words are of immense value on the ways in which to glorify the Father and take confidence in Him. Borrowing from Judith MacNutt's powerful and beautiful analysis of them, I encourage you to make your own the following reasons for Jesus's confidence in the Father at his darkest time: Jesus knew he had come from the Father, Jesus knew that he had the authority to do the work

---

253 Marmion, *Monk*, 394–95.
254 "Devotions to the Blessed Trinity" in *The Daily Roman Missal*, 2353–55; cf. *Catechism of the Catholic Church*, n. 2473.
255 Cf. Marmion, *Priest*, 363.

of his mission, and Jesus knew that he would return to the Father.[256] With this analysis in mind, let us return to Timothy Radcliffe's words about the cross: "[On the cross] we see a throne of glory which is also a void, an absence, as a man dies crying out for the God who seems to have deserted him. The ultimate throne of glory is an empty tomb, where there is no body."[257] The story does not end at the cross; the Father's blessing includes the resurrection and giving Jesus "the glory which [he] had with [the Father] before the world was made" (Jn 17:5). If you are facing death, take courage in Jesus and in the ongoing aspects of the Father's blessing. If you have time left here below, know that you too have a mission to accomplish and blessings appropriate to it while you journey towards a yet fuller blessing in heaven.

Marmion on Union with God

We are now prepared to close our reflections with Marmion's description of the state of union with God that can begin in this life here below:

> God acts towards us as we act towards Him; God, as it were, measures His Providence according to our attitude in relation to Him: and the more we give ourselves to Him, the more we look upon Him as our Father, as the Spouse of our souls, the more His Providence enters into the least details and circumstances of our life. For a soul totally surrendered to Him, God has ineffable delicacies which show that His gaze is ever fixed upon it; never has mother cared for her child, never has friend gladdened his friend, as God cares for and gladdens this soul.

> This soul is perfectly free and detached from self and from creatures. It is the captive of nothing whatsoever, neither of an employment, nor of a charge. It seeks and desires God, *Revera quaerit Deum* (Rule of Saint Benedict, 58:7), and when it has found Him, its every desire is fulfilled. God is the sovereign Master of this soul; nothing in it disputes this sovereignty: it procures Him incomparable glory by the continual homage of utter self-surrender; the Lord works great things through it, and its life has the most wonderful repercussion in the spiritual world.

---

256 Cf. Judith MacNutt, "Level 2, Lesson 9: Healing the Wounds of Divorce," in *School of Healing Prayer DVDs*, Founders Edition, DVD (N.p.: Christian Healing Ministries, date unknown), last accessed September 4, 2021. https://www.christianhealingmin.org/.
257 Radcliffe, "The Throne of God," in *I Call You Friends* (London: Continuum, 2001), 100.

The liberty possessed by souls thus given to God, brings them great peace and deep joy: they know that God is a Father full of goodness, that He loves them and wills to bring them to Himself. What have they to fear? God guides them, nothing is wanting to them, neither light nor grace: *Dominus regit me, et* NIHIL *mihi deerit* [The Lord is my Shepherd, I shall not want] (Ps 22:1). They live in the abundance of Divine gifts and in an inward peace passing all understanding. [258]

To be "captive of nothing whatsoever" and to have an "inward peace passing all understanding" are, according to Marmion, the traits of a soul who has attained union with God. [259] This transformation is what occurs for a person who — note the citation of Saint Benedict's words — "truly seeks God" ("*Revera quaerit Deum*"), [260] or "[tends] to God in Himself." [261] Furthermore, to be "captive of nothing whatsoever" [262] is to act merely for the love of God peaceably and without fear. It is a representation of Saint John's and later Saint Benedict's "perfect love of God [that] casts out fear" (1 Jn 4:18). [263]

A soul intimately connected with God and ruled by Him knows the peace that springs from having accepted God's love. This recognition brings peace because you can then properly integrate your loves without being captivated by any lower ones. To verify this truth with another saint, let us look at a brief comment by Saint Thérèse on this topic:

All creatures can bow toward her, admire her, and shower praises upon her. I don't know why this is, but none of this could add one single drop of false joy to the true joy she experiences in her heart. Here she sees herself as she really is in God's eyes: a poor little thing, nothing at all. [264]

Notice that Saint Thérèse is not captivated by the praises of others, for she knows deeply the greatest praise from the One who matters most. God constantly loves her, even in her nothingness, and his love for her is always enough. Let us think here of an art exhibition. The artist wins the admiration

258 Marmion, *Monk*, 395.
259 Ibid.
260 Ibid. Benedict of Nursia, *The Rule of Saint Benedict*, chap. 58, no. 7.
261 Marmion, *Union*, 197.
262 Marmion, *Monk*, 395.
263 Benedict of Nursia, *The Rule of Saint Benedict*, chap. 7, no. 67.
264 St. Thérèse of Lisieux, "Manuscript C, 02r," in *Archives du Carmel de Lisieux*, last accessed June 20, 2020. http://www.archives-carmel-lisieux.fr/english/carmel/index.php/c01-10/c02/c02r.

of the greatest aesthetes and connoisseurs; she receives the acceptance of her gift by her family and friends; she has brought the inspiration within her to masterful conclusion. Yet most importantly, she recognizes that the Grand Master Artist has always been at work in her.

In conclusion, if you follow the above advice, then you have nothing left to fear. Before coming to this peace, you are held captive by the various fears associated with your false pursuits of importance[265] — by trying to be perfect for God, to please others unnecessarily, to please yourself unnecessarily, to appear to be a saint (even by coyly trying not to appear to be a saint), etc. What fears most hold you captive? You are most held captive by those very fears that threaten to make you feel your nothingness. By God's grace, though, you can embrace God's constant love in ever deeper and more liberating ways, coming thereby to a perfect love of God, yourself, and others.

While other aspects of Catholic spirituality must form the basis for this simple scheme for interior development, it is nonetheless a practical approach by which you can avoid the most common difficulties associated with over-complicating the process. In short, it keeps your attention on the Father (*in sinu Patris*), rather than on a measure of success that will eventually distract you from coming to perfect love, freedom, peace, intimate union with God, and your most gifted self. God wills these blessings perfectly, if you but let Him accomplish them in you. If God truly finds you tending toward union with Him and accepting your nothingness with absolute confidence in Him, then God will care for and gladden you in such a way that "never has mother cared for her child, never has friend gladdened his friend."[266]

---

265 Burrows, *Guidelines for Mystical Prayer*, 128.
266 Marmion, *Monk*, 395.

APPENDIX I:

CHRIST IN HIS MYSTERIES, 455–56

*Feelings that ought to animate our seeking to be
holy: a deep humility and an absolute confidence*

FROM THIS TEACHING ARE BORN THE FEELINGS THAT
ought to animate us in seeking to be holy: a deep humility because of our
feebleness, and an absolute confidence in Christ Jesus. Our super-natural
life wings backwards and forwards between two poles: on the one hand, we
should have an inner conviction of our powerlessness to attain perfection
without the help of God; on the other hand, we should be filled with an
unshakeable hope of finding everything in the grace of Christ Jesus.

Because it is super-natural, because God — sovereignly Master of His
designs and of His gifts — has placed it above what the whole of our created nature requires, above the rights of that created nature, the holiness
to which we are called is inaccessible without divine grace. Our Lord said
to us: "without me you can do nothing" (Jn 15:5). St Augustine remarks
that Christ Jesus did not say, "without me you cannot do great things"; He
said: "without me you can do nothing that will lead you to life eternal."
St Paul has explained in detail this teaching of our Divine Master. Paul
has assurance through Christ, but he adds: "not that we are sufficient of
ourselves to think anything, as from ourselves, but our sufficiency is from
God" (2 Cor 3:5). "Our sufficiency is from God": it is He who gives us
the power of willing and bring all things to that super-natural end: "It
is God who of his good pleasure works in you both the will and the per-
formance" (Phil 2:13). And so, we cannot, for our holiness, do anything
without divine grace.

Should we, therefore, be disheartened? Quite the contrary! The inner
conviction of our powerlessness should neither drive us to discouragement
nor serve as an excuse for sitting back and not making an effort ourselves.
Though we can do nothing without Christ, with Him we can do everything: "I can do all things in Him who strengthens me" (Phil 4:13). I can
do all things (it is Paul again who tells us), not by myself but "in Him who
strengthens me." Whatever be our trials, our difficulties, our weaknesses,
we can, through Christ, reach the highest sanctity.

Why is it? Because in Him are amassed "all the treasures of wisdom and knowledge" (Col 2:3), because "in Him dwells the fullness of the God-head bodily" (Col 2:9); and because being our head, He has the power to make us sharers in all this. It is "of His fullness" — fullness of life and holiness — "that we draw" (Jn 1:16), so much so that we "lack no grace" (1 Cor 1:7)!

What great assurance is engendered in us by faith in these truths! Christ Jesus is ours, and in Him we find everything: "How can He (the Father) fail to grant us . . . all things with Him" (Rom 8:32). What, then, can prevent us from becoming saints? If, on the day of the Last Judgment God asks us: "Why have you not reached the height of your vocation? Why have you not attained the holiness to which I was calling you?" we shall not be able to reply: "Lord, my weakness was too great, the difficulties were insurmountable, the trials beyond my strength." God would reply to us: "On your own, it is but too true that you could do nothing. But I have given you my Son; in Him you lacked nothing of what was necessary for you. His grace is all-powerful, and through Him you could have united yourself to the very source of life."[1]

---

1 Marmion, *Mysteries*, 455–56.

PRAYER 6

of

SAINT THÉRÈSE OF LISIEUX

"Offering of myself as a Victim of Holocaust to God's Merciful Love"

O MY GOD! MOST BLESSED TRINITY, I DESIRE TO LOVE you and make you Loved, to work for the glory of Holy Church by saving souls on earth and liberating those suffering in purgatory. I desire to accomplish your will perfectly and to reach the degree of glory you have prepared for me in your kingdom. I desire, in a word, to be a Saint, but I feel my helplessness and I beg you, O my God! to be yourself my Sanctity!

Since You loved me so much as to give me your only Son as my Savior and my Spouse, the infinite treasures of his merits are mine. I offer them to you with gladness, begging you to look on me only through the Face of Jesus and in his Heart burning with Love.

I offer you, too, all the merits of the Saints (in Heaven and on earth), their acts of Love, and those of the Holy Angels. Finally, I offer you, O Blessed Trinity! the Love and merits of the Blessed Virgin, my dear Mother. It is to her I abandon my offering, begging her to present it to you. Her Divine Son, my Beloved Spouse, told us in the days of his mortal life: "Whatsoever you ask the Father in my name he will give it to you!" I am certain, then, that you will grant my desires; I know, O my God, that the more you want to give, the more you make us desire. I feel in my heart immense desires and it is with confidence I ask you to come and take possession of my soul. Ah! I cannot receive Holy Communion as often as I desire, but, Lord, are you not All-Powerful? Remain in me as in a tabernacle and never separate yourself from your little host.

I want to console you for the ingratitude of the wicked, and I beg of you to take away my freedom to displease you. If through weakness I sometimes fall, may your Divine Glance cleanse my soul immediately, consuming all my imperfections like the fire that transforms everything into itself.

I thank you, O my God! for all the graces you have granted me, especially the grace of making me pass through the crucible of suffering. It is with joy I shall contemplate You on the last day carrying the scepter of your Cross. Since you deigned to give me a share in this very precious Cross, I hope in Heaven to resemble you and to see shining in my glorified body the sacred stigmata of Your Passion...

After earth's exile, I hope to go and enjoy you in the Fatherland, but I do not want to lay up merits for Heaven. I want to work for your Love alone with the one purpose of pleasing you, consoling your Sacred Heart, and saving souls who will love you eternally.

In the evening of this life, I shall appear before you with empty hands, for I do not ask you, Lord, to count my works. All our justice is stained in your eyes. I wish, then, to be clothed in your own Justice and to receive from your Love the eternal possession of Yourself. I want no other Throne, no other Crown but You, my Beloved!

Time is nothing in your eyes, and a single day is like a thousand years; you can, then, in one instant prepare me to appear before you...

In order to live in one single act of perfect Love, I offer myself as a victim of holocaust to your merciful love, asking you to consume me incessantly, allowing the waves of infinite tenderness shut up within you to overflow into my soul, and that thus I may become a Martyr of your Love, O my God!...

May this martyrdom, after having prepared me to appear before you, finally cause me to die and may my soul take its flight without any delay into the eternal embrace of Your Merciful Love...

I want, O my Beloved, at each beat of my heart to renew this offering to you an infinite number of times, until the shadows having disappeared I may be able to tell you of my Love in an Eternal Face to Face!...

Marie, Françoise, Thérèse of the Child Jesus and the Holy Face
unworthy Carmelite religious
Feast of the Most Holy Trinity
The 9th day of June in the year of grace 1895.[2]

---

2   Thérèse of Lisieux, "Prayer 6," in *Archives du Carmel de Lisieux*, last accessed August 16, 2014. http://www.archives-carmel-lisieux.fr/english/carmel/index.php/pri-6.

BIBLIOGRAPHY

WORKS BY MARMION

IN FRENCH

Marmion, Columba. *Le Christ Vie de l'Âme*. 17e mille ed. Paris: Desclée, De Brouwer, 1919.

———. *Le Christ dans Ses Mystéres*. 36e mille ed. Paris: Desclée, De Brouwer, 1926.

———. *Le Christ, Idéal du Moine*. 17e mille ed. Lille: Desclée, De Brouwer, 1924.

———. *Le Christ, Idéal du Prêtre*. 11e mille ed. Namur: Abbaye de Maredsous, 1952.

———. *Sponsa Verbi: La Vierge consacrée au Christ*. 65e mille ed. Namur: Abbaye de Maredsous, 1955.

———. *L'Union a Dieu: D'apres les Lettres de Direction de Dom Columba Marmion*, selected and annotated by Raymond Thibaut. Paris: Desclée, De Brouwer, 1934.

———. *Correspondance: 1881–1923*. Paris: Francois-Xavier de Guibert, 2008.

IN ENGLISH

Marmion, Columba. *Christ the Life of the Soul*. Translated by Nun of Tyburn. Tacoma, WA: Angelico, 2012.

———. *Christ in his Mysteries*. Translated by Alan Bancroft. British ed. Leominster: Gracewing, 2009.

———. *Christ the Ideal of the Monk*. Translator unknown. Ridgefield, CT: Roger A. McCaffrey, n.d.

———. *Christ: The Ideal of the Priest*. Translated by Matthew Dillon. San Francisco: Ignatius, 2005.

———. *Sponsa Verbi: The Virgin Consecrated to Christ*. Translated by Francis Izard. Saint Louis, MO: B. Herder, 1925.

———. *Union with God: Letters of Spiritual Direction by Blessed Columba Marmion*. Selected and annotated by Raymond Thibaut. Translated by Mary St. Thomas. Bethesda, MD: Zaccheus Press, 2006.

———. *The English Letters of Abbot Marmion, 1858–1923*. Baltimore: Helicon, 1962.

WORKS ABOUT MARMION

Boylan, Eugene. "Benedictine Influence in the Doctrine of Abbot Marmion." In *Abbot Marmion: An Irish Tribute*. Edited by the Monks of Glenstall. Westminster, MD: Newman Press, 1948.

Connell, Desmond. Homily at S. Agatha Dei Gothi, September 4, 2000. marmion. be/marm3108.html.

Gionta, Paolo Maria. *Le Virtù Teologali nel Pensiero di Dom Columba Marmion*. Rome: STD diss., Santa Croce, 1998.

Monk of Maredsous. *Une Ame Bénédictine: Dom Pie de Hemptinne*. 5th ed. Paris: Desclée, De Brouwer, 1922.

———. *Dom Pie de Hemptinne, Moine de Maredsous: Un Disciple de Dom Marmion*. 9th ed. Namur: Maredsous, 1941. [A revised and expanded version of the above book.]

Monks of Glenstall, eds. *Abbot Marmion: An Irish Tribute*. Westminster, MD: Newman Press, 1948.

O'Herlihy, T. "Abbot Marmion as Spiritual Director." In *Abbot Marmion: An Irish Tribute*. Edited by the Monks of Glenstall. Westminster, MD: Newman Press, 1948.

Philipon, M. M. *The Spiritual Doctrine of Dom Marmion*. Translated by Matthew Dillon. London: Sands & Co., 1956.

Poswick, R. Ferdinand. *Prier 15 Jours avec Columba Marmion: Abbé de Maredsous*. Montrouge: Nouvelle Cité, 2004.

Thibaut, R. *Dom Columba Marmion: Un Maitre de la Vie Spirituelle*. New ed. 50e mille ed. Namur: Maredsous, 1953.

———. *L'Idée Maîtresse de la Doctrine de Dom Marmion*. Namur: Maredsous, 1947.

———. Preface to *In Union with God: Letters of Spiritual Direction by Blessed Columba Marmion*. Selected and annotated by Raymond Thibaut. Translated by Mary St. Thomas. Bethesda, MD: Zaccheus Press, 2006.

Tierney, Mark. *Blessed Columba Marmion: A Short Biography*. Dublin: Columba, 2000.

Toups, David. Foreword to *In Union with God: Letters of Spiritual Direction by Blessed Columba Marmion*. Selected and annotated by Raymond Thibaut. Translated by Mary St. Thomas. Bethesda, MD: Zaccheus Press, 2006.

OTHER PRIMARY SOURCES

Angela of Foligno. *Book of Divine Consolation*. Translated by Mark Steegman. London: Chatto and Windus, 1909. archive.org/stream/divineconsolatioooangeuoft#page/n5/mode/2up.

Aquinas, Thomas. *Summa Theologica*. Complete English edition. Translated by English Dominican Province. Notre Dame, IN: Ave Maria, 1948.

Arnáiz Barón, Rafael. *Opere Complete*. Siena: Cantagalli, 2009.

Augustine of Hippo. *Augustini De Civitate Dei*. N.p.: Publisher Unknown, Date Unknown. Last accessed October 17, 2014. thelatinlibrary.com/augustine/civ5.shtml.

———. *The City of God: Books I–VII*. In *Fathers of the Church: A New Translation: Writings of Saint Augustine*, vol. 6. Translated by Demetrius Zema and Gerald Walsh. Washington, DC: Catholic University of America Press, 1950.

———. *City of God: Books VIII–XVI*. In *Fathers of the Church: A New Translation: Writings of Saint Augustine*, vol. 7. Translated by Gerald Walsh and Grace Monahan. Washington, DC: Catholic University of America Press, 1952.

———. *Confessions*. Translated by J.G. Pilkington. Garden City, NY: International Collectors Library, 1900. archive.org/details/confessionsofstaooaugu.

——. *Saint Augustine on Genesis: Two Books on Genesis against the Manichees and On the Literal Interpretation of Genesis: An Unfinished Book*. In *The Fathers of the Church: A New Translation*, vol. 84. Translated by Roland J. Teske. Washington, DC: Catholic University of America Press, 1991.

——. "Tractate 81 (John 15:4–7)." In *Tractates on John*. Translated by John Gibb. In *Nicene and Post-Nicene Fathers, First Series*, vol. 7. Edited by Philip Schaff. Buffalo, NY: Christian Literature Publishing Co., 1888. Revised and edited for New Advent by Kevin Knight. Last accessed August 13, 2014. newadvent.org/fathers/1701081.htm.

Barsinuphius and John. *Letters*, vol. 2. In *Fathers of the Church*, vol. 114. Translated by John Chryssavgis. Washington, DC: CUA Press, 2007.

Benedict of Nursia. *RB 1980: The Rule of Saint Benedict in English*. Edited by Timothy Fry. Collegeville, MN: Liturgical Press, 1981.

Bernard of Clairvaux. *Commentary on the Song of Songs*. Arranged by Darrel Wright. Last accessed August 14, 2014. ia600500.us.archive.org/20/items/StBernards CommentaryOnTheSongOfSongs/StBernardOnTheSongOfSongsall.pdf.

——. *Sermons for Advent and the Christmas Season*, Translated by Irene Edmonds et al. Kalamazoo, MI: Cistercian Publications, 2007.

Blosius. *A Book of Spiritual Instruction* [*Institutio spiritualis*]. Translated by Bertrand Wilberforce. Edited by a Benedictine of Stanbrook. London: Burns and Oats, 1955.

Brother Lawrence of the Resurrection. *The Practice of the Presence of God*. Translated by Donald Attwater. Springfield, IL: Templegate, 1974.

Cassian, John. *The Conferences*. In *The Works of the Fathers in Translation*, vol. 57. Translated by Boniface Ramsey. New York: Newman Press, 1997.

——. *The Institutes*. In *The Works of the Fathers in Translation*, vol. 58. Translated by Boniface Ramsey. New York: Newman Press, 2000.

Catechism of the Catholic Church. Washington: Libreria Editrice Vaticana, 1994.

Catherine of Siena, *Le Orazioni*. Rome: Centro Internazionali di Studi Caceriniani. Last accessed February 13, 2015. centrostudicateriniani.it/download/Le%20 Orazioni.pdf.

Christian Prayer: The Liturgy of the Hours. New York: Catholic Book Publishing Co, 1976.

Church Music Association of America. *Parish Book of Chant*. Expanded second ed. N.p.: CMAA, 2012. /media.musicasacra.com/books/pbc_2nd.pdf.

Chrysostom, John. *Homilies of S. Chrysostom: Philippians, Colossians, Thessalonians*. Oxford: John Henry Parker, 1843.

The Daily Roman Missal: Complete with Readings in One Volume. 7th ed. Woodridge, IL: Midwest Theological Forum, 2012.

The Daily Missal and Liturgical Manual (1962). Summorum Pontificum ed. London: Baronius Press, 2008.

Denzinger, Heinrich. *Enchiridion symbolorum definitionum et declarationum de rebus fidei et morum: Compendium of Creeds, Definitions, and Declarations on Matters of Faith and*

Morals. 43rd ed. Latin-English ed. Edited by Peter Hünermann, Robert Fastiggi, and Anne Englund Nash. San Francisco: Ignatius, 2012.

The Documents of Vatican II: With Notes and Index. Vatican City: Libreria Editrice Vaticana / Saint Pauls, 2009.

Francis de Sales. *Introduction to the Devout Life*. Translated by Michael Day. London: Burns & Oats, 1956.

Francis of Assisi. *The Little Flowers of St. Francis*. Translated by Raphael Brown. Garden City, NY: Hanover House, 1958.

John of the Cross. *Collected Works*. Translated by Kieran Kavanaugh and Otilio Rodriguez. Rev. ed. Washington, DC: ICS Publications, 1991.

John Paul II. Homily, 17th World Youth Day, Toronto, July 28, 2002. vatican.va/content/john-paul-ii/en/homilies/2002/documents/hf_jp- ii_hom_20020728_xvii-wyd.html.

———. *Salvifici Doloris: On the Christian Meaning of Human Suffering*. Last accessed July 21, 2020. Vatican.va.

Lozano, Neal. *Unbound*. Grand Rapids, MI: Chosen, 2010.

Teresa of Avila, *The Collected Works*, vol. 1. Translated by Kieran Kavanaugh and Otilio Rodriguez. 2nd ed. Washington, DC: ICS Publications, 1987.

———. *The Collected Works*, vol. 2. Translated by Kieran Kavanaugh and Otilio Rodriguez. Washington, DC: ICS Publications, 1980.

Teresa of Calcutta. *Come Be My Light: The Private Writings of the "Saint of Calcutta."* Edited with commentary by Brian Kolodiejchuk. New York: Image/Doubleday, 2007.

Thérèse of Lisieux. *Novissima Verba: The Last Conversations of St Thérèse of the Child Jesus*. London: Burns Oates & Washbourne, 1929.

———. *Oeuvres Completes*. 36e mille ed. N.p.: Cerf et Desclée de Brouwer, 1992.

———. *Story of a Soul: The Autobiography of Saint Thérèse of Lisieux*. Translated by John Clarke. 3rd ed. Washington, DC: ICS Publications, 1996.

———. *Archives du Carmel de Lisieux*. Last accessed February 28, 2015. archives-carmel-lisieux.fr/english/carmel/.

——— Last Conversations, Yellow Notebook, August 3, no. 5.

——— "Letter 109, to Marie Guérin, July 27–29, 1890"

——— "Letter 197, to Sister Marie of the Sacred Heart, September 17, 1896"

——— "Letter 226, to Fr. Roulland, May 9, 1897"

——— "Letter 243, to Sister Geneviève, June 7, 1897"

——— "Letter 247, to Father Bellière, June 21, 1897"

——— "Letter 261: to Fr. Bellière, July 26, 1897"

——— Manuscript A

——— Manuscript C 02r

——— "Prayer 6"

Thomas à Kempis. *The Imitation of Christ*. Translated by Leo Sherley-Price. London: Penguin Books, 1952.

OTHER WORKS CONSULTED

Arintero, Juan. *Mystical Evolution in the Development and Vitality of the Church*, vol. 2. Translated by Jordan Aumann. Rockford, IL: TAN, 1978.

Aumann, Jordan. *Christian Spirituality in the Catholic Tradition.* London: Sheed & Ward, 1985.

———. *Spiritual Theology.* 7th ed. London: Continuum, 1993.

Bacci, Giacomo Pietro. *Vita di S. Filippo Neri, Apostolo di Roma.* Edition with added contributions from some companions. Roma: Tipografia Marini e Compagno, 1837. books.google.it/books/reader?id=kX0002h5FlMC&printsec=frontcover&output=read er&pg=GBS.PP7.

Barclay, J. "2 Corinthians." In *Eerdmans Commentary on the Bible.* Edited by J. D. Dunn. Grand Rapids, MI: William B. Eerdmans, 2003.

Barnett, Paul. *The Second Epistle to the Corinthians.* Grand Rapids, MI: William B. Eerdmans, 1997.

Bauer, Walter. *A Greek-English Lexicon of the New Testament and Other Early Christian Literature.* Translated by W. Arndt and F. W. Gingrich. 2nd ed. Chicago: University of Chicago Press, 1979.

Bennett, Art and Lorainne Bennett. *The Temperament God Gave You: The Classic Key to Knowing Yourself, Getting Along with Others, and Growing Closer to the Lord.* Manchester, NH: Sophia Institute Press, 2005.

Blount, James. "On the Flame of Love." Lecture, March 22, 2018. youtube.com/watch?v=Cyqeg_NEx-0.

Brown, Brené. "Listening to Shame." Lecture, Vancouver Convention Center, Vancouver, 2010. ted.com/talks/brene_brown_listening_to_shame?language=.

———. "The Power of Vulnerability." Lecture, Vancouver Convention Center, Vancouver, 2010. ted.com/talks/brene_brown_the_power_of_vulnerability?language=en.

Bultmann, Rudolf. *The Second Letter to the Corinthians.* Translated by Roy Harrisville. Minneapolis: Augsburg Publishing House, 1985.

Burrows, Ruth. *Guidelines for Mystical Prayer.* 7th ed. London: Bloomsbury, 2007.

Cohen, Leonard. "Halleluiah." Last accessed August 12, 2020. leonardcohen.com/video/hallelujah.

Delgado, Jesús. "La Cultura di Romero." In *Oscar Romero: Un Vescovo Centroamericano tra Guerra Fredda e Rivoluzione.* Edited by Roberto Morozzo della Rocca. Milano: San Paolo, 2003.

De Meester, Conrad. *With Empty Hands: The Message of Saint Thérèse of Lisieux.* London: Burns and Oats, 2002.

Finley, James. "Spirituality and Healing: Transforming Trauma (#5)." Lecture, Retreat on Spiritual Healing: Transforming Trauma, Tucson, AZ, June 20–22, 2014. youtube.com/watch?v=Kc2XVSpkoeA.

Fox, James. "Divine Attributes." In *The Catholic Encyclopedia*, vol. 2. New York: Robert Appleton Company, 1907. newadvent.org/cathen/02062e.htm.

Furnish, Victor Paul. II Corinthians. The Anchor Bible, vol. 32A. Garden City, NY: Doubleday, 1985.

Garrigou-Lagrange, Reginald. The Three Ages of the Interior Life: Prelude of Eternal Life, vol. 2. Translated by M. Timothea Doyle. Rockford, IL: TAN, 1989.

——. The Three Ways of the Spiritual Life. London: Burns, Oats, and Washbourne, 1938.

——. Christian Perfection and Contemplation: According to St. Thomas Aquinas and St. John of the Cross. Translated by M. Timothea Doyle. Saint Louis, MO: B. Herder, 1937.

Genz, Henning. Nothingness: The Science of Empty Space. Translated by Karin Heusch. Cambridge, MA: Perseus, 1999.

Hugh, Henry. "Veni Sancte Spiritus et Emitte Coelitus." In The Catholic Encyclopedia, vol. 15. New York: Robert Appleton Company, 1912. newadvent.org/cathen/15342a.htm.

Jamart, François. Complete Spiritual Doctrine of St. Thérèse of Lisieux. Translated by Walter van de Putte. New York: Alba House, 1961.

Kurian, Alex. Ascent to Nothingness: The Ascent to God according to John of the Cross. Edited by Andrew Tulloch. London: St. Paul's, 2000.

Macdonald, Margaret. "2 Corinthians." In The Oxford Bible Commentary. Edited by J. Barton and J. Muddiman. Oxford: Oxford University Press, 2001.

MacNutt, Francis, Judith MacNutt, and Christian Healing Ministries. "Prayer to be set free." N.p.: Christian Healing Ministries. Last accessed June 19, 2020. christianhealingmin.org/index.php?option=com_content&view=article&id=647&Itemid=389.

——. "Level 2, Lesson 9: Healing the Wounds of Divorce." In School of Healing Prayer DVDs, Founders Edition. DVD. N.p.: Christian Healing Ministries. Last accessed September 4, 2021. christianhealingmin.org/.

——. "Worship in Community: Healing Conference, Session 3: Inner Healing, Sept. 21, 2007." Lecture, Asbury Theological Seminary, Healing Conference, 2007. vimeo.com/341085381.

Marie Eugene. I Want To See God: A Practical Synthesis of Carmelite Spirituality, vol. 1. Translated by M. Verda Clare. Chicago: FIDES Publishers, 1953.

Mather, Michael. Having Nothing, Possessing Everything: Finding Abundant Communities in Unexpected Places. Grand Rapids: William B. Eerdmans, 2018.

Matthew, Iain. The Impact of God: Soundings from St John of the Cross. London: Hodder, 2010.

Maurer, Armand. Medieval Philosophy. A History of Philosophy, vol. 2. Edited by Etienne Gilson. New York: Random House, 1962.

May, Gerald G., M.D. Addiction and Grace: Love and Spirituality in the Healing of Addictions. New York: HarperCollins, 1988.

Meyer, Heinrich. Critical and Exegetical Commentary on the New Testament: Corinthians, vol. 2. Translated by W. A. Dickson and W. Stewart. Edinburgh: T. & T. Clark, 1879.

Murphy-O'Connor, J. "The First and Second Letters to the Corinthians." In New Jerome Biblical Commentary. Edited by R. Brown. Englewood Cliffs, NJ: Prentice Hall, 1990.

Murray, Paul. *Aquinas at Prayer: The Bible, Mysticism, and Poetry.* London: Bloomsbury, 2013.

———. *I Loved Jesus in the Night: Teresa of Calcutta, A Secret Revealed.* London: Darton,
Longman, and Todd, 2010.

Noffke, Suzanne. *The Prayers of Catherine of Siena.* 2nd ed. Translated and edited by
Suzanne Noffke. San Jose, CA: Authors Choice, 2001.

Ocáriz, F., L. F. Mateo Seco, and J. A. Riestra. *The Mystery of Jesus Christ: A Christology and Soteriology Textbook.* Translated by Michael Adams and James Gavigan.
Dublin: Four Courts, 1994.

Peake, Artur. *Peake's Commentary on the Bible.* Edited by Matthew Black. London:
Thomas Nelson, 1962.

Pio of Pietrelcina. *Epistolario III, Correspondenza con le figlie spirituali.* Edited by Gerardo
di Flumeri. 4th ed. San Giovani Rotondo: Edizioni, 2012.

———. *Correspondence with His Spiritual Daughters,* vol. 3. Translated by Geraldine Nolan.
Edited by Gerardo Di Flumeri. 2nd ed. San Giovani Rotondo: Edizioni, 2001.

Philippe, Jacques. *Searching for and Maintaining Peace: A Small Treatise on Peace of Heart.*
Translated by George Driscoll and Jannic Driscoll. New York: St. Paul's, 2002.

———. *Time for God: A Guide to Prayer.* Translated by Sinag Tala. London: St. Paul's,
2005.

Pohle, Joseph. "Justification." In *The Catholic Encyclopedia,* vol. 8. New York: Robert
Appleton Company, 1910. newadvent.org/cathen/08573a.htm.

———. "Sanctifying Grace." In *The Catholic Encyclopedia,* vol. 6. New York: Robert
Appleton Company, 1909. newadvent.org/cathen/06701a.htm.

——— "Semipelagianism." In *The Catholic Encyclopedia,* vol. 13. New York: Robert
Appleton Company, 1912. newadvent.org/cathen/13703a.htm.

Radcliffe, Timothy. *I Call You Friends.* London: Continuum, 2001.

Raymond of Capua. *The Life of St Catherine of Siena.* Translated by George Lamb.
New York: PJ. Kennedy & Sons, 1960.

Rodenberg, Patsy. *Presence: How to Use Positive Energy for Success.* London: Penguin,
2009.

Rolling Stone. "How Leonard Cohen's 'Hallelujah' Brilliantly Mingled Sex, Religion." *Rolling Stone,* December 12, 2019. rollingstone.com/music/music-news/
how-leonard-cohens-hallelujah-brilliantly-mingled-sex-religion-194516/.

Tanquerey, Adolphe. *The Spiritual Life: A Treatise on Ascetical and Mystical Theology.*
Translated by Herman Branderis. 2nd revised ed. Tournai: Desclée, De Brouwer:
1930.

Thrall, Margaret. *A Critical and Exegetical Commentary on the Second Epistle to the Corinthians,* vol. 2. In *The International Critical Commentary.* Edinburgh: T & T Clark, 2000.

Zerwick, Max and Mary Grosvenor. *A Grammatical Analysis of the Greek New Testament.*
5th ed. Rome: Editrice Pontificio Istituto Biblico, 1996.

Made in the USA
Monee, IL
26 August 2023

41665511R00111